ANYTHING FOR A VOTE

BY
JOSEPH CUMMINS

DIRTY TRICKS, CHEAP SHOTS, and OCTOBER
SURPRISES in U.S. PRESIDENTIAL CAMPAIGNS

QUIRK BOOKS
PHILADELPHIA

Library of Congress Cataloging in Publication Number: 2007925761

ISBN: 978-1-59474-156-2
Printed in China

Typeset in Gill Sans and Mrs. Eaves Roman

Designed by Doogie Horner
Illustrations by Mike Fink

Cover photos courtesy AP Images

Distributed in North America by Chronicle Books
680 Second Street
San Francisco, CA 94107

10 9 8 7 6 5 4 3 2 1

Quirk Books
215 Church Street
Philadelphia, PA 19106
www.quirkbooks.com

★ ★ ★ ★ ★ ★ ★ ★ ★ ★

FOR DEDE AND CARSON,
WHO GET MY VOTE EVERY TIME.

★ ★ ★ ★ ★ ★ ★ ★ ★ ★

CONTENTS

★ ★ ★ INTRODUCTION ★ ★ ★

"What do men gain by elective governments, if fools and knaves have the same chance to obtain the highest office, as honest men?"
—Noah Webster to Thomas Jefferson, 1801

The idea for this book was born shortly after the 2004 presidential election. In that contentious contest, Democratic candidate and war hero John Kerry was vilified as a coward by an organization called the Swift Boat Veterans for Truth, while incumbent president George W. Bush was rumored to be such a dunce that he had to be wired to a transmitter to participate in a public debate.

During election postmortems, I listened as pundits moaned about how sleazy the campaign had become, how the candidates had stooped to new lows of dirty tricks and vicious discourse. Yet, it seemed to me that I'd heard this same tune played after every presidential contest I'd lived through. So I asked myself, are things really getting worse? Have presidential campaigns truly turned more vicious?

After a year and a half spent researching and writing *Anything for a Vote: Dirty Tricks, Cheap Shots, and October Surprises In U.S. Presidential Campaigns*, I can happily answer that question with a resounding *No*. Presidential elections haven't gotten worse—they're just as dirty now as they've always been. Democracy has never been for the faint of heart. Every dirty election in current times can easily be matched by one further back in history. What party stole a close presidential election from the Democrats in Florida? The Republicans in 1876, during the Hayes-Tilden face-off. Which presidential candidate kept company with a "smoking bimbo" and was rumored to have sired a love child? That would be Warren Harding in 1920. What president bugged his opponent's headquarters? Why Richard Nixon, of course—but also Lyndon Johnson, whose 1964 campaign against Barry Goldwater is one of the dirtiest on record.

Probably the only clean election in American history was the first one, in 1789, in which George Washington ran unopposed. By the next ballot, in 1792, the nation's first political parties had begun to form. Four years later, the two rivals were going at it full force . . . and they haven't stopped since.

During the past 220 years of Americans voting for their presidents, much has changed. In the beginning, the framers of the Constitution dictated that there would be no direct popular vote; instead, the president was chosen by electors appointed by state legislatures. Each elector could cast two votes for president: the top vote-getter became president, the runner-up vice president. This made it possible for a president to have a vice president from a different party, as happened in 1796 when Thomas Jefferson became John Adams's White House partner. (For a contemporary reference, imagine George W. Bush with John Kerry as his veep, and you'll have some idea of the trouble caused.)

In 1824, however, Americans began electing their president by popular vote, and over the next century, presidential electioneering became the country's favorite spectator sport. Nineteenth-century customs dictated that candidates maintain a dignified public silence during the campaign, but that didn't keep members of both parties from fighting like pigs over truffles. Huge rallies were held in candidates' honor, and newspapers—usually aligned with a political party, a practice that ended only in the mid-twentieth century—hurled lavish insults at the presidential hopefuls. (You haven't lived until you've been trashed by a nineteenth-century tabloid.) Voter turnout was extraordinary—consistently in the high seventieth percentile. Note that today, depending on which statistics you believe, it ranges from 49 to 55 percent.

As I wrote this book, many people (hidden agendas gleaming in their eyes) asked me which party had resorted to the dirtiest tricks. Depends on the situation, I would usually reply. Frankly, they've both acted pretty badly at different times throughout our nation's history.

In general, my research revealed two things:

1) Incumbent parties are more likely to wage dirty presidential campaigns, probably because they have more money and influence.

2) Parties with the strongest ideologies—be they Democratic or Republican—tend to wage the nastiest battles. If you sincerely believe that you have a better candidate and a superior life philosophy, you're more willing to pull out all the stops to ensure your party wins.

And dirty tricks do influence the outcome of presidential elections. In some of the ugliest elections of all time—from the Jefferson-Adams bloodbath of 1800 through the Hoover-Smith smearfest of 1928 to the Bush-Gore millennial madness—the party responsible for the dirtiest tricks usually won.

If all this sounds pretty grim, cheer up. Without smears, innuendo, and thievery tainting our electoral system, what would we have to connect us to our quickly vanishing past? Believe me: You could take any Whig or Federalist of yore, plunk him down in a modern presidential campaign, and (once accustomed to television and the Internet) he'd be up and shrieking with the best of us.

We're Americans, after all. A nice, dirty election runs in our blood.

1789

GEORGE WASHINGTON

★ ★ ★ ★ ★ ★ ★ ★ ★ ★ ★ VS. ★ ★ ★ ★ ★ ★ ★ ★ ★ ★ ★

HIMSELF

"Welcome, mighty chief! Once more
Welcome to this mighty shore
Now no mercenary foe—
Aims at thee the fatal blow!"

—Ode to George Washington performed by thirteen girls (one for each of
the new states) as Washington journeyed to his first inauguration

SLEAZE-O-METER

10
9
8
7
6
5
4
3
2
1

I n the very beginning—before primaries, spin control, PACs, sound bites, hanging chads, and talking heads—electing a president was a clean, sober, and dignified business.

Before the first presidential election in 1789, Alexander Hamilton envisioned future candidates as men "most likely to possess the information and discernment requisite to such complicated investigations." Those who chose such men would, by definition, be men of high seriousness and probity, the kind of men who might pick a pastor for a church or select the head of a new university.

And the first time, it worked out pretty much that way.

★ ★ ★ THE CAMPAIGN (SUCH AS IT WAS) ★ ★ ★

In 1789, America was like a newborn babe, and since the birth pains included a bloody and divisive war, a calming paternal figure was needed. The only one who really fit the bill was Commander-in-Chief George Washington, who was even then being called the father of his country.

Washington was not happy about being the anointed one. He was a genuinely reluctant leader who, at the age of fifty-six, thought he was too far past his prime to undertake such a challenge. (He told his future secretary of war, Henry Knox: "My movement to the chair of Government will be accompanied by feelings not unlike those of a culprit who is going to the place of his execution.")

But Washington had presided over the Constitutional Convention, which met in Philadelphia in 1787 to create a coherent democratic governing system. His friends Alexander Hamilton and James Madison convinced him that America needed his presence—if only to make sure that the gains of the Revolution did not disappear in factional infighting between state's rights advocates and those who favored a strong central government.

Never mind that the general had some decidedly undemocratic ways about him, such as his habit of referring to himself in the third person like an eighteenth-century Julius Caesar, and his dislike of shaking hands (he preferred bowing). Washington was the man, all the way.

In the very beginning, electing a president was a clean, sober, and dignified business.

The first presidential election in American history was also the quickest. There was no popular vote and there would not be one until 1824. Instead, following rules set down in the newly ratified Constitution, each state appointed presidential electors in January 1789 (except New York, which failed to appoint its allotted eight electors in time and thus sat out this first election). With the first Electoral College thus established, the electors cast two votes for two different people—a point that would become extremely controversial in early American history. The man who received the most votes would become president; the man coming in second would be vice president.

The only hint of skullduggery came from the crafty Alexander Hamilton. He urged electors to "waste" their second votes on candidates who were not even in the running, so that his rival John Adams—patriot and framer of the Declaration of Independence—would have absolutely no chance of becoming president.

★ ★ THE WINNER: GEORGE WASHINGTON ★ ★

Hamilton's strategy was quite unnecessary, for Washington had everything sewn up from the beginning and walked away with all sixty-nine electoral votes. All Hamilton really accomplished was to royally tick off John Adams; he would later complain about the "scurvy manner" in which he had been made vice president.

These grumblings foreshadowed things to come—but for the time being, all was wonderful. Washington made his triumphal entry into New York City, the nation's temporary capital, on April 30, 1789. Thousands of spectators thronged the road that led from Mount Vernon, cheering and tossing flowers. The first president was ferried across the Hudson River on an enormous barge manned by thirteen white-smocked sailors; the barge was surrounded by a veritable flotilla of ships, filled to the gunwales with celebrants who sang Washington's praises to the spring skies.

In more ways than one, the election of 1789 was the smoothest sailing an American presidential candidate would ever have.

★ ★

OF COURSE, THE SAILING WASN'T COMPLETELY SMOOTH The acerbic John Adams did claim that the only reason Washington was chosen for everything was that he was taller than anyone else in the room.

1792

WASHINGTON

* * * * * * * * * * * * * VS. * * * * * * * * * * * * *

HIMSELF (AGAIN)

"Damn 'em, damn 'em, damn 'em. You see—an elective government won't do!"

—John Adams

SLEAZE-O-METER

10
9
8
7
6
5
4
3
2
1

In 1792, things got just a little worse. Being the first president meant that Washington had a lot of ceremonial stuff to figure out, for example, what he should be called ("Mr. President" was finally settled on, although John Adams grumbled that the term *president* recalled such commoners as "presidents of fire companies and clubs"). But there was much more substantial fare on the presidential menu, including the ever-delicate matter of relations with Great Britain and how the administration was to react to the French Revolution (Washington was all for it, until the Terror brought up the fearful specter of mob rule).

As Father of the Nation, Washington also had to deal with quarreling kids. The children in this case were cabinet members Alexander Hamilton and Thomas Jefferson, and their dispute helped create something the framers of the Constitution hadn't quite bargained for: the first American political parties.

Hamilton, in spite of (or because of) his impoverished origins, had no great trust in the common people. He believed in a strong, firm-handed central government and, as secretary of treasury under Washington, created a federal bank and sponsored measures that helped the rich merchants, bankers, and manufacturers of the cities in the Northeast. People who shared Hamilton's views came to be called Federalists.

Secretary of State Jefferson, although a landed aristocrat by birth, believed in the power of the people—the people preferably being farmers in an idealized agrarian society. He thought that Hamilton's form of government meant too much power vested in too few hands. Those who agreed with Jefferson's point of view called themselves Republicans.

★ ★ ★ THE CAMPAIGN ★ ★ ★

With his first term nearing completion, Washington wanted nothing more than to return to Mount Vernon to spend his remaining years in bucolic retreat with his wife, Martha. But with the country starting to split, he decided to run one more time, as a unifying figure.

Fifteen states participated in the 1792 election, compared with only ten in 1789. North Carolina and Rhode Island had finally ratified the constitution; New York, which had abstained the first time around, added its vote; and two new states joined the Union: Vermont and Kentucky.

Since Washington was considered a shoo-in, the only remaining question was whether Federalist Vice President John Adams would get a second term. Republican congressmen from five states convened in the fall and proposed New York Governor George Clinton as their veep candidate. Federalists perceived this as such a threat that even Alexander Hamilton, Adams's own sworn enemy, saw fit to coach the vice president in spin control, advising Adams to tone down some of his more inflammatory Federalist pronouncements. For instance, Adams had written that the country would be a better place if ruled by "the rich [and] well-born." This may have been an honest summation of his feelings, but it was terrible PR.

★ ★ ★   THE WINNER: GEORGE, AGAIN   ★ ★ ★

No one was surprised when all 132 electors gave their first vote for Washington. Adams received 77 votes to Governor Clinton's 50. He considered this a sign of disrespect and thus the stage was set for 1796 and the first truly contested presidential election in American history.

★ ★

IF YOU CAN'T BEAT 'EM, START YOUR OWN NEWSPAPER Hamilton and his pal John Fenno, editor of the *Gazette of the United States*, took aim at Jefferson and Republican supporters like James Madison at every opportunity. They claimed that Jefferson (whom Hamilton was fond of addressing sardonically in print as "Generalissimo") was a man of "profound ambition and violent passions" who would do anything to become president.

Jefferson responded by funding a rag called the *National Gazette*, in whose pages James Madison wrote nineteen different articles designed to fan anti-

Federalist flames. Hamilton's adherents, Madison said, were "monied men of influence." With broad sarcasm, he told his readers that, under Hamilton's plan, citizens "should think of nothing but obedience, leaving the care of their liberties to their wiser rulers."

GET THEM DRUNK, AND THEY WILL COME These days, presidential candidates go on television and urge citizens, in the most sober of tones, to do their civic duty and vote. In 1792, candidates had a different idea—get voters hammered on your tab and naturally they'd vote for you. The *Gazette of the United States* reported that "a bystander, observing the particular situation of a great number of electors, who had been regaled at the expense of one of the candidates, remarked . . . that the Voice of the People was the Voice of Grog."

Getting voters drunk was a surefire way to earn their support.

1796

JOHN ADAMS

★ ★ ★ ★ ★ ★ ★ ★ ★ ★ ★ ★ **VS.** ★ ★ ★ ★ ★ ★ ★ ★ ★ ★ ★

THOMAS JEFFERSON

"*[I pray] that your administration may be filled with glory and happiness . . .*"

—Thomas Jefferson, in an unsent letter to John Adams

SLEAZE-O-METER

10
9
8
7
6
5
4
3
2
1

No man can be president for long without becoming, as John Adams so nicely put it, "the Butt of Party Malevolence," and George Washington was no exception. During his last term of office, Washington often wished he were back home with Martha, swilling Madeira on the front porch.

Every day brought a new headache. When a few farmers in western Pennsylvania refused to pay an excise tax on whiskey, Washington put down the so-called Whiskey Rebellion with what freedom-loving early Americans thought was excessive force. Perhaps predictably, Republicans began calling our first president a tyrant and a dictator.

Then there was the issue of relations with Great Britain—a touchy subject, to say the least. American sympathies with France—a country then at war with Britain—caused friction in London, and it seemed as though further hostilities between the former mother country and her colonies might be inevitable.

Washington sent Chief Justice John Jay to London to hammer out a treaty; he came back with a document that, while not perfect, gave America peace with Great Britain. Washington signed it, and Republicans howled, calling it a cop-out to Federalist "monarchist" tendencies and supposed desire to return America to England.

Throughout his career, Washington benefited from a superb sense of timing, and 1796 was no exception. That winter, he began to hint that he was going to leave office; on September 19 of the same year, he had published his "Farewell Address," in which he warned against divisive political parties. This was all to no avail—as soon as the farewell was released, hungry politicians began scheming to fill Washington's shoes.

One of these men—Thomas Jefferson, Washington's former secretary of state—couldn't resist a parting shot at his old boss and Revolutionary comrade: "The president is fortunate to get off just as the bubble is bursting, leaving others to hold the bag."

It's nice to know that even the author of the Declaration of Independence occasionally fell prey to mixed metaphors.

★ ★ ★ THE CANDIDATES ★ ★ ★

FEDERALIST: JOHN ADAMS John Adams was a two-term vice president and getting on in years (he would turn sixty-one during the campaign). His acerbic personality won him admirers and enemies in equal measure. While pretending he was planning on leaving public life—he liked to discourse on the "foul fiend" of electoral degeneracy—Adams highly desired becoming president. "Hi! Ho! Oh, Dear!" he gaily started off one letter to his wife, Abigail, when it became apparent that Washington would not seek a third term.

REPUBLICAN: THOMAS JEFFERSON Jefferson had retired from his secretary of state position in 1793 to return to Monticello and attend to his affairs (including the one he had with Sally Hemings, the slave by whom he sired several children). As 1796 approached, he still maintained that life in politics—what was even then being called the "game"—was "a useless waste of time." But it was clear to everyone where his ambitions lay.

★ ★ ★ THE CAMPAIGN ★ ★ ★

The ten weeks after the publication of Washington's farewell address were filled with feverish activity and loud proclamations by both parties—except for the candidates. Following what would generally be the custom for the next century, Jefferson and Adams maintained an aloof and dignified public silence.

Even though a good deal of campaigning was already under way, there was no official manner of picking the candidates. The Constitution said nothing on the issue, and the first national nominating convention was more than thirty years away. Until then, prominent members of each party decided on the candidates and then tried to convince their fellow members to follow suit.

They achieved varying degrees of success. Since the parties themselves were barely formed, party discipline was a joke: Electors often voted based on local enmity, personal friendship, or mere whimsy. (In 1796, nearly 40 percent of the 138 electors voted for candidates not in their own parties or for candidates not even on the ballot!)

What the parties lacked in organization, they made up for in vicious character assassination. For anyone who loves the democratic process, it's reassuring to see how immediately and full-heartedly politicians in early America launched malicious attacks through handbills, pamphlets, and articles in various party journals.

In the Republican newspaper *Aurora*, editor Benjamin Franklin Bache (grandson of Benjamin Franklin) immediately went for the throat—or rather, the tummy—by referring to the chubby Adams's "sesquipedality of belly." (This meant, literally, that his stomach was 18 inches long.) Bache also warned that Adams was "champion of kings, ranks, and titles."

Not to be outdone, Federalists cited Jefferson for his supposed "atheistic" tendencies and his love of the French Revolution, especially the bloody, screaming mob. Jefferson's Republican followers became "cut-throats who walk in rags and sleep amidst filth and vermin."

Meanwhile, in the first examples of balancing a national ticket by the judicious selection of a vice-presidential candidate, Federalists nominated southern diplomat Thomas Pinckney to offset New Englander Adams, while Republicans paired the Virginian Jefferson with Aaron Burr, the up-and-coming New York lawyer and early Tammany operative.

As usual, Alexander Hamilton acted the spoiler. Taking advantage once again of what was rapidly being acknowledged as a defect in the Constitution—the fact that electors voted for two candidates—he urged certain Federalist voters to withhold their votes for Adams entirely and vote only for Pinckney. If his plan had succeeded, Pinckney (whom Hamilton rightly considered far easier to manipulate than Adams) would have become president and Hamilton the power behind the throne.

Federalists warned that Thomas Jefferson was "soft on France" and supported bloody, screaming mobs.

THE WINNER: JOHN ADAMS

The electors cast their ballots in their respective state capitals on the first Wednesday in December. At this time in American history, there was an odd law stipulating that ballots could not be opened until the second Wednesday in February, when both houses of Congress were in session. It seemed like weeks of rumor and wild speculation would ensue—but by the middle of December, the cat was out of the bag and everyone knew that John Adams had squeaked into the presidency, seventy-one votes to Jefferson's sixty-eight. He was president, indeed, but the wisdom of the framers of the Constitution had ensured that he had a member of the opposition party as his vice president.

Over the next four years, this would mean nothing but trouble.

★ ★

FRANCOMANIAC VS. THE ANGLOMAN In charges that foreshadowed the "egghead" slurs thrown at future presidential candidates such as Adlai Stevenson and Eugene McCarthy, Federalists smeared Jefferson as a "philosopher" and, worse, a "visionary." Jefferson, harrumphed one writer, was "fit to be professor in a college ... but certainly not first magistrate of a great nation." Just to make sure people got the point, Jefferson was also called an anarchist and a Francomaniac.

Of course, Adams had his own share of detractors and bizarre nicknames (including "Monoman" and "Angloman"). The Republican *Boston Chronicle* wrote quite seriously that if Adams were elected, hereditary succession would be foisted upon America in the form of his son, John Quincy. (With Jefferson, the paper added, who needed to worry? Even if he had hidden monarchist intentions, the man had only daughters.)

1800

THOMAS JEFFERSON
★ ★ ★ ★ ★ ★ ★ ★ ★ ★ ★ ★ VS. ★ ★ ★ ★ ★ ★ ★ ★ ★ ★ ★ ★ ★
JOHN ADAMS

"The Republic is safe. . . . The [Federalist] party is in rage and despair."

—John Dawson, Republican Congressman, Virginia

SLEAZE-O-METER

10
9
8
7
6
5
4
3
2
1

By 1800, the American population had increased to 5.3 million; Washington, D.C., had replaced Philadelphia as the new "Federal City"; and a mellow dude named John Chapman, a.k.a. Johnny Appleseed, was wandering through Ohio Territory, dispensing wisdom as well as gardening tips.

And in a harbinger of things to come, America had its first presidential free-for-all—the first election in which, at the end of the day, bodies lay strewn everywhere. Forget Bush vs. Gore, forget Nixon vs. Kennedy, forget most of the really nasty national elections you've experienced in your lifetime. The 1800 contest between John Adams and Thomas Jefferson can be ranked as one of the top five dirtiest elections of all time—and all because of two reasons:

One: It is hard to think of two parties in the history of American politics who hated and vilified each other more than John Adams's Federalists and Thomas Jefferson's Republicans.

Two: For the first and last time in American history, a president was running against his own vice president.

What a way to begin a century.

★ ★ ★ THE CANDIDATES ★ ★ ★

FEDERALIST: JOHN ADAMS The chief foreign policy issue of Adams's presidency was America's relationship with France. Since the French and the British were at war and America had signed the Jay Treaty with Britain, the new French Republic declared that any American trade with Great Britain was an act of war, and French seamen began boarding American ships and seizing goods.

When Adams tried to raise money for a larger navy to counter the threat, he was attacked by the Republicans for being a warmonger. When he attempted negotiations with France, Hamilton's gang called him an appeaser. The guy just couldn't win.

Another factor in the 1800 campaign was the Alien and Sedition Acts, steered through Congress by the Federalists during the height of war fever. Under the Sedition Act, anyone who criticized or sought to undermine the U.S. government or the president could be fined or thrown in jail, and many were. Republicans reviled the law as a violation of Constitutional rights. People weren't even safe in the neighborhood bar—a New Jersey tavern patron was arrested and fined for drunkenly noting that the president had, to put it indelicately, a big ass.

Despite Federalist reservations about Adams (and "reservations" may be a mild word, as one prominent Federalist prayed openly that the president might suffer a carriage accident), he was the only candidate they had. For his vice-presidential running mate, the party picked General Charles Cotesworth Pinckney, brother of Adams's 1796 veep nominee, a seasoned diplomat, and Southern ticket balancer.

REPUBLICAN: THOMAS JEFFERSON Thomas Jefferson had spent most of the four years of his vice presidency adroitly keeping a safe distance between himself and his boss, John Adams. Therefore, almost nothing with which Adams was associated—including the Sedition Act, which Jefferson had done little to keep from passage in Congress—rubbed off on his vice president, and he was in a strong position to run.

As Jefferson's vice-presidential candidate, the Republicans once again picked Aaron Burr, whose star had continued to rise since the '96 elections.

★ ★ ★ THE CAMPAIGN ★ ★ ★

What a difference four years can make. The 1796 presidential campaigns had begun roughly one hundred days before the election. But by 1800, the parties were launching attacks a full year before any votes were cast.

The first strike against Adams came from Jefferson himself, who secretly hired a writer named James Callender (the kind of hack one pictures skulking in the back of foul taverns, cackling as he scratches away with his quill) to assail the president in print. Callender set to work with a vengeance. Adams, he wrote, was "a repulsive pedant," a "gross hypocrite," and, most interesting, "a hideous hermaphroditical character which has neither the force and firmness of a man, nor the gentleness and sensibility of a woman." Not surprisingly, Callender was jailed for nine months under the Sedition Act, which gave the Republicans a convenient martyr.

The Federalists fired back, spreading rumors that Jefferson had swindled his legal clients, that he was a godless atheist from whom one had to hide one's Bibles, that he had been a coward during the Revolutionary War, and that he slept with slaves while at home in Monticello. A few mischievous Federalists even spread the rumor that Jefferson was dead, knowing full well that it was actually a Monticello slave by the same name who was deceased.

The vicious sallies increased, and by fall both parties had reached a peak of character assassination. The Republicans, in particular, had discovered the power of the press—their attacks ran in single-page circulars, newspapers, and pamphlets as long as fifty pages. In one of the first attempts at true national organization, Jefferson's party set up Committees of Correspondence that were responsible for producing these broadsides and disseminating them to voters.

But an election this boisterous could not simply take place in print. Federalists liked to hold military parades; Republicans planted liberty poles. Both parties threw picnics and barbecues, where they plied voters with huge amounts of alcohol. At a Republican dinner in Lancaster, Pennsylvania, everyone drank sixteen toasts—one for each state of the Union—before tying into a half-ton of beef and pork.

Although Adams held out hope for a great victory, most politicians at the time considered Jefferson almost a sure winner. The ubiquitous Alexander Hamilton, Adams's nemesis, tried to make sure of it. In October, Hamilton published a most astonishing document, the *Letter from Alexander Hamilton Concerning the Public Conduct and Character of John Adams, Esq., President of the United States*, fifty-four pages of what one historian has called unremitting vilification. "If we must have an enemy at the head of the government, let it be one whom we can oppose . . . who will not involve our party in the disgrace of his foolish and bad measures," wrote Hamilton.

Although Hamilton had long been known for his machinations, the letter was a shock to everyone. To try to understand the impact, imagine if Senator John McCain sent an E-mail to Republican Party faithfuls under the subject heading "e-mail from John McCain concerning the Public Content and Character of George W. Bush" and go on to accuse the president—the nominal leader of his party—of suffering from "distempered jealousy," "extreme egotism," and an "ungovernable temper."

Some historians feel that Hamilton had temporarily lost his mind; others think the publication was a calculated ploy to throw votes away from Adams and to Charles Pinckney, who would be more sympathetic to Hamilton's extreme Federalist agenda. There is even the possibility that the letter was stolen from Hamilton and published without his consent. In any event, Hamilton was attacked by both parties, and he retired from politics after the election. Four years later, he was shot and killed in a duel by Vice President Aaron Burr.

★ ★ ★ THE WINNER (EVENTUALLY): ★ ★ ★
THOMAS JEFFERSON

Election Day was December 3, and electors met in their respective state capitals to cast their votes. Once again, the law stipulated that ballots would not be opened until early February, when both houses of Congress were in session. And once again, word leaked out early—Jefferson was the winner. "The Jig Is Up!" cheered one Republican Party newspaper. Another writer declared: "Here ends the 18th century. The 19th begins with a fine, clear morning."

There was just one small problem. By the end of December, it became clear that Republican candidates Jefferson and Burr had actually tied for the presidency at seventy-three votes each (Adams received only sixty-five). The problem with the two-vote system now became more apparent than ever. In past elections, Republican electors might have "wasted" a handful of votes on Adams or Pinckney, or even a minor candidate, just to make sure Burr did not receive an equal number as Jefferson (ensuring his position as VP). But in such a close contest, every vote mattered, so every Republican voted for Jefferson and Burr. The result was a tie.

To make matters worse, the Constitution dictated that the Republican runoff election should be resolved by the House of Representatives—which, ironically enough, was controlled by the Federalists!

Burr initially declared he would be happy to serve under Jefferson, but this was only because he mistakenly thought he had lost the election by one vote. His spirit of cooperation vanished when he realized that he had a pretty fair shot at becoming president. In fact, many Federalists came to him, offering their backing—anything to keep Jefferson out—and Burr's chances of winning rose exponentially.

On February 11, during a massive snowstorm, the House of Representatives met in Washington, D.C., to vote for the president. All members were there, even one who was so ill he had to be carried on a stretcher for two miles through the snow and then placed in a bed in an adjoining chamber. Vice President Jefferson, who was the Senate president, counted the electoral ballots and certified the vote at seventy-three apiece for him and Burr. Then the House deliberated on who would be the next president.

The slate was now blank. Each of the sixteen states had a single vote, and the winner needed a majority of nine states to take the prize. Over the course of six days, thirty-six ballots were recorded. For the first thirty-five, the results were the same: eight states for Jefferson, six for Burr, two undecided—no winner. In the back rooms of taverns and the antechambers of the House, the behind-the-scenes maneuvering was intense. Federalists wooed Burr, but he wouldn't agree to their agenda in exchange for a chance to become president. The deadlock continued.

Finally, on February 17, a Federalist congressman from Delaware who opposed Jefferson abstained in the voting, as did Federalists from Maryland, Vermont, and South Carolina. With these states out of the balloting, Jefferson was quickly elected, winning ten out of sixteen votes, with Aaron Burr as his vice president.

No records survive to confirm what happened because almost everything important that occurred during those six historic days took place in the utmost secrecy. But many suspected that Thomas Jefferson cut a deal with the Federalist party to become president of the United States.

Jefferson would always deny this, but his policies while in office—which included continuing the Bank of the United States set up by Hamilton, financing a national debt, and keeping certain Federalists in office—seemed to confirm that a secret agreement had been made with the opposition party.

★ ★

THE ONLY THING MISSING IS MONICA . . . The Federalists couldn't get enough of attacking Jefferson in a very, very personal way—their assaults sound like the insults leveled at Bill Clinton, another Southerner, almost 200 years later. "Jefferson is a mean-spirited, low-lived fellow, the son of a half-breed Indian squaw, sired by a Virginia mulatto father," said one leaflet. A Connecticut paper raised the specter of the French Revolution, supposedly beloved by Jefferson: "Are you prepared to see your dwellings in flames . . . female chastity violated, [your] children writhing on the pike? GREAT GOD OF COMPASSION AND JUSTICE, SHIELD MY COUNTRY FROM DESTRUCTION."

KING JOHN Republicans claimed that Adams planned to marry one of his sons to a daughter of King George III of England in order to start an American royal dynasty and reunite England and America. And if that wasn't enough to make Anglophobes panic, Republicans also claimed that Adams sent his running mate, Charles Pinckney, to England to pick up four pretty mistresses—two for the president, two for Pinckney. (When Adams heard about this, he exclaimed, "If this be true, General Pinckney has kept them all for himself and cheated me out of my two!")

FIRST BLAME-IT-ALL-ON-THE-MEDIA ATTACK After the election, one Federalist poet decided that his party's defeat could be blamed entirely on the media, which (in his opinion) clearly favored the Republican Party:

Republicans claimed that John Adams and running mate Charles Pinckney shared a total of four mistresses—all imported from England.

"And lo! In meretricious dress,
Forth comes a strumpet called 'THE PRESS.'
Whose haggard, unrequested charms
Rush into every blaggard's arms."

WHO'S YOUR DADDY? Alexander Hamilton was born illegitimate, a fact that John Adams—who had good reason to hate Hamilton's guts—never let him forget. On various occasions, Adams referred to Hamilton as "a Creole bastard," "the bastard brat of a Scotch peddlar," and "a man devoid of every Moral principle—a bastard."

NEVER AGAIN In the election's aftermath, all Republicans and Federalists agreed on one thing: Another election like that of 1800 was to be avoided if at all possible. Therefore, Congress passed a resolution for a constitutional amendment stating that electors would henceforth vote separately for president and vice president, rather than allowing the two top vote-getters to take all. The resolution was quickly ratified and became the Twelfth Amendment.

THOMAS JEFFERSON
vs. CHARLES PINCKNEY

Since Thomas Jefferson proved to be a highly skilled middle-of-the-road president, the election of 1804 was a bit of a snoozer. Despite Federalist howls, Jefferson did not turn the country into an atheistic society, instigate a Jacobian bloodbath, or abandon the New England merchant class. In fact, the new president made a number of popular decisions during his first term—most notably the Louisiana Purchase, in which Jefferson doubled the size of the United States for a mere fifteen million bucks (amounting to roughly three cents an acre).

On February 25, 1804, in what was the first official nominating caucus for a U.S. president, Republican congressmen met and re-nominated Thomas Jefferson for president, naming New York Governor George Clinton as his veep candidate.

The Federalists chose Charles Cotesworth Pinckney, Adams's 1800 running mate, as their candidate. Pinckney was a large, jowly man, respected by both parties but half-deaf and not terribly exciting. New York Senator Rufus King got the nod for vice president.

THE CAMPAIGN Everyone could see that Jefferson and the Republicans had a lock on the election, but the Federalists—desperate to salvage votes in their base of New England—fought as hard as they could. The usual anti-Jefferson slurs were trotted out—he was an atheist, he had an affair with his slave, and so on.

THE WINNER: THOMAS JEFFERSON It was absolutely no contest: 162 votes for Jefferson, 14 for Pinckney. The Federalists carried only two states: Connecticut and Delaware. Even Massachusetts voted Republican.

1808

AT A GLANCE

JAMES MADISON
vs. CHARLES PINCKNEY

Thomas Jefferson's second term was a much different story than his first, primarily because of escalating hostilities between the French and the British. The powerful British navy had returned to its extremely antagonistic practice of stopping American ships on the pretext of looking for English deserters, but actually to impress American seamen into duty. After one particularly nasty incident when a British warship attacked an American frigate just off the coast of Virginia, killing and wounding twenty-one sailors, Jefferson prevailed upon Congress to pass the Embargo Act, which kept Americans from trading with not just Great Britain and France but all of Europe.

Unfortunately, the biggest victims of the embargo were American farmers who exported grain overseas and New England merchants, whose lively trade in goods to Europe was now cut off. Instead of being the shining hero, Jefferson became, as one newspaper put it, "an infernal villain."

Like Washington before him, Jefferson knew when to shuffle off the public stage. Declaring that it was time to retire to "my family, my books, and farms," he recommended his close friend and secretary of state, James Madison, as the next Republican presidential candidate. Vice President George Clinton would remain as running mate.

Despite his résumé, the fifty-seven-year-old Madison did not necessarily make a good first impression. He was five-feet-four-inches tall, weighed less than one hundred pounds (his contemporaries referred to him as Little Jemmy), and suffered from numerous health complaints. He didn't like to make eye contact and his expression was generally dour; most portraits seem to capture him having just bitten into a lemon.

Yet first impressions could be deceiving, for Little Jemmy was extremely bright, with an astute grasp of the problems that faced the nation. And, if he lacked Jefferson's political charm and savvy, he did have another, quite valuable, asset: his wife, Dolley, who was seventeen years younger than he, beautiful, and vivacious—the Jackie Kennedy of her day.

As for the Federalists, they brought back Charles Pinckney and Rufus King—the less-than-dynamic duo of 1804. This time around, they didn't have to face off against the charismatic Thomas Jefferson. But in picking the same stolid candidates all over again, the Federalists showed they were a party in need of fresh talent.

THE CAMPAIGN By the summer of 1808, things were not looking great for the Republicans, mainly because of the embargo (many opponents called it the "Dambargo"). But with a possible war against Great Britain on the horizon, the country rallied around the party in office.

THE WINNER: JAMES MADISON Madison received 122 electoral votes, Pinckney received a mere 47. And, on March 1, 1809, the departing Thomas Jefferson gave Little Jemmy a gift—he signed a bill repealing the Embargo Act.

1812

AT A GLANCE

JAMES MADISON
vs. DEWITT CLINTON

J ames Madison was not a colorful man; he was often eclipsed during his presidency by his wife, Dolley. Historically speaking, the same holds true. In America's litmus test of enduring presidential fame—otherwise known as Show Me the Money—Madison's likeness can be found only on the $5,000 bill, a unit of currency that has been discontinued.

But much to the delight of giggling high-school students everywhere, Madison is renowned for the Non-Intercourse Act. Despite its name, this new law, pushed through Congress by Madison, took the place of the repealed Embargo Act. The much more sensible Non-Intercourse Act allowed Americans to trade with the whole world except for England and France; thus American merchants found other markets, particularly in the Netherlands, and prospered.

War with Great Britain was definitely in the air as the election season of 1812 heated up. In the congressional elections of 1810–11, a revolution had taken place. Half the admittedly creaky and aging House members were voted out, replaced by idealistic younger men like Henry Clay and John C. Calhoun. These War Hawks wanted England to pay for her insults over the years.

Madison understood that most of the country, along with the War Hawks, wanted to engage in hostilities with Great Britain and that it might behoove him to go along. He was nominated by the Republicans in May 1812. Since VP George Clinton had died in office just a few weeks earlier, the Republicans nominated Elbridge Gerry, former governor of Massachusetts, as their new vice president. (Gerry's energetic redistricting of Federalist voting areas is how we got the term *gerrymandering*.)

What happened—or didn't happen—with the Federalist nominating process provides the only thing that really passes for suspense in the election of 1812. The Federalists decided not to nominate their own candidate. Instead, they gave their support to . . . a Republican.

That Republican was DeWitt Clinton, mayor of New York City, nephew of the deceased George Clinton, and implacable enemy of James Madison. Like another Clinton after him, DeWitt figured he could be all things to all people. He would appeal as an antiwar candidate to Federalists, yet would also be attractive to New England Republicans sick of the "Virginia Dynasty" (that's how many described the choke hold the South seemed to have on the White House after the Washington, Jefferson, and Madison administrations). In August of 1812, the Federalists met in great secrecy and decided to tacitly throw their support his way.

THE CAMPAIGN Clinton's supporters presented themselves as the peace ticket, but they assured voters that, if Clinton were elected, he would still prosecute the war—only far more wisely than Madison (if you were paying attention in the election of 2004, this line of thinking ought to sound familiar). Clinton's supporters called the sitting president "a base wretch . . . who is for WAR," attempting to pound the drum of popular indignation. But since the war against Great Britain had plenty of supporters, the ploy was unsuccessful.

THE WINNER: JAMES MADISON After the electoral votes from the eighteen states of the Union were counted, James Madison was declared the winner, with 128 votes to Clinton's 89. Not then—not ever—would Americans turn a "war president" out of office.

This election heralded the beginning of the end for the Federalist Party. Over the next few years, it faded from the political scene. Ironically, this was partially because so many of the Federalist ideas had already been, or would soon be, incorporated into the fabric of American life—including a national bank, a standing army, and a strong central government to ride herd on unruly states. But, ultimately, the Federalist Party had allowed itself to become too narrowly defined—as the party of the rich and the powerful, as a group who cared only about northern New England states. As Americans began spreading out across the continent, they sought political representation that reflected a broader and more democratic view of the burgeoning new country.

1816

AT A GLANCE

JAMES MONROE
vs. RUFUS KING

E ven though the War of 1812 ended on a satisfactory note in 1814 with an American victory, Madison announced that he would follow the custom of leaving after two terms. James Monroe stood ready behind the throne.

Monroe was the last of the revolutionary generation of Virginians—Washington, Jefferson, Madison—to become president. He had quite a résumé: Continental Congress, U.S. Senate, minister to France under both Washington and Jefferson, secretary of state, and acting secretary of war under Madison.

Despite all that, Monroe elicited a general dearth of enthusiasm. He may have been honest and hardworking, but he clearly lacked charisma. Still, in the absence of fierce party rivalries, there was no need to trumpet Monroe's virtues (or those of his vice president, Daniel Tompkins). Voters didn't have much of an alternative.

The Federalists didn't even bother to make an official nomination, although three or four northern states got together and decided it might be a good idea if Rufus King, the perennial vice-presidential candidate, ran for president against Monroe. It was a half-hearted gesture from a dying political party. "Federalists our age must be content with the past," King sadly told a friend even before the election was over.

THE CAMPAIGN There was none. Rufus King sniped that Monroe had "the zealous support of nobody, and he was exempt from the hostility of everybody." This was accurate, but beside the point.

THE WINNER: JAMES MONROE A snap: 183 votes for Monroe, 34 for Rufus King. The "Era of Good Feelings" was about to begin.

1820

AT A GLANCE

JAMES MONROE
vs. HIMSELF

I n the inaugural address delivered by James Monroe in March 1817, he remarked how gratifying it was "to witness the increased harmony of opinion which pervades our Union. Discord does not belong to our system."

Spoken like a true Founding Father—they never did like those pesky political parties.

There's nothing like a successful war, economic prosperity, and a lack of Federalists to make a Republican circa 1820 feel good. As in the wilderness when the natural enemy of a species is removed, the predator-free creatures thrive.

The most contentious issue facing the country was that the North was rapidly outstripping the South in terms of population and therefore political clout. If the new states entering the Union from the Louisiana Purchase were admitted without slaves, the South would quickly become marginalized. The Missouri Compromise signed by Monroe divvied things up—states south of the 36°30' latitude could own slaves—but set the scene for further strife.

For now, however, all was well. Republicans nominated James Monroe for president, with Vice President Daniel Tompkins continuing in his role.

The Federalist Party, since it had ceased to exist, nominated no one. For the third—and last—time in history, a presidential candidate ran unopposed.

THE WINNER: JAMES MONROE James Monroe received all the electoral votes—well, all but one. A curmudgeon in New Hampshire gave his one vote to John Quincy Adams, Monroe's secretary of state, so that George Washington would remain the only president ever elected unanimously.

1824

JOHN QUINCY ADAMS

★ ★ ★ ★ ★ ★ ★ ★ ★ ★ VS. ★ ★ ★ ★ ★ ★ ★ ★ ★ ★ ★

ANDREW JACKSON

"Every liar and calumniator was at work day and night to destroy my reputation."

—John Quincy Adams

SLEAZE-O-METER

10
9
8
7
6
5
4
3
2
1

Like many presidents, James Monroe seemed to grow into the presidency just as it was time to leave office. His second term reached an apex in 1823 when he issued the historic Monroe Doctrine, in which he declared the Western Hemisphere closed to colonization by other powers. But despite this foreign relations coup, the real excitement during the second Monroe administration concerned the naming of his successor.

The election of 1824 had much in common with the elections of today, especially in that candidates began unofficially running almost the minute Monroe was inaugurated in 1821. One newspaper, the *Niles Register*, counted seventeen men who had thrown their hats in the ring; among them were some pretty influential personalities, including Secretary of War John C. Calhoun, Secretary of the Treasury William Crawford, former Speaker of the House Henry Clay, and Andrew Jackson, hero of New Orleans and supposed "friend of the common man." And then there was Secretary of State John Quincy Adams, the brilliant but aloof son of America's second president.

Crawford was considered the front-runner—Monroe himself favored him—and he was certain that when it came time for the Congressional caucus, he would receive the nomination over his rivals. But a funny thing happened on the way to the caucus.

Since 1804, small groups—or caucuses—of influential congressmen had picked the Republican Party nominee for president, but public sentiment was changing. Many Americans perceived the caucuses as elitist. Residents of new Western states such as Missouri, Kentucky, Tennessee, Ohio, and Illinois wanted a more direct say in electing the president and thus voted in congressmen who more truly represented their wishes. Certain states began to let citizens choose their electors by popular vote. Tennessee sent the half-literate coonskin-capped Davy Crockett to Congress, declaring he was every bit as good as some bewigged aristocrat from Virginia.

Realizing the times were a-changing, all the candidates except Crawford simply boycotted the caucus procedure, lined up their own support, and started campaigning. The caucus did choose Crawford as the presidential nominee, but it didn't matter. These were wild and woolly times; the American electoral system was reinventing itself, and no one recognized Crawford as the sole candidate. The so-called King Caucus system was officially dead, and it would never be used to choose a presidential candidate again.

★ ★ ★ THE CANDIDATES ★ ★ ★

ANDREW JACKSON Jackson was born in 1767 in South Carolina to poor Irish immigrant parents who worked a hardscrabble farm out in the boondocks, thus making him that most-coveted nineteenth-century commodity—a true "backwoods" presidential candidate (the first in American history). He was orphaned by the age of fourteen but became a successful lawyer, politician, and general; after destroying the British at New Orleans in 1815, Jackson became a bona fide national celebrity. He was tall, handsome, and—as many of his opponents on the battle-field and campaign trail discovered—extremely ruthless.

WILLIAM CRAWFORD Talk about a dream candidate: During Crawford's distinguished career, he had served as U.S. senator, minister to France, secretary of war (under Madison), and secretary of treasury (under Monroe). He was robust, good-looking, affable, and gregarious. Unfortunately, soon after being nominated, he suffered a stroke that left him paralyzed and nearly blind. Crawford eventually returned to work in his cabinet post, but he was no longer the front-runner for president.

HENRY CLAY A native Kentuckian, Clay had been the leader of the War Hawks in 1812 and was now a brilliant Speaker of the House. He was an ardent patriot who wanted a national bank and a standing army. He was also a debonair gambler known for holding card games that lasted until all hours.

JOHN QUINCY ADAMS Adams boasted distinguished bloodlines—his father was the second president of the United States—as well as a notable career. He helped negotiate the Treaty of Ghent, ending the War of 1812, and had labored tirelessly as James Monroe's secretary of state. Unlike his handsome opponents, however, Adams was short, bald, and had a constantly running eye. Even he described himself as "a man of reserved, cold, austere, and forbidding manners."

★ ★ ★ THE CAMPAIGN ★ ★ ★

In a word, nasty. Rumors were spread in particular about Adams—that his father, the aging former president, had broken with him politically and that he was selling future patronage appointments in return for votes. Yet people smiled to his face. "My complaint," he wrote, "is not that attempts were made to tear my reputation to pieces," but that such slanders "were accompanied by professions of great respect and esteem."

After twenty years of sleepy presidential elections, the pamphleteers were relieved to be slinging mud again. They satirized Adams's sartorial inelegance (he was, admittedly, an eccentric dresser—when he couldn't find his cravat, he'd sometimes tie a black ribbon around his neck), called Clay a drunkard, and accused Jackson of murder for having executed mutineers in 1813 (charges that would follow Jackson into the next election). Crawford—still running, even though paralyzed and sightless—was accused of malfeasance in his role as treasury secretary.

If all these charges were true, one politician said, "our presidents, secretaries, and senators are all traitors and pirates."

★ ★ ★ THE WINNER (EVENTUALLY): ★ ★ ★
JOHN QUINCY ADAMS

The voting of the presidential electors was completed in early December, and it soon became clear that there was still quite a horse race going on. Andrew Jackson pulled ninety-nine electoral votes (he also led in the first popular vote ever, although six out of twenty-four states were still appointing electors in their state legislatures). In close pursuit were Adams with eighty-four electoral votes, William Crawford with forty-one, and Henry Clay at thirty-seven. Since no single candidate had a majority, the outcome of the race would be decided in the House of Representatives, with each state delegation casting one vote. (John C. Calhoun did win the majority of votes for vice president, so his position was a lock regardless of who became president.)

The voting was scheduled for February 9, 1825, and the candidates set busily to work lining up support in Congress. Since Jackson had received the most electoral votes, many were saying that he should be president, even if the Constitution disagreed.

The matter was finally resolved when Henry Clay pulled out of the race. He would throw the three states that had voted for him—Ohio, Missouri, and Kentucky—to John Quincy Adams. Clay had probably decided that between Jackson and Adams, the latter would be more likely to strengthen the West by providing money for constructing roads and canals—projects badly needed in the outlying states. Of course, many speculated that the two men had embarked on a "corrupt bargain"—votes for Adams in return for a cabinet position for Clay—but Adams always swore this was not true.

In any event, when the vote came down on February 9, Adams squeaked out a majority with thirteen states, as opposed to Jackson's seven and Crawford's four. He would be president—and the next four years would turn out to be an almost unmitigated disaster.

★ ★

TO BE, OR NOT TO BE—PRESIDENT? Like a medieval prince or modern analysand, John Quincy Adams was prone to a deep ambivalence about success. At no time was this more evident than in the election of 1824. "Oh, the winding of the human heart," he wrote in his diary. "Whether I ought to wish for success is among the greatest uncertainties of the election." On the one hand, "the object nearest to my heart [is] to bring the whole people of the Union to harmonize together." On the other hand, winning and losing "are distressing in prospect, and the most formidable is that of success. The humiliation of failure will be so much more than com-

Fashion-conscious opponents argued that John Quincy Adams dressed too poorly to be president.

pensated by the safety in which it will leave me that I ought to regard it as a con-summation devoutly to be wished."

Somehow, one cannot picture opponent Andrew Jackson (who preferred beating up other people to beating up on himself) muttering away in like fashion.

CLAY VS. JACKSON Henry Clay did not like Andrew Jackson—in fact, he thought he was a rash and boneheaded military thug—and made no secret of the fact: "I cannot believe that killing 2,500 Englishmen at New Orleans qualifies for the various, difficult, and complicated duties of the Chief Magistracy."

JACKSON VS. CLAY When Adams announced shortly after the election that Henry Clay would be his secretary of state, Jackson told a friend: "So you see, the Judas of the West [Clay] has closed the contract and will receive the thirty pieces of silver. His end will be the same. Was there ever witnessed such a bare-faced cor-ruption in any country before?"

THE DUEL The election of 1824 was so contentious that a duel resulted from it. In April of 1826, the hot-tempered Virginian Senator John Randolph made a speech on the Senate floor accusing Henry Clay of throwing the election to John Quincy Adams—specifically, he called him a blackleg, slang for a cheating gambler. This was too much for Clay, who challenged Randolph to a duel.

The two met early in the morning at a deserted spot along the Potomac River. They took their positions, backed up by seconds who included Senator Thomas Hart Benton, but a comedy of errors ensued. First, Randolph accidentally discharged his gun and had to be given another. Then both men shot and missed. They reloaded, and Clay fired. His bullet pierced Randolph's coat without hurting him. Randolph paused a moment, then turned and deliberately fired his pistol straight up into the air.

"I do not fire at you, Mr. Clay," he said. The two men shook hands and were thereafter friendly acquaintances. Senator Benton dryly remarked that it was "about the last high-toned duel" he ever saw.

1828

ANDREW JACKSON

★ ★ ★ ★ ★ ★ ★ ★ ★ ★ VS. ★ ★ ★ ★ ★ ★ ★ ★ ★ ★

JOHN QUINCY ADAMS

"To the Polls! To the Polls! The faithful sentinel must not sleep—Let no one stay home—Let every man go to the Polls!"

—United States Telegraph

SLEAZE-O-METER

10
9
8
7
6
5
4
3
2
1

The election of 1828 begins with Andrew Jackson's anger. Jackson—the six-foot-tall ex-frontiersman hero of New Orleans, the man who as a boy of thirteen in the Revolutionary War received a saber slash across the head for refusing to shine the boots of a British officer, and who then survived smallpox and the deaths of his mother and two brothers, and who grew up to defeat not only the British in 1814 but also the Creeks, Seminoles, and Spanish—well, Jackson was not a guy you wanted to piss off.

But Jackson was convinced that John Quincy Adams had entered into a "corrupt bargain" with Henry Clay to win the presidency, and he was determined to make things right. Enthusiastically backed by his Tennessee delegation, which in its eagerness nominated him for president in 1825, Jackson resigned his Senate seat and went after the presidency with renewed fervor.

This spelled bad news for John Quincy Adams, whose presidency was off to a rocky start. On his inauguration day, Adams had to compete for attention with a traveling circus that had come into town—not an easy thing to do in the early 1800s. Then he and his wife, Louisa, discovered that the Monroes had left the White House in a shambles— the furniture was so battered, the place such a horrible mess, that Louisa actually invited members of the public in to take a look, lest she be blamed.

Adams began his administration with a number of blunders. In his first State of the Union address, he focused not on foreign affairs or the future of westward expansion, but on establishing a national observatory, a series of astronomical outposts that would be "the lighthouses of the sky." To his credit, Adams was far ahead of his time (he used the same speech to lobby for a regulated system of weights and measures), but this was akin to a contemporary president giving an hour-long State of the Union address passionately advocating the adoption of the metric system.

Things quickly went from bad to worse. The whole Adams administration, according to a sympathetic biographer, "was a hapless failure and best forgotten, save for the personal anguish it cost him." With cries of "Corruption and Bargain" ringing from Jackson allies in the West (who now included Adams's own vice president, John C.

Calhoun), Adams was on the defensive at every turn. No wonder he began to feel that he was surrounded by "conspirators," that he was being tried by a "secret inquisition." He was. A spiteful opposition in Congress thwarted him in matters both foreign and domestic.

With so much conflict and strife, it's no surprise that the Republican Party split into two factions. The National Republicans supported Adams and his vice-presidential pick, Treasury Secretary Richard Rush. They were the party of the old-line Republicans, the wealthy merchant classes, and the landed aristocracy.

Opposing them were Andrew Jackson and his running mate, John C. Calhoun; they were backed largely by the western small farmers and the eastern laboring men. At first they called themselves the Friends of Andrew Jackson, then Democratic-Republicans, and finally Democrats. This group would form the core of the future Democratic Party.

And in 1828, both groups would have to contend with a major change to the electoral process—the widespread use of the popular vote. The election of 1828 saw four times as many people casting their vote for president as in the election of 1824. All but two states (Delaware and South Carolina) would use this form of voting to select their candidates, which meant that presidential campaigns—crazy enough to begin with—were about to get a whole lot crazier.

★ ★ ★ THE CANDIDATES ★ ★ ★

DEMOCRAT-REPUBLICAN: ANDREW JACKSON The general—now sixty-one years old— was probably at the peak of his power. Driven by a belief that the White House had been stolen from him in 1824, as well as a sincere, life-long desire to wrest power from the privileged and place it in the hands of the people, Jackson envisioned himself as a president for the common man, leading with his beloved wife, Rachel, by his side. Sadly, only one part of this dream would come true.

NATIONAL-REPUBLICAN: JOHN QUINCY ADAMS It was possible that John Quincy Adams—also sixty-one—was running for president just for the sheer, stubborn pride of it, because the previous years had been no picnic. At one point, he was stalked by the first would-be presidential assassin, a crazed doctor who (in a day when any citizen could and did just walk into the White House to see the president) talked openly about killing Adams. To his credit, Adams met with the lunatic and gave him a stern talking-to. Not surprisingly, many historians now speculate that Adams was clinically depressed going into the 1828 campaign.

★ ★ ★ **THE CAMPAIGN** ★ ★ ★

With one party claiming to defend the nation against "howling Democracy" and the other battling "a lordly, purse-proud aristocracy," is it any wonder things soon became very, very malicious?

The campaign began in September of 1827, after both candidates were nominated (since each party still operated without national nominating conventions, Jackson and Adams were put forward in a series of special state nominating conventions and mass meetings).

Jackson had the immediate edge because he had understood the need for party organizations in each state. ("You must avail yourself of the physical force of an organized body of men," he told supporters.) Soon "Friends of Jackson" in all parts of the country were pushing for Old Hickory, the Hero of New Orleans. These "Hurra Boys" wrote political songs, printed pamphlets, and attacked Adams with a vengeance. "[Adams's] habits and principles are not congenial with . . . the notions of a democratic people," one Jackson supporter wrote. They spread rumors about his mysterious "foreign wife" (Louisa was English). When the president bought a billiard table and set of ivory chessmen for the White House, Jackson supporters accused him of purchasing a "gaming table and gambling furniture." They called Adams a monarchist and anti-religious because he traveled on the Sabbath. And of course he was smeared by his association and friendship with

Secretary of State Henry Clay, who supposedly owed his position to the "corrupt bargain." (Clay was not a statesman, snarled the *New Hampshire Patriot*, but "a shyster, pettifogging in a bastard suit before a country squire [Adams].")

Adams supporters organized themselves and returned fire. Jackson, they said, had aided Aaron Burr when the latter conspired against the union in 1806, invading Florida and nearly starting an international incident. They claimed Jackson had the personality of a dictator. And that he couldn't spell (he supposedly spelled Europe as "Urope").

The Republicans also published an extremely nasty but delightfully titled pamphlet called "Reminiscences; or, an Extract from the Catalogue of General Jackson's Youthful Indiscretions between the Age of Twenty-three and Sixty." It enumerated all of Jackson's purported fights, duels, brawls, and shoot-outs. It described him as an adulterer, a gambler, a cockfighter, a slave trader, a drunkard, a thief, a liar, and the husband of a really fat wife.

There was very little serious examination of the issues, such as rural America's desperate need of public works projects or tariff protection for New England manufacturers. Jackson was known for being evasive about his opinions—a fact that he tried to turn into a virtue: "My real friends want no information from me on the subject of internal improvement and manufactories. . . . Was I now to come forward and reiterate my public opinions on these subjects, I would be charged with electioneering for selfish purposes."

Adams's positions were well-known—he was pro-tariff and pro-public works—but his voice was lost in the din of battle. No wonder the guy was depressed.

★ ★ ★ THE WINNER: ANDREW JACKSON ★ ★ ★

Balloting took place on different days in different states, from September through November of 1828. Results indicated a clear victory for Jackson, with 642,553 votes compared to 500,897 for Adams. The campaign had been so bitter that neither candidate made the customary post-election courtesy calls on the other (and John Quincy Adams became the second American president, after his father, not to attend his successor's inauguration).

Jackson took the oath of office in March; the streets of Washington were filled with massive crowds of common people who had come from hundreds of miles away to view this historic day. Jackson supporters famously surged into the White House, wiped their feet on delicate rugs, broke antique chairs, and ate and drank everything in sight. Thousands of dollars worth of glass and china were broken, fights ensued, and women feared for their virtue. In the end, the exhausted Jackson slipped out the back door to a local inn to get some sleep.

★ ★

JOHN Q. ADAMS, PIMP When people really want to get dirty, they hit below the belt. In this case, Jackson supporters claimed with utter seriousness that the prudish Adams, when serving as minister to the Russian court of Czar Alexander I, had offered his wife's maid to the czar as a concubine. That there was a kernel of innocent truth here—Adams had introduced the young woman to the czar—made the lie easier to swallow.

ANDREW JACKSON, BIGAMIST The Republicans returned fire with a vengeance—targeting not only Jackson but also his wife, Rachel. She had been previously married to the abusive and pathologically jealous Lewis Robards, who had finally left her in 1790 to get a divorce. Jackson had married Rachel in 1791, under the impression that the divorce was final—only it wasn't, because Robards had delayed getting the divorce decree. This clerical oversight went undiscovered for nearly two years, and once it surfaced, Jackson and Rachel were forced to remarry, just to make everything legal.

Because of this history, Rachel—whom Jackson loved deeply—fell victim to the ugliest slanders imaginable. Republicans said that she was a "whore" and a "dirty, black wench" given to "open and notorious lewdness." "Ought a convicted adulteress and her paramour husband be placed in the highest office of this free and Christian land?" asked the *Cincinnati Gazette*.

Adams supporters hoped that Jackson might lose his cool and challenge

Bible-thumping Republicans described Andrew Jackson's wife as a
"dirty black wench" and worse.

someone to a duel—perhaps even kill one of his tormentors. But what happened was that Rachel, who was overweight and had some health problems, took these attacks quite literally to heart. In December 1828, after Jackson had won the election, she died of a heart attack. Jackson grieved profoundly and was as wrathful as an Old Testament prophet. At her funeral, he intoned: "In the presence of this dear saint I can and do forgive all my enemies. But those vile wretches who have slandered her must look to God for mercy."

MOST VICIOUS BROADSIDE Perhaps the nastiest political attack on Jackson was the infamous Coffin Handbill, a widely circulated broadside displaying six coffins under the headline: "Some account of some of the Bloody Deeds of General Jackson." It went on to tell the story of the six militiamen whose order of execution Jackson had approved during the War of 1812. The men were the leaders of a mutiny of 200 militiamen who thought their terms of service were up. The army disagreed. The men were court-martialed; nearly all were merely fined, but the six ringleaders were sentenced to death. Jackson signed the execution papers, and at the time, few objected. During the campaign, however, the Coffin Handbill painted Jackson out to be bloodthirsty and merciless: "Sure he will spare! Sure JACKSON yet / Will all reprieve but one— / O hark! Those shrieks! That cry of death! / The deadly deed is done!"

MOST COMPREHENSIVE WHY-YOU-SHOULDN'T-VOTE-FOR-HIM STATEMENT

This, from an anti-Jackson pamphlet, pretty much covers it all: "You know that Jackson is no jurist, no statesman, no politician; that he is destitute of historical, political, or statistical knowledge, that he is unacquainted with the orthography, concord, and government of his language; you know that he is a man of no labor, no patience, no investigation; in short that his whole recommendation is animal fierceness and organic energy. He is wholly unqualified by education, habit, and temper for the station of the President."

1832

ANDREW JACKSON

★ ★ ★ ★ ★ ★ ★ ★ ★ ★ VS. ★ ★ ★ ★ ★ ★ ★ ★ ★ ★

HENRY CLAY

"*THE KING UPON THE THRONE:*
THE PEOPLE IN THE DUST!!!"

—Anti-Jackson headline

SLEAZE-O-METER

10
9
8
7
6
5
4
3
2
1

One of the supreme ironies about Andrew Jackson is that although he was the first president to be born in a log cabin and saw himself primarily as the champion of the common man, his enemies in the 1832 election claimed he was a dictator.

After Jackson paid for the damage to the Executive Mansion caused by the *Animal House*–style antics of his inauguration, one of his first acts was to try to rid the Civil Service of incompetent bureaucrats with lifelong sinecures. Claiming that "the duties of all public officers . . . are so plain and simple that men of intelligence may readily qualify themselves for their performance" (translation: any idiot can do these jobs), he initiated what he called rotation in office. His opponents dubbed it the spoils system since, naturally, any fired officeholder was replaced by a Democrat. Only some 10 percent of federal officeholders actually lost their jobs, but the new president became feared throughout the bureaucracy.

The 1832 election would change the political landscape by introducing the first national party conventions—an attempt to regulate nominations currently being held by state legislatures, which tended to fracture into local, sectional disputes.

The first convention was held by the Antimasons, a third political party that had sprung up in opposition to such powerful secret societies as the Masons. Their candidate was the well-known orator William Wirt; the party was also the first to introduce such lasting convention features as the party platform and rules committee.

The National-Republicans—soon to start calling themselves the Whigs—held their convention in December 1831. They nominated Congressman Henry Clay for president, with former Attorney General John Sergeant as his running mate.

The Democrats met in a hotel saloon in Baltimore in May 1832, and naturally they renominated Jackson for president. Martin Van Buren was Jackson's handpicked VP. The Democrats also came up with an innovation in political conventions, declaring that the majority of delegates from each state would henceforth designate the single nominee.

★ ★ ★ THE CANDIDATES ★ ★ ★

DEMOCRAT: ANDREW JACKSON In many ways, Andrew Jackson was a hollow man without his beloved Rachel. Although he could be chivalrous and courteous in private, his public persona was increasingly cold, unbending, and given to fits of rage. In fact, much of the time Jackson's opponents gave in to him because they were afraid of his temper.

NATIONAL-REPUBLICAN: HENRY CLAY Clay was the silver-tongued senator from Kentucky who had been a bitter enemy of the Democrats ever since the election of 1824, when Jackson accused him of entering into a "corrupt bargain." He and Jackson had something in common, however. Both were dueling men—Clay had fought one against Senator John Randolph, while Jackson fought anywhere from two to (if you believed the smears proffered by his opponents) more than one hundred.

★ ★ ★ THE CAMPAIGN ★ ★ ★

The American public was decidedly uninterested in the election of 1832, and for two reasons. First, a deadly cholera epidemic had struck the eastern United States in the summer of 1832; most people found it hard to focus on politics with a plague in the land. Second, the main issue of the election was Jackson's attack on the Bank of the United States—an important concern, but not something that really drove voter turnout.

Alexander Hamilton, the first secretary of the treasury, had established the Bank of the United States to accept tax revenue deposits to fund the national debt and issue paper money. But Jackson liked coins that clinked and rattled in his pocket; he hated the Bank of the United States and, in particular, its president, Nicholas Biddle, a Republican old-money man. Jackson (with some accuracy) felt the bank was an elitist institution with too much power, one that made "the rich richer and the potent more powerful."

Republicans accused Andrew Jackson of being a petty tyrant—but not to his face.

He vetoed the bank's recharter, essentially trying to put it out of business. None of this made Republican Party hounds very happy. They began baying. "A more deranging, radical, law-upsetting document was never promulgated by the wildest Roman fanatic," wrote one New England editor about Jackson's veto. A mob of anti-Jacksonians went to the bank's headquarters in Philadelphia to announce that Jackson had "wantonly trampled upon the interests of his fellow citizens." Noah Webster proclaimed that in vetoing the Bank recharter, Jackson had announced: "I AM THE STATE!"

But Jackson continued the attack. He hated banks that issued paper money, or, as he put it, "wretched rag money." Jackson's followers made toasts to "Gold and silver, the only currency recognized by the Constitution." Jackson branded Nicholas Biddle as Czar Nick. (No wonder Biddle used funds from the bank—money deposited there by the U.S. government—to support Jackson's enemies, including Henry Clay.)

Republicans responded by tagging Jackson as King Andrew I. They also spread stories about Jackson's illnesses—his health, in the blunt phrase of former Vice President John C. Calhoun, was "deranged"—and attacked him for traveling on Sunday (ironic, since the same slur had been used against John Quincy Adams by the Democrats).

But Jackson's party organization won the day. One visiting French official saw a torchlight parade for Jackson in New York City that was a mile long. Jackson even won over Clay's home state of Kentucky, where one disheartened Clay supporter reported that large crowds of people held hickory bushes and sticks in honor of Old Hickory.

★ ★ ★ THE WINNER: ANDREW JACKSON ★ ★ ★

In the end, Jackson ran away with the election—he won 701,780 votes to Clay's 484,205. He had defeated "the overwhelming influence" of the "corrupt Aristocracy" of the Bank of the United States and continued—in a way that would influence the way Americans thought about their future presidents—to amass executive power for himself.

★ ★

LAMPOONING JACKSON Commercial lithography had taken hold in America in the 1820s, making it easier to turn out newspaper cartoons (before that, all illustrations had to be engraved or cut into wood or copper). And something in Andrew Jackson's tall, spare demeanor, with his Woody Woodpecker thatch of gray hair, made Republican cartoonists salivate.

During the campaign of 1832, Jackson was painted as a pig about to be dissected at a barbecue by a ravenous Clay and Webster; a decrepit old man playing poker with opposition candidates Clay and William Wirt (the cards in Jackson's hand read "Intrigue," "Corruption," and "Imbecility"); and as a king with a crown and scepter and royal robes, stomping on the Constitution and Bank Charter, under the heading "Born to Command."

ZOUNDS! Much like Thurston Howell III on the television show *Gilligan's Island*, Andrew Jackson was given to wonderfully apocalyptic oaths. "By Almighty God!" "By the Eternal!" and the Shakespearian "S'blood!" (God's Blood!). The only other president to match him for such rich cursing was probably Lyndon Johnson—in some ways, Jackson's twentieth-century counterpart—who was known to rip off a few really choice phrases from time to time (see page 229).

THE GALLANT JACKSON During his first term, Jackson lost almost his entire cabinet to the so-called Peggy Eaton Affair. When Jackson's close friend and Secretary of War John Henry Eaton married Peg O'Neale, the beautiful but notoriously not virtuous daughter of a Washington tavern keeper, the wives of Jackson's cabinet members and Vice President John C. Calhoun shunned her. Jackson—still hurting from the attacks made against his wife, Rachel—defended Peg as "chaste as a virgin," causing much hilarity among his enemies. However, Secretary of State Martin Van Buren saw this as a wonderful opportunity to forward his own ambitions for the presidency and so defended Peg Eaton at every turn.

The colorful Peg Eaton continued to be a legend in her own time. Her husband died, leaving her a fortune; later, as a much older woman, she married an Italian ballet master who turned around and ran off with her granddaughter.

1836

MARTIN VAN BUREN

★ ★ ★ ★ ★ ★ ★ ★ ★ ★ VS. ★ ★ ★ ★ ★ ★ ★ ★ ★ ★ ★

WILLIAM HENRY HARRISON

"... his [Martin Van Buren's] mind
beats round like a tame bear tied to a
stake, in a little circle."

—Davy Crockett

SLEAZE-O-METER

10
9
8
7
6
5
4
3
2
1

Congressman Davy Crockett accused Martin Van Buren of wearing women's corsets.
How would Davy know?

The year 1836 was a volatile time in American history. Davy Crockett fought at the Alamo in March; Samuel Colt received a patent for what would soon be America's favorite "peacemaker," the Colt revolver; and Andrew Jackson, gaunter and more pissed-off than ever, continued his campaign against Nicholas Biddle and the Bank of the United States. He refused to deposit tax revenues into the bank's coffers and instead placed the money into his own "pet" banks—institutions run by his cronies. (Naturally, many of these banks made unwise loans, and the government revenues were lost.) When his first two treasury secretaries protested against this plan, Jackson fired them and eventually found one who would cooperate.

Jackson followed the tradition of leaving office after two terms and made sure that Democrats nominated Martin Van Buren, his hand-picked successor. To do this, he insisted that the Democrats hold a national convention in Baltimore, in May 1835, a good year and three-quarters before the election. Van Buren was nominated in good order, although there were problems when Jackson pushed through the nomination of the vice-presidential candidate, Richard M. Johnson. Johnson was a hero of the War of 1812 Battle of the Thames, where he supposedly killed the Indian leader Tecumseh. But he had openly lived with a black woman named Julia Chinn and had two daughters with her. Because Johnson actually had the nerve to present his family in public, he was reviled by Southern Democrats who "hissed most ungraciously" when his name was presented.

Meanwhile, Jackson's enemies, the Republicans, had coalesced into a new party. The Whigs were composed of Republicans, Antimasons, and disaffected Democrats who shared one thing in common: their dislike of Andrew Jackson and his policies. The Whigs (named after the British Reform Party that battled for the supremacy of Parliament over the king) skipped a nominating convention and instead threw three candidates at Van Buren and Johnson, hoping to keep Van Buren from a majority victory and force the election into the House of Representatives. The Whig candidates were Massachusetts Senator Daniel Webster, Tennessee Senator Hugh White, and William Henry Harrison, the sixty-three-year-old former Indiana Territory governor and hero of the Battle of Tippecanoe. Of the three, Harrison was by far the strongest contender.

★ ★ ★ THE CANDIDATES ★ ★ ★

DEMOCRAT: MARTIN VAN BUREN Fifty-three years old, Van Buren had been New York's governor and senator and was a bit of a dandy who took on aristocratic airs, even though (or because) he had come from a very middle-class family—his father had been a popular tavernkeeper near Albany, New York. His chief qualities, according to both his friends and enemies, were his loyalty to Andrew Jackson, whom he served well as vice president, and his political astuteness (which is how he earned the nickname "Little Magician").

WHIG: WILLIAM HENRY HARRISON Harrison, a congressman and senator from Ohio, was the son of a signer of the Declaration of Independence. Despite a tendency to get into personal financial trouble, he was picked to run for president because he was a hero of the War of 1812; destroying the Shawnee Indians at the Battle of Tippecanoe had earned him the nickname "Old Tip." And having three or more Anglo-Saxon names has never hurt a presidential candidate—consider John Fitzgerald Kennedy and Lyndon Baines Johnson and George Herbert Walker Bush and . . . well, you get the picture.

★ ★ ★ THE CAMPAIGN ★ ★ ★

The campaign kicked into high gear early in 1835 as the Whig rag the *New York Courier* and the *Enquirer* got beastly on Van Buren, comparing him to "the fox prowling near the barn; the mole burrowing near the ground; the pilot fish who plunges deep in the ocean in one spot and comes up in another to breathe the air." One cartoon shows Van Buren and Harrison, both bare-chested and boxing. Van Buren, getting the worst of it, cries: "Stand by me Old Hickory or I'm a gone Chicken!"

Feeling confident of victory, Democrats had a hard time rousing their ire against the Whig triumvirate of candidates. They labeled them as "Federalists, nullifiers, and bank men," but otherwise depended, as usual, on their superb state organizations to carry the day for Van Buren.

But as with many elections that follow the presidency of a popular and charismatic chief executive, the 1836 contest was not so much about Van Buren or Harrison as it was about Andrew Jackson. If you liked him, you voted for Van Buren. If not, you went for Harrison or one of the other Whig candidates.

★ ★ THE WINNER: MARTIN VAN BUREN ★ ★

It was an easy victory for Van Buren, who pulled 764,176 votes to a total of 738,124 for all the Whig candidates combined. (The Whigs did manage to confuse the vice-presidential contest; since a clear majority was not attained by any one candidate, the outcome was decided by the Senate. They voted for Richard Johnson.)

The Whigs, however, were encouraged by William Henry Harrison's 550,816 vote count. And they knew that Van Buren's election win was a triumph of party politics and the power of Andrew Jackson—Van Buren himself did not inspire passion. It all boded well for the election of 1840.

★ ★

DAVY CROCKETT, ATTACK DOG When one reads about Davy Crockett's career in politics, one gets a very different picture than that of the honorable homespun hero of 1950s TV coonskin cap fame. Crockett was a Whig attack dog, the Ann Coulter of his time. In his insanely spurious *The Life of Martin Van Buren, Heir-Apparent to the 'Government,' and the Appointed Successor of General Andrew Jackson. Containing Every Authentic Particular by Which His Extraordinary Character Has Been Formed. With a Concise History of the Events That Have Occasioned His Unparalleled Elevation; Together with a Review of His Policy as a Statesman,* Crockett (or his ghost-writer) claims that Martin Van Buren "is fifty-three years old; and notwithstanding his baldness, which reaches all round and over half down his head, like a white pitch plaster, leaving a few white floating locks, he is only three years older than I am. His face is a good deal shrivelled, and he looks sorry, not for any thing he has gained, but what he may lose."

Crockett goes on to administer the coup de grace thusly: "Martin Van Buren is laced up in corsets, such as women in a town wear, and if possible tighter than the best of them. It would be difficult to say from his personal appearance, whether he was a man or a woman, but for his large red and gray whiskers."

Davy, unfortunately, was skewered on a Mexican bayonet before he could observe whether his skewering of Van Buren hit home.

OLD EXECUTIONERS NEVER DIE, THEY JUST . . . WISH THEY HAD KILLED MORE On the day after Van Buren's inauguration, Andrew Jackson sat reminiscing over his presidency with a friend. He remarked that he had only two regrets. One, he should have shot Henry Clay. Two, it would have been nice if he'd had a chance to hang John C. Calhoun.

1840

WILLIAM HENRY HARRISON

★ ★ ★ ★ ★ ★ ★ ★ ★ ★ VS. ★ ★ ★ ★ ★ ★ ★ ★ ★ ★

MARTIN VAN BUREN

"Passion and prejudice properly aroused and directed would do about as well as principle and reason in a party contest."

—Thomas Elder, Whig politician

SLEAZE-O-METER

10
9
8
7
6
5
4
3
2
1

M artin Van Buren didn't know it when he entered the presidency, but he was a "gone chicken" before he had barely begun—all thanks to the Panic of 1837, the worst economic recession the country had yet seen, and the reason why the Whigs started joking about Martin Van Ruin.

That this panic was partially the result of Andrew Jackson's monetary policies made things even worse for Van Buren. Under Jackson, the United States government made millions of dollars by selling land to speculators. The government then deposited the money in Jackson's "pet" banks—run by his cronies—instead of the Bank of the United States, which Jackson had gutted. These local banks made large loans, often to speculators who bought even more land from the government. Add to this vicious circle high inflation, a crop failure in 1835, and a new "hard money" law forcing banks to repay money borrowed from the government in specie rather than currency, and by the summer of 1837 America's economic life had ground to a standstill. The panic would last several years, forcing factories to close and sending families to beg on the streets.

The Whigs held their first national nominating convention in December of 1839, in Harrisburg, Pennsylvania. A strange thing happened—the boisterous convention, attended by farmers, disgruntled bankers, protariff and antitariff forces, slaveholders and abolitionists, resembled nothing more than a passionate Democratic rally. Henry Clay hoped to be the Whig candidate (a young Illinois lawyer in attendance, Abraham Lincoln, pronounced him the "beau ideal of a statesman"), but because Clay was a Mason, the Antimasons would not vote for him. The nomination instead went to Old Tip, William Henry Harrison. His vice-presidential ticket-balancer was Virginia Senator John Tyler.

The Democrats knew they were in trouble when they met in Baltimore in May to pick their candidate—and thousands of Whigs were waiting for them in the streets, marching and chanting:

With Tip and Tyler
We'll bust Van's biler.

Well, maybe you had to be there, but the demonstration certainly got the Democrats' attention. The times they were a-changin' but Van Buren won the nomination anyway. Many Democrats balked once again at Richard Johnson (who "openly and shamefully lives in adultery with a buxom young negro," as one anonymous letter writer had it), but in the end, Johnson was nominated as well.

★ ★ ★ THE CANDIDATES ★ ★ ★

DEMOCRAT: MARTIN VAN BUREN Van Buren was basically a decent guy with a lot of government experience who didn't know how to handle an economic crisis. And after four years in the presidency, many people still perceived him as Andrew Jackson's lackey. The first cartoon portraying the Democratic Party as a donkey appeared during this election. Jackson rode the beast, Van Buren walked behind it, hat in hand, saying obsequiously, "I shall tread in the footsteps of my illustrious predecessor."

WHIG: WILLIAM HENRY HARRISON At age sixty-eight, Harrison was getting up there in years, but his reputation as war hero still inspired a great deal of loyalty. And much like George Herbert Bush would one day transform himself from New England preppie to Texas "aw-shucks" oilman, this Virginia aristocrat portrayed himself as a "just-folks" guy with a log cabin constituency. Voters bought it.

★ ★ ★ THE CAMPAIGN ★ ★ ★

The Whigs were handed a wonderful gift at the beginning of the 1840 campaign. Just after their convention, the *Baltimore Republican* published a remark supposedly made by a Whig backer of Henry Clay about Harrison: "Give him a barrel of hard cider and settle a pension of two thousand a year on him and, my word for it, he would sit the remainder of his days in a log cabin, by the side of a 'sea-coal' fire, and study moral philosophy."

Whigs claimed that their candidate, Virginia aristocrat William Henry Harrison, was just a good ol' country boy.

This was meant to be an insult, but the Whigs turned it into the campaign's greatest asset. In almost no time, Harrison became the "log cabin and hard cider" candidate, a guy who hung out with the coonskin cap boys, plowed the back forty with his own hands, and was always ready to raise a glass of cider. Never mind his Virginia ancestry and ownership of at least 2,000 acres—Harrison was now a man of the people. The Whigs organized huge rallies attended by thousands of people and held parades four and five miles long. The log cabin symbol was everywhere: There were log-cabin-shaped newspapers, songbooks, pamphlets, and badges. You could buy Log Cabin Emollient or whiskey in log-cabin-shaped bottles from the E.C. Booz distillery (incidentally, this is how the word *booze* entered the English language).

The Democrats protested, mostly in vain, that Harrison wasn't born in a log cabin, didn't drink hard cider, and, when you came right down to it, wasn't much of a war hero (a mediocre strategist, Harrison sustained heavy casualties in the fight at Tippecanoe). It didn't do a bit of good. Crying "Tippecanoe and Tyler, too!" the Whigs charged onward. Because Democrats whispered that Harrison did nothing without his political handlers—that he was "An Old Gentleman in Leading Strings"—the Whigs had their candidate make a few stump speeches (he was the first presidential candidate ever to do so). Democrats groaned that the man talked about nothing at all, but crowds gathered everywhere to hear him.

★ THE WINNER: WILLIAM HENRY HARRISON ★

The popular vote was closer than some people expected: Harrison's 1,275,390 votes won out over Van Buren's 1,128,854. But Old Tip killed in the Electoral College, 234 votes to the president's 60. An incredible 78 percent of eligible voters turned out.

The contest had been so vitriolic that there was no kissing and making up afterward. "We have been sung down, lied down, and drunk down," wrote the *Wheeling Times*. "Right joyous are we that the campaign of 1840 is closed." The Whigs were not exactly gracious in victory.

Harrison's election, they proclaimed, was proof that voters had "placed their seal of condemnation upon a band of the most desperate, aspiring and unprincipled demagogues that ever graced the annals of despotism."

★ ★

RUNNING OFF AT THE MOUTH A congressman named Charles Ogle made a three-day-long speech in the House of Representatives, arguing that the White House was "as splendid as that of the Caesars, and as richly adorned as the proudest Asiatic mansion." According to Ogle, Van Buren had mirrors nine feet high, slept on fine French linens, ate from silver plates with forks of gold, and—most incredibly—constructed on the White House grounds a pair of "clever sized hills" that resembled "an Amazon's bosom, with a miniature knoll on its apex, to denote the nipple."

These were, as Democrats and even some horrified Whigs protested, some of the strangest and most twisted lies that were ever argued in the House of Representatives. Nevertheless, the speech was distributed nationwide and further set up the dichotomy between the supposedly aristocratic Van Buren and his supposedly countrified opponent Harrison.

MUM'S THE WORD The Democrats attacked Harrison for the way his handlers—among them Thurlow Weed, the brilliant Tammany operative who was managing the campaign—kept him from replying to even the most innocuous queries about political issues. Was "Granny Harrison" senile? Was he a "man in an iron cage"? The Whigs denied these charges, but in private, the prominent Whig Nicholas Biddle cautioned, "Let the use of pen and ink be wholly forbidden [to Harrison] as if he were a mad poet in Bedlam."

OLD KINDERHOOK, OKAY? The election of 1840 may have given America its enduring expression "okay." Since Van Buren hailed from Kinderhook, New York, some of his supporters started a new organization called the O.K. Club to promote Van Buren's candidacy—O.K. standing for Old Kinderhook. Some etymologists believe that the phrase existed before Van Buren's campaign (many believe that it began as an abbreviation of "all correct"), but the boy from Old Kinderhook certainly helped popularize the expression.

1844

JAMES K. POLK

★ ★ ★ ★ ★ ★ ★ ★ ★ ★ VS. ★ ★ ★ ★ ★ ★ ★ ★ ★ ★ ★ ★

HENRY CLAY

"A more ridiculous, contemptible, and forlorn candidate was never put forth by any party."

—*New York Herald*, on James Polk

SLEAZE-O-METER

10
9
8
7
6
5
4
3
2
1

U nfortunately for the Whigs, the good times stopped rolling very, very quickly. One month into his term, William Henry Harrison was dead of pneumonia supposedly brought on by speaking for more than one hundred minutes without hat or coat as he made his inaugural address on a blustery March day.

The Whigs were bereft, the Democrats joyous. So strong still were the ill feelings lingering from 1840 that most Democrats did not even pause for a hypocritical moment of silence for the fallen president. Poet William Cullen Bryant said he regretted Harrison's death only because "he did not live long enough to prove his incapacity for the office of President." And former president Andrew Jackson turned his eyes heavenward, calling Harrison's death "the deed of a kind and over-ruling Providence."

The Whigs turned to John Tyler, the first vice president ever to replace a sitting president, a man whom John Quincy Adams tartly dubbed "His Accidency." What occured proved to future political generations that choosing a vice-presidential candidate is a lot like picking a spouse—after the honeymoon, things change.

Once in power, Tyler started acting far more like a Democrat than the "firm and decided" Whig he had declared himself to be. He vetoed a Whig bill for a new Bank of the United States (to replace the one Jackson had gutted) and went head-to-head with Whig leader Henry Clay, who resigned his Senate seat in protest. All but one member of Tyler's cabinet would soon quit; essentially, the party disowned its own president, declaring in an extraordinary statement: "Those who bought the President into power can no longer, in any manner or degree, be justly held responsible or blamed for [his actions]."

Naturally, Tyler's chances of being Whig candidate for president in 1844 were less than zero. He made overtures to the Democrats, but they didn't trust him either, and so he was left out in the cold. But he still had one surprise up his sleeve. In 1843, Tyler negotiated a treaty to annex the slaveholding Republic of Texas (heretofore, because of the volatile slavery issue, the Texas situation had been sidestepped by both parties). But Tyler put a patriotic spin on the debate—if we don't grab Texas, he proclaimed, Mexico will. Although his treaty was vetoed by the

Senate in 1844, the issue of annexation was the pivot around which the election revolved.

The Whigs assembled in Baltimore on May 1, 1844, and nominated Henry Clay for president. For vice president they picked New Jersey politician Theodore Frelinghuysen, a so-called Christian gentleman who was supposed to balance Clay's reputation for high living, boozing, and playing cards.

The Democrats met a month later, also in Baltimore. Their convention was stormy, to say the least. Martin Van Buren was considered the front-running candidate, but many didn't like that he opposed the annexation of Texas. Finally, after eight rounds of balloting, former Speaker of the House and Andrew Jackson protégé James K. Polk was picked as a compromise candidate. The vice-presidential nod went to Pennsylvania lawyer George M. Dallas.

★ ★ ★ THE CANDIDATES ★ ★ ★

DEMOCRAT: JAMES K. POLK James K. Who? That's what most Americans were saying after the Democratic pick was announced. But Polk, former governor of Tennessee as well as House Speaker, was admired by many Democrats as a solid and loyal party member. Not surprisingly, the Whigs hated him. On Polk's last day as Speaker, Henry Clay had made a special trip over from the Senate to shout from the visitor's gallery: "Go home, God damn you. Go home where you belong!"

WHIG: HENRY CLAY Clay had influenced American politics for twenty-five years as Speaker, senator, and party leader. This was his third try for the presidency, after 1824 and 1832, and he wanted it badly.

★ ★ ★ THE CAMPAIGN ★ ★ ★

The Whigs immediately targeted Polk's obscurity and made derisive comments to newspaper editors all over the country: "Who is James K.

Democrats warned that Henry Clay spent "his days at a gambling table and his nights in a brothel."

Polk?" they cried. "Good God, what a nomination!" They claimed that the very raccoons in the forests of Tennessee were now singing: "Ha, ha, ha, what a nominee / Is Jimmy Polk of Tennessee!"

You couldn't call Henry Clay obscure, but the Democrats fired back at something else—the candidate's supposed baggage train of gambling, dueling, womanizing, and "By the Eternal!" swearing. An alleged Protestant minister wrote a letter published in numerous Democratic papers claiming to have heard Clay curse extensively during a steamboat trip. A popular leaflet titled *Twenty-One Reasons Why Clay Should Not Be Elected* listed as reason two that "Clay spends his days at the gambling table and his nights in a brothel." Clay was also accused of being a white slaver, and the Democrats hammered again at the "corrupt bargain" that he and John Quincy Adams supposedly had made to steal the presidency from Jackson in 1824. Not much was true, but Clay played enough cards and drank enough liquor for the mud to stick. It was much harder to slander James K. Polk, a man so thoroughly colorless that his nickname was "Polk the Plodder."

The Whigs tried to brand Polk as a man who owned slaves to elicit votes from abolitionists, but this was a little tricky since both Polk and Clay were slave owners. The Whigs got around this technicality by claiming that it was all a matter of degree—that Polk was really an *ultra* slaveholder, in slavery "up to his ears." One Whig newspaper claimed that Polk had branded the initials J.K.P onto the shoulders of a group of forty of his slaves. This was so patently untrue that the paper later printed a retraction.

★ ★ ★ **THE WINNER: JAMES K. POLK** ★ ★ ★

The term *Manifest Destiny* was not coined by New York journalist John L. O'Sullivan until 1845, but that's what the 1844 election was all about. Polk was firmly in favor of annexation—not only of Texas but of Oregon Territory as well—hence his famous campaign slogan, "Fifty-four Forty or Fight!" which referred to the northernmost latitude to which America should extend. Clay waffled on annexation, which cost

Southern votes and annoyed Northerners. And there was one other factor, an effective third party outing by the Liberty Party of New York— a group of Abolitionists and radicals—who garnered 62,000 votes nationwide.

In the end, Polk beat Clay by only about 39,000 popular votes, although he bested him in the Electoral College 170 to 105.

★ ★

THE NASTY PERSONAL SMEAR THAT HENRY CLAY ONLY WISHED WERE TRUE Democrats accused Clay, an admitted lover of gambling, of having invented poker. In fact, Clay was only a superb practitioner of the newfangled bluffing card game, which was based on the English game of brag.

HEY, GO EASY ON THAT STUFF! In desperation to find something to smear Polk with, Sam Houston, hero of the Texas war against Mexico, proclaimed that moderate drinker Polk was "victim of the use of water as a beverage." This tactic— attacking a candidate for not drinking enough—was unsuccessful and rarely used in subsequent presidential smear campaigns.

VOTER FRAUD, 1844-STYLE Since Polk had Scotch-Irish heritage, a group of key New York City Democrats used their influence to naturalize thousands of Irish immigrants, eager to have them vote in the election. The Whigs quickly pounced on these newly registered voters, telling them that Clay's name was actually "Patrick O'Clay."

And in what is probably the first incident of floating voter fraud, a Democratic Party boss in New Orleans sent a boatload of Democrats up the Mississippi River. They stopped and voted in three different places.

ZACHARY TAYLOR
vs. LEWIS CASS

Historians may say that Jimmy Polk lacked personality (all right, they actually say that he was "colorless and methodical," "a loner," "not well liked," a "stern task-master," "inflexible," and "Puritanical"), but they all agree he worked his butt off. Elected at the age of forty-nine, Polk was the youngest president to date; he regularly put in ten to twelve hours a day and held two cabinet meetings a week. Polk put it this way: "No President who performs his duty faithfully and conscientiously can have any leisure."

Just how faithfully Polk performed can be judged by the fact that of the four goals he set for himself in the presidency—reducing the tariff, re-establishing an independent treasury (a way to get money out of the hands of private banks without a national bank), acquiring Oregon from the British, and acquiring California from Mexico—he accomplished the first three in a year.

The last required a "small war," as Polk called it, against Mexico. It turned out to be bigger and bloodier than Polk expected. The Mexicans lost all the major battles but simply would not surrender. The nation grew increasingly tired of dead bodies coming back home. By 1848, the war was won and the United States was significantly larger—but the damage to Polk's popularity was considerable.

Big and bloody conflicts such as the war with Mexico often make heroes out of military men—who then run for president. This was the case with General Zachary Taylor, "Old Rough and Ready," hero of the battle of Buena Vista. The Whigs nominated Taylor for president when they convened in Philadelphia in June of 1847. His running mate was Millard Fillmore, former congressman and comptroller of New York State.

The Democrats were having a much harder time finding a candidate. Polk had made few friends in his own party and decided not to run for re-election. The best the Democrats could come up with was Lewis Cass, former Michigan governor and U.S. senator, who picked General William O. Butler, another Mexican war hero, as his vice president.

THE CAMPAIGN The sixty-four-year-old Taylor had the perfect voting record for a presidential candidate—he had never voted once, for anyone. He was as middle-of-the-road as you could get. He was a Southerner but not too much of a slaveholder; he was a war hero but not a man who started a war; he was a Whig but, as Taylor himself put it, "not an ultra Whig." No one could tell what "Old Rough and Ready" was thinking, but a few suspected the answer was "not much."

Lewis Cass was a nice enough fellow and had a distinguished career, but his name rhymed with both "ass" and "gas." Predictably enough, he was depicted in cartoons as "General Gass," with cannons farting noxious fumes out of his belly, or as "The Gas Bag," with an enormous rear end, ready to lift off into the sky, like a hot-air balloon. Whigs claimed that Cass had sold white men into slavery (not true). Whigs also said that he was guilty of graft in a previous job as superintendent of Indian Affairs—another lie. Finally, they just gave up and called him a "pot-bellied, mutton-headed cucumber," which seemed to sum it all up.

Taylor also received his fair share of abuse. One cartoon showed a phrenologist measuring his head with a pair of calipers. The good scientist's judgment? Taylor was "Obstinate and Mulish" as well as "Utterly wanting in all Sympathy."

THE WINNER: ZACHARY TAYLOR With everyone now voting on November 7 because of a newly enacted federal law, Taylor was the victor, winning the election 1,361,393 votes to Cass's 1,223,460. It was close, though mainly because Martin Van Buren had leapt into the race with an antislavery splinter party, the Free Soilers, and garnered more than 290,000 votes. The campaign issue of slavery was quickly coming of age.

Interesting footnote: When the Whigs won, a Democratic appointee named Nathaniel Hawthorne was fired from his civil service position at the Salem Custom House. At which point the poor man had no choice but to write *The Scarlet Letter*.

1852

FRANKLIN PIERCE

★ ★ ★ ★ ★ ★ ★ ★ ★ ★ VS. ★ ★ ★ ★ ★ ★ ★ ★ ★ ★ ★ ★

WINFIELD SCOTT

*"Tis said that when in Mexico,
While leading on his force,
Pierce took a sudden fainting fit,
And tumbled off his horse."*

—Whig campaign song

SLEAZE-O-METER

10
9
8
7
6
5
4
3
2
1

Wow, those Whigs—they sure know how to kill a good party! Just a few years after William Henry Harrison became the first president to die in office, Zachary Taylor became the second. "Old Rough and Ready" gave his inauguration address on a raw, windy day in March 1849 and then settled in for about sixteen months worth of presidenting. On July 9, 1850, Taylor died of gastroenteritis supposedly brought on by eating tainted fruit and chugging iced milk and water after a blazing hot Fourth of July ceremony. Rumors lingered for years that he had been poisoned with arsenic, but these were disproved in 1991 when Taylor's body—now much more rough than ready—was exhumed, and samples of his hair and fingernail tissue tested negative for large amounts of the toxic substance.

During his brief tenure, Taylor faced issues regarding new American territories that would permeate presidential politics for the next ten years. The Gold Rush began in 1849, the population of California swelled, clamoring for admission to the Union. Henry Clay introduced his famous Compromise of 1850, which suggested that California be admitted as a free state, that New Mexico (which included present-day Utah and Arizona) be admitted "with no mention of slavery," and that a more vigorous Fugitive Slave Law be enacted.

Clay's Compromise pleased neither Northern radicals, who abhorred the Fugitive Slave Law, nor Southern ones, who were already talking about secession. After Taylor died, his vice president, Millard Fillmore, took over and supported the Compromise measures. Big mistake. In June of 1852, the Whigs held their national convention in Baltimore. A splinter group of more than sixty delegates opposed to the Clay Compromise threw their votes to the Virginian and Mexican War hero General Winfield Scott. Chaos ensued. It took fifty-three ballots, but, in the end, Scott triumphed over both Millard Fillmore and Nathaniel Webster. Secretary of the Navy William Graham would run as his VP.

Typically, the Whigs did not run firmly on an antislavery platform but waffled, saying they would support the compromise "until time and experience shall demonstrate the necessity of further legislation."

Things were equally chaotic on the Democratic side when the party met, also in Baltimore, to pick its nominee. This time, delegates bypassed party warhorses like Lewis Cass and James Buchanan and, after much boisterous debate, picked the little-known Franklin Pierce of New Hampshire. His running mate was Senator William King of Alabama. The Democrats came out firmly in favor of the compromise.

★ ★ ★ THE CANDIDATES ★ ★ ★

DEMOCRAT: FRANKLIN PIERCE Pierce, the son of a New Hampshire governor, was a good-looking and well-liked congressman and senator. He had fought in the Mexican War and, at forty-eight years old, was a relatively youthful presidential candidate. Yet he was dogged by alcoholism and tragedy, which (at this point) included the deaths of two of his three children. Pierce pledged, along with his party, to execute all the provisions of the compromise, including the Fugitive Slave Law.

WHIG: WINFIELD SCOTT The good general was sixty-six years old, six-feet-five-inches tall, and looked every bit the Mexican War hero he was. Scott was essentially against the compromise but waffled on his public pronouncements. Like Clay before him, and many a presidential candidate after, he would pay the price for being afraid to come down clearly on one side or the other of an important issue.

★ ★ ★ THE CAMPAIGN ★ ★ ★

Everyone is quick to congratulate a war veteran for bravely serving his country, until that same war veteran decides to run for president. Once your name appears on a ballot, all your so-called heroism is suddenly questionable. Franklin Pierce was attacked with as much vehemence in 1852 as John Kerry was excoriated by Bush supporters in 2004.

The attacks centered on an apparent "fainting fit" that Pierce had suffered during a battle in Mexico, after which he had to be carried to safety. Ignoring the fact that Pierce was in severe pain from a knee injury he had suffered the previous day, the Whigs had a field day. They called Pierce the Fainting General and asked voters if they wanted a coward for a president. In a Whig cartoon, General Scott rides a proud cock, Pierce a goose, while Scott sneers at his rival, "What's the matter, Pierce? Feel 'Faint'?"

The Democrats, for their part, assailed Scott as "Old Fuss and Feathers," a nickname given to the general by his officers, who saw first-hand that Scott was, to put it mildly, a bit of a pompous ass. Using his waffling on the compromise issue, they also took him to task for supposedly being a puppet of New York Senator William H. Seward, a radical antislavery Whig.

With the growing number of Irish immigrants in the country, Catholicism had also become a campaign issue. Democrats laughed at Scott's attempts to curry favor with Irish Catholics by telling them that one of his daughters, now dead, had been a nun. (The story was true, but it was such blatant pandering that it sounded like a lie.) The Whigs retaliated by digging up a clause in the New Hampshire constitution that prohibited Catholics from holding public office—and then they accused Pierce of writing it.

Scott went a step further by embarking on a speaking tour (still not common practice for candidates) to address crowds of immigrants. He spoke to his listeners with all the unctuousness of the most politically correct twenty-first-century presidential candidate: "Fellow citizens. When I say fellow citizens I mean native and adopted as well as those who intend to become citizens." When Scott heard an Irish accent, he would exclaim: "I hear that rich brogue. It makes me remember the noble deeds of Irishmen, many of whom I have led to battle and victory."

★ ★ ★ THE WINNER: FRANKLIN PIERCE ★ ★ ★

Scott's wearing of the green did him little good. In the end, Americans preferred someone who at least said what he thought—and perhaps some wished that Henry Clay's compromise might put an end to the battling over slavery in America. With thirty-one states voting, Franklin Pierce

During the War with Mexico, Franklin Pierce fainted in the heat of battle—and his political opponents never let him forget it.

took all but four, receiving 1,607,510 votes to Scott's 1,386,942. At his inauguration, the new president said: "I fervently hope that the question [of slavery] is at rest, and that no sectional or ambitious or fanatical excitement may again threaten the durability of our institutions."

★ ★ ★ ★ ★ ★ ★ ★ ★ ★ ★ ★ ★★ ★ ★ ★ ★ ★ ★ ★ ★ ★ ★ ★ ★ ★ ★ ★ ★ ★

THE WELL-FOUGHT BOTTLE Franklin Pierce was known to have a drinking problem, which he kept at bay as a congressman and senator by joining the Temperance League. But his alcoholism was fair game in the election campaign, just as Senator Thomas Eagleton's alcoholism and "nervous exhaustion" became an issue in 1972. The Whigs called Pierce the "hero of many a well-fought bottle" and kept at the issue ferociously during the entire campaign.

Ultimately, Pierce's well-fought bottle was a losing one—he died of cirrhosis in 1869.

IT HELPS TO HAVE A GREAT AMERICAN AUTHOR ON YOUR SIDE. OR DOES IT?

Franklin Pierce and Nathaniel Hawthorne were college buddies from Bowdoin and lifelong friends. In 1852, Hawthorne—thrown out of work by the Whig victory in the last election—wrote a campaign biography for Pierce, who rewarded him with the job of consul to Liverpool. Unfortunately, having the dark and self-doubting Hawthorne write a campaign biography is a little bit like hiring Franz Kafka to pen press releases for the Junior League. Below is an excerpt from the preface to *The Life of Franklin Pierce:*

"THE AUTHOR of this memoir—being so little of a politician that he scarcely feels entitled to call himself a member of any party—would not voluntarily have undertaken the work here offered to the public. Neither can he flatter himself that he has been remarkably successful in the performance of his task, viewing it in the light of a political biography . . . intended to operate upon the minds of multitudes, during a presidential canvass. This species of writing is too remote from his customary occupations—and, he may, add, from his tastes—to be very satisfactorily done, without more time and practice than he would be willing to expend for such a purpose."

Uh, thanks, Nathaniel.

1856

JAMES BUCHANAN

★ ★ ★ ★ ★ ★ ★ ★ ★ ★ VS. ★ ★ ★ ★ ★ ★ ★ ★ ★ ★ ★

JOHN FRÉMONT

"I did not intend to kill him, but I did intend to whip him!"

—South Carolina Congressmen Preston Brooks, after nearly beating to death Massachusetts Senator Sumner in the Senate chambers

SLEAZE-O-METER

10
9
8
7
6
5
4
3
2
1

P ierce was sworn in on a biting and blustery March day, with snow swirling through the air. Only weeks before, he and his family had been in a train accident. The only casualty was his eleven-year-old son, Bennie, the last of his children, who died in front of his eyes. His wife, unable to recover from the blow, did not accompany him to Washington, and Pierce, though deeply religious, became the only president in U.S history who refused to place his hand on the Bible during the swearing-in. Pierce's vice president—elect, William King, was not at the inauguration either. He was in Cuba, ill with tuberculosis, and died a month later.

Pierce took to drinking again, hard, and soon revealed himself to be a weak president who was unable to hold his party together. Democrat Senator Stephen A. Douglas of Illinois—interested in pushing through a transcontinental railroad that would please his powerful Chicago constituency—persuaded Pierce to go along with a bill that reorganized land west of Missouri into the Kansas and Nebraska Territories (soon to be divided into two states, Kansas and Nebraska).

In his desire to accomplish his goal, Douglas made the mistake of bowing to powerful Southern interests. At their behest, he pushed through what became known as the Kansas-Nebraska Act, which completely abrogated the Missouri Compromise (wherein slavery was kept to a line below latitude 36°30'). Instead, the states of Kansas and Nebraska would decide by "popular sovereignty" if they would be free or slave-holding.

All hell broke loose. The political parties split along slavery and antislavery lines. In fact, the Whig party simply disintegrated. Disgusted by election losses and the party's inability to take a firm stance against slavery, dissident Whigs and antislavery Democrats met in February 1854 in Ripon, Wisconsin, and formed a new political organization known as the Republicans, named in honor of Jefferson's old party. Gaining strength as more former Whigs (mainly from the North and West) joined them, the Republicans held their national convention in Philadelphia in June of 1856. For president they nominated John C. Frémont, hero of Western exploration, with Senator William L. Dayton of New Jersey as his running mate. The Republican platform was based on admission of Kansas as a free state and opposition to any new slave states.

The Democrats met in Cincinnati in June and ruled out any pos-sibility of reelecting the current president (one popular campaign slo-gan at the convention was "Anyone but Pierce!"). Instead, they eventu-ally settled upon James Buchanan, secretary of state under James Polk and Pierce's minister to England. Buchanan, helpfully, had been out of the country during most of the Kansas-Nebraska Act fight, and thus the public did not associate him with it.

★ ★ ★ THE CANDIDATES ★ ★ ★

DEMOCRAT: JAMES BUCHANAN Buchanan was a sixty-five-year-old bachelor and a frequent presidential contender. He had been a possible candidate for president in 1844, 1848, and 1852, but each time someone else had gotten the nod. This time he was, as one promi-nent Democrat said, "the most available and most unobjectionable choice." His VP was Kentucky Senator John C. Breckinridge.

REPUBLICAN: JOHN C. FRÉMONT Frémont was forty-three, handsome and dashing, and a former army officer whose pioneering exploration of the West earned him the nickname "The Pathfinder." The Republicans were determined to make Frémont into a political matinee idol; they sold poster-size colored lithographs of him for a buck apiece. John Greenleaf Whittier even wrote an adoring poem called "The Pass of the Sierras." His vice president was William Dayton, a former senator from New Jersey.

★ ★ ★ THE CAMPAIGN ★ ★ ★

The campaign of 1856 revolved around the very serious matter of slavery—not until the Vietnam War would one single issue so polarize presidential politics. The subject aroused so much passion among Americans that out-bursts of violence were common. Proslavery forces had made a bloody raid on an antislavery newspaper office in the town of Lawrenceville, Kansas, killing five men. In response, John Brown and his men attacked a proslavery town, killing five more—an eye for an eye, a tooth for a tooth.

Republicans held mass meetings and marched through the streets. They were joined by Northern thinkers and writers like Ralph Waldo Emerson and Henry Wadsworth Longfellow. Abraham Lincoln, who had been a potential Republican candidate for vice president, beat the drums for the party.

The Democrats responded by hurling the usual assortment of insults at Frémont. They said he was a drunkard, a slave owner, guilty of brutal treatment of California Indians, and that he had lied or exaggerated certain of his discoveries in the West. They parodied his election slogan of "Free Soil, Free Men, Fremont, and Victory!" chanting: "Free Soilers, Fremonters, Free Niggers, and Freebooters!"

But one thing they said about Frémont made sense to a lot of people: He was a polarizing candidate, too radically proslavery, and that his election would cause the South to secede from the Union.

★ ★ ★ THE WINNER: JAMES BUCHANAN ★ ★ ★

Almost 80 percent of eligible voters participated in this election, the third highest turnout in American history (1876 holds the record with 81.8 percent, followed by 1860 and 81.2 percent). James Buchanan won with 1,836,072 votes, compared to Frémont's 1,342,345. For the new and underfunded Republican Party, however, Frémont's very respectable tally suggested that 1860 might hold great promise.

★ ★

GAY BASHING, NINETEENTH-CENTURY-STYLE James Buchanan never married. His longtime roommate in Washington (then, as now, many congressmen shared apartments to cut down on costs) was Senator William Rufus King of Alabama. As far back as the Jackson administration, rumors circulated about a possible homosexual liaison between Buchanan and King. Andrew Jackson called Buchanan "Miss Nancy," and the nickname stuck. (Buchanan was a Jackson supporter, but Jackson disliked him in the extreme. He made him minister to Russia only because, he told a friend, "it was as far as I could send him out of my sight.") And Henry Clay liked to taunt fellow senator Buchanan to his face, saying, "I wish I had a more ladylike manner of expressing myself."

THE CRIME OF CATHOLICISM William T. Seward once said that John C. Frémont was "nearly convicted of being a Catholic." Frémont's wife (the daughter of Senator Thomas Hart Benton) was a Catholic, and in fact, Frémont had allowed a priest to marry them—for want of any other clergyman available. But Frémont himself was a staunch Episcopalian.

But in pamphlets like Frémont's "Romanism Established," the candidate was attacked as a secret Catholic, one who would surface after his election with allegiances to the Roman Pope. At the time, these were serious charges, and they hurt Frémont in certain political circles. But he felt that to respond to the slurs would be to give them credence, and thus he suffered in silence.

HANG IT ALL! James Buchanan suffered from congenital palsy that caused his head to tilt slightly to the left. Frémont supporters claimed the tilt was really a result of Buchanan's bungled attempt to hang himself—and a man who couldn't even do away with himself could not be president, could he?

Republicans claimed that James Buchanan had attempted suicide but was too incompetent to finish the job.

1860

ABRAHAM LINCOLN

★ ★ ★ ★ ★ ★ ★ ★ ★ ★ ★ VS. ★ ★ ★ ★ ★ ★ ★ ★ ★ ★ ★

STEPHEN DOUGLAS

"The conduct of the Republican party in this [Lincoln's] nomination is a remarkable indication of a small intellect, growing smaller."

—*New York Herald*

SLEAZE-O-METER

10
9
8
7
6
5
4
3
2
1

In 1860, the U.S. population was just over thirty-one million—and every man, woman, and child was waiting for the coming storm of a terrible war.

From the beginning, James Buchanan's administration was effectively held hostage by the boiling factional dispute over slavery. Two days after his inauguration, the Supreme Court handed down its judgment in the Dred Scott case, in which it declared that a freed slave who had moved back to Mississippi could be legally enslaved.

This meant that when it came to new states, all bets were off. No more Missouri Compromise, no more "popular sovereignty." If a man in Kansas or Nebraska wanted to own a slave, he could—no ifs, ands, or buts. The South was ecstatic, the North enraged, and political debate became tinged with violence.

The Democrats held their convention in Charleston, South Carolina, in April. Senator Stephen A. Douglas from Illinois—proponent of popular sovereignty, famous for his 1858 Senate race debates with his old buddy and adversary Abraham Lincoln—was the leading candidate of moderate Democrats. He refused to put a proslavery plank in the party platform. But the radical Southern delegates vowed that they would not apologize for slavery—in fact they would "declare it right" and "advocate its extension." Refusing to support Douglas, the delegates of Alabama, Mississippi, Florida, Texas, and most of Louisiana, South Carolina, Arkansas, Delaware, and Georgia withdrew from the convention—45 delegates in all.

Without the two-thirds majority required to elect a candidate, the Democrats were forced to adjourn the convention until June, when they met again in Baltimore. This time, they nominated Douglas for president, with Herschel Johnson, former governor of Georgia, as his running mate. The Democrats would run on a relatively moderate popular sovereignty platform.

When the Republicans met in Chicago—at the "Wigwam," a massive two-story wooden structure that could accommodate ten thousand people and was the first-ever building constructed especially for a political convention—they knew they were in a great position to win the election, thanks to all the disarray among the Democrats. As the convention began, the chief contender was William Seward, the former governor of New York and a powerful antislavery speaker, who had the backing of New York City boss Thurlow Weed and his Tammany machinery. So sure of victory were Seward's supporters that a cannon had been set up on Seward's lawn in Albany, ready to blast a celebratory shot at the right time.

But then conventioneers began to wonder whether a tall, skinny former congressman named Abraham Lincoln might be a good compromise. Lincoln, who was remembered for his debates against Douglas in an 1858 senatorial race, was the more moderate candidate that many of the delegates were seeking.

As the nomination battle heated up, dirty tricks abounded. Thurlow Weed promised $100,000 to the Indiana and Illinois delegations (which supported Lincoln) if they threw their votes to Seward. No deal. In return, Lincoln backers waited until Seward's delegates were outside marching in demonstration around the convention hall, then distributed counterfeit tickets to other Lincoln backers waiting outside. When Seward's men returned, they found they could not get back into the Wigwam to vote.

The Wigwam was set for a rocking, rolling, reeling ride such as would not be seen again in Chicago until 1968. When the voting began, ten thousand people were inside the hall, and another twenty thousand screaming and chanting on the streets. One observer described the noise inside the place: "Imagine all the hogs ever slaughtered in Cincinnati giving their death squeals together, plus a score of steam whistles going." After four rounds of balloting, the vote went to Abraham Lincoln.

Lincoln, waiting anxiously in Springfield, was informed by telegram of his victory but advised not to come to Chicago—Seward backers, many of them weeping profusely, were in such a state that it was not advisable for the new presidential nominee to meet with them. The party's judicious choice for Lincoln's vice president would be Hannibal Hamlin, senator from Maine and a friend of the defeated Seward.

The stage was now set for the most important presidential campaign in the country's history.

★ ★ ★ THE CANDIDATES ★ ★ ★

REPUBLICAN: ABRAHAM LINCOLN The six-foot-four Lincoln capitalized on his humble upbringing—unlike William Henry Harrison, he actually had been born in a log cabin. Living the hard-scrabble life in Kentucky, Indiana, and finally Illinois, he received minimal formal schooling but worked his way up to become a circuit lawyer, Illinois legislator, and congressman. His folksy exterior concealed a brilliant political mind that would prove to be his most valuable campaign asset.

DEMOCRAT: STEPHEN A. DOUGLAS Officially five-feet-four, although some estimates put him at no taller than five feet, Stephen

The Mutt and Jeff of 1860: The Little Giant and the Railsplitter.

Douglas was as short as Lincoln was tall. In fact, the senator from Illinois was known as the Little Giant. He earned the nickname as much for his bulky, boxlike torso and head as for his declamatory abilities and outsized political stances. "Let the people rule!" was his famous cry, and this meant allowing each state to decide whether slavery should be allowed within its territory. But for much of his political career, he had to keep hidden the fact that he had married a North Carolina woman who owned a large, slavery-driven cotton plantation.

★ ★ ★ THE CAMPAIGN ★ ★ ★

The Republicans held massive rallies and marches several miles long, with hordes of Wide Awakes—Republican faithful who would save the Union—marching with torches and likenesses of "Honest Abe." The Wide Awakes wore oilcloth capes and strange black enamel caps to protect themselves from dripping torch oil. In surviving lithographs, they bear a weird resemblance to certain members of the Village People. Boston Republicans organized a rail-splitter's battalion—in homage to Lincoln, every member stood exactly six-feet-four-inches tall. And throughout the campaign, Republican newspapers published countless jokes at Douglas's expense, such as: "Lincoln is like a rail; Douglas is the reverse—rail spelled backwards—liar."

The Democrats, at a disadvantage to begin with, tried to answer back. Lincoln, they said, had participated in duels. As a congressman during the Mexican War (which Lincoln opposed), he had failed to vote for provisions for the troops. There was a claim that he had slandered Thomas Jefferson by saying that Jefferson had sold his own children (by Sally Hemings) into slavery.

Lincoln denied these lies privately but was too smart to be lured into public debate. He remained in Springfield, while Douglas stumped mightily, riding a railcar all over the country. Douglas told audiences that a Republican win would mean secession. If only Andrew Jackson were alive, he bellowed, "he might hang Northern and Southern traitors on the same gallows."

★ ★ ★ THE WINNER: ABRAHAM LINCOLN ★ ★ ★

After November 7, when the votes were counted, Lincoln was the president-elect, with 1,865,908 votes to Douglas's 1,380,202. It was a
strong victory for Lincoln, but with a powerful quotient of caution—he
had not received a single vote from a Southern state.

★ ★

THEY'RE GRRRREAT! Lincoln did not debate Douglas during the 1860 campaign; if their 1858 debates were any indication, Lincoln would have come out on
top. Honest Abe could be quite droll; he had the habit of mocking Douglas's rolling
stentorian tones, sounding like Tony the Tiger as he satirized the Little Giant's "gr-r-
r-r-r-r-reat pur-r-rinciple" of popular sovereignty. What popular sovereignty really
meant, Lincoln pointed out, was that "if one man chooses to make a slave of another
man, neither that other man nor anybody else has a right to object."

THE LOST BOY Douglas took a lot of heat for his whistle-stop tour during the
election. In the next century, of course, such journeys would become a standard for
any presidential candidates—but back in 1860, they still felt unseemly. Douglas didn't
help matters by claiming that he wasn't so much electioneering as making a few
stops on the way to visit his dear mother in New York. It took him about a month
to finally see her, and Republicans wouldn't let him forget it. One pamphlet purported to be a "Lost Boy" handbill. "Left Washington, D.C., some time in July, to go
home to his mother . . . who is very anxious about him. Seen in Philadelphia, New
York City, Hartford, Conn., [and] at a clambake in Rhode Island. Answers to the
name of Little Giant. Talks a great deal, very loud, always about himself."

MUTT AND JEFF SQUARE OFF Lincoln took some hard hits because of his
appearance—he was gaunt and far taller than most people of his day. Photographs made
him look dreadfully serious, almost spectral. It's little wonder that Democratic papers
caricatured him with a vengeance. "[He is] a horrid-looking wretch," wrote the
Charleston *Mercury*, "sooty and scoundrelly in aspect, a cross between the nutmeg
dealer, the horse-swapper, and the nightman."

The Houston *Telegraph* added: "Lincoln is leanest, lankest, most ungainly mass of legs and arms and hatchet face ever strung on a single frame."

Not to be outdone, Republicans described Douglas as "about five feet nothing in height and about the same in diameter the other way. He has a red face, short legs, and a large belly."

THE RACE CARD
While Douglas waffled on the slavery issue, making such strange pronouncements as, "I am for the negro against the crocodile, but for the white man against the negro," Lincoln was plainly antislavery, which left him open to attack from racist elements of the Democratic Party. In one Democratic poster, he was pictured being carried into the lunatic asylum by numerous "supporters." One was a black man dressed in fancy clothes who was saying: "Da white man hab no rights at collud pussuns am bound to spect." And just to make the whole poster a little more offensive, the artist also included a feminist screeching: "I want women's rights enforced and man reduced in subjugation to her authority!"

1864

ABRAHAM LINCOLN
★ ★ ★ ★ ★ ★ ★ ★ ★ ★ VS. ★ ★ ★ ★ ★ ★ ★ ★ ★ ★
GEORGE MCCLELLAN

"It is not best to swap horses
while crossing the river."

—Abraham Lincoln

SLEAZE-O-METER

10
9
8
7
6
5
4
3
2
1

A braham Lincoln took office under stresses felt by no other president, before or since. A month after his inauguration, Confederate batteries opened up on Fort Sumter, in South Carolina, and the Civil War began.

America had had only one wartime president—James Madison—and the War of 1812 was nothing compared to this bloody struggle that threatened to destroy the American republic. Lincoln was forced to learn on the job; early results were mixed. As the war heated up, partisan politics in the North reached a temporary cease-fire. Lincoln's opponent in the 1860 election, Stephen Douglas, supported him wholeheartedly. But as the war continued and casualties increased, opposition to Lincoln was inevitable.

His chief critic among the Democrats was General George G. McClellan, commander-in-chief of the Army of the Potomac and the youngest of the Union generals. Lincoln had appointed "Little Mac" early in the war to replace General Winfield Scott, the aging Mexican War hero, who had a habit of napping during major battles. But McClellan turned out to be a disaster. He consistently overestimated enemy strength and moved at such a glacial pace that Lincoln once sent him a note that read: "If you don't want to use the army, I should like to borrow it for a while."

In 1862, after the bloody battle of Antietam, Lincoln fired McClellan, and the Democrats immediately starting talking up the embittered Little Mac as their candidate.

Lincoln now had problems within his own party as well. Many so-called Radical Republicans disagreed with his conduct of the war. They called him a dictator—and not a very good one. ("How vain to have the power of a god and not use it godlike," Senator Charles Sumner wrote.) They pointed out that in the previous thirty years, since Andrew Jackson, no president had served more than one term—so why should Lincoln be any different?

Even Union victories at Gettysburg and Vicksburg in 1863 didn't satisfy the Radical Republicans. They eventually splintered away to form a party they called Radical Democracy. Meeting in Cleveland in May of 1864, they chose the 1856 Republican candidate John C. Frémont as their nominee. Their platform demanded one-term limits on the presidency and congressional participation in wartime and reconstruction decision-making.

The Republican Convention was held in June, in Baltimore, and Lincoln was renominated. Still, no one was at all sure that he could win the presidency again. Despite Union victories in the summer of 1863, the war seemed to be turning in the Confederacy's favor. Countless party luminaries asked Lincoln to step aside, including Horace Greeley ("Mr. Lincoln is already beaten") and Boss Thurlow Weed ("I told Mr. Lincoln that his election was an impossibility"). Lincoln, understandably nervous, chose his running mate carefully—he picked Andrew Johnson, former Democrat and senator from Tennessee, as a ticket-balancer who might win votes in the border states.

The Democrats met in Chicago in August; the convention was controlled by antiwar Democrats known as the Copperheads. George McClellan was nominated as their presidential candidate, although he wisely refused to endorse the "peace at any cost" plank that Copperheads had inserted into their platform. His vice-presidential nominee was George Pendleton, a congressman from Ohio.

★ ★ ★ THE CANDIDATES ★ ★ ★

REPUBLICAN: ABRAHAM LINCOLN The fifty-five-year-old Lincoln looked much older than his age. He was worn down not only by the war but also by the death of his young son Willie, in 1862. Yet he fervently pursued his goals, issuing the Emancipation Proclamation in 1862 as he sought to find the right generals to conduct the war.

DEMOCRAT: GEORGE B. MCCLELLAN When George McClellan was first appointed commander-in-chief of the Army of the Potomac, at the remarkably young age of thirty-four, the handsome and dashing general wrote to his wife: "I find myself in a new and strange position here—Presdt., Cabinet . . . & all deferring to me—by some strange operation of magic I seem to have become the power of the land. . . . I almost think that were I to win some small success now

I could become Dictator." No wonder McClellan earned the nickname "Little Napoleon."

But the reality of McClellan was at odds with his image. He was a plodding general, insubordinate to Lincoln (whom he openly despised), and a divisive presence in the army.

★ ★ ★ THE CAMPAIGN ★ ★ ★

McClellan started things off with a bang: "The President is nothing more than a well-meaning baboon," he roared. "He is the original gorilla. What a specimen to be at the head of our affairs now!"

It was hard to match this level of rhetoric, but other Democrats tried their best. "Honest Abe has few honest men to defend his honesty," wrote the New York *World*, accusing Lincoln of corruption. They published a truly perfidious campaign biography, *The Only Authentic Life of Abraham Lincoln, Alias Old Abe*, that accused Lincoln of being interested only in the money: "Abraham thought [being president] was a good chance to make twenty-five thousand a year." The same circular went on to describe him personally: "Mr. Lincoln stands six-feet-twelve in his socks, which he changes once every ten days. His anatomy is composed mostly of bones, and when walking he resembles the offspring of a happy marriage between a derrick and a windmill."

A pamphlet war ensued between the two parties. In "The Lincoln Catechism, Wherein the Eccentricities & Beauties of Despotism Are Fully Set Forth," Democrats asked a series of mock questions:

Q. What is the constitution?
A. A compact with hell, now obsolete.
Q. By whom hath the constitution been made obsolete?
A. By Abraham Africanus the First.

Republicans fired back with "The Copperhead Catechism":
Q. What is chief Aim of a Copperhead in life?
A. To abuse the President, vilify the administration, and glorify himself.

In July, Confederate forces under Jubal Early came within five miles of the White House. Lincoln himself stood on a parapet to watch their battle with Union forces and was told repeatedly to seek shelter as bullets flew and the men around him were wounded. Despite his show of bravery, Early's raid was bad political news for the president, and he began to despair of winning the election. Late in August, he even made each member of his cabinet sign a note he had written indicating that they would cooperate with the new president-elect, whoever that person might be.

★ ★ ★ THE WINNER: ABRAHAM LINCOLN ★ ★ ★

Fortunately for Lincoln—or not so fortunately, considering that he would be assassinated in six months—the gods of battle finally smiled on the Union. In early September, Admiral Farragut captured Mobile Bay ("Damn the torpedoes, full speed ahead!") and Sherman marched into Atlanta.

When the tide of war turned, so did the election. In November, Lincoln easily beat McClellan 2,218,388 votes to 1,812,807. The soldiers of the Army of the Potomac, whom McClellan bragged would vote for him to a man, went for Lincoln by a margin of almost four to one.

★ ★

LINCOLN'S DIRTY TRICKS Most history textbooks portray Lincoln as a martyred American icon, but Honest Abe was not above a little double-dealing.

In 1864, Lincoln feared that John C. Frémont's third-party candidacy would drain votes away from the Republican ticket. With Senator Zachariah Chandler of Michigan acting as broker, a deal was struck—Frémont would withdraw his presidential bid if Lincoln would fire his controversial Postmaster General Montgomery Blair, who hated Frémont and the Radical Republicans. There is some doubt whether Lincoln knew about Chandler's actions ahead of time, but he certainly acquiesced once the deal was brought to him. On September 22, Frémont quit the election. On September 23, Lincoln fired Blair, using the excuse that the volatile Blair, on numerous occasions, had offered to resign. "You have generously said to me more than

According to one Democratic newspaper, Abraham Lincoln changed his socks only once every ten days!

once that whenever your resignation could be a relief to me, it was at my disposal." Thus was Blair disposed of.

Lincoln still, however, needed to please powerful Tammany boss Thurlow Weed and his New York City conservative Republicans, who in general were not fans of the president. To help his cause, therefore, Lincoln ousted several appointees in New York's Port and Custom Houses and replaced them with Weed's handpicked men. The New York *Herald* dryly pointed out: "It is remarkable to note the change which has taken place in the political sentiments of some of these gentlemen in the last forty-eight hours—in fact, an anti-Lincoln man could not be found in any of the departments yesterday."

Lincoln was also a man who believed in getting out the vote, in whatever way he could. On Election Day, he sent a federal steamer down the Mississippi to collect the ballots of gunboat sailors and furloughed federal employees in Washington, D.C.

IS NOTHING SACRED? After Lincoln delivered his famous Gettysburg Address, the *Harrisburg Patriot and Union* wrote: "We pass over the silly remarks of the President; for the credit of the nation we are willing that the veil of oblivion shall be dropped over them."

MIXED MARRIAGES Only Lincoln could have the charm to joke about interracial marriage during the Civil War and get away with it. Responding to continuous Democratic smear charges that Republicans favored intermarriage of blacks and whites, Lincoln joked: "It's a democratic mode of producing good Union men, and I don't propose to infringe on the patent."

LITTLE MAC TO THE REAR Republicans noted how far Little Mac kept to the rear of his army during any combat. Lincoln called the Army of the Potomac McClellan's bodyguard, and another Republican said that, during a retreat, "McClellan for the first time in his life was found in the front."

This was mainly a canard—McClellan had performed bravely during the Mexican War—but it was true that, compared to some Civil War generals, he did spend a good deal of time back with the camp wagons.

1868

ULYSSES S. GRANT

★ ★ ★ ★ ★ ★ ★ ★ ★ ★ ★ VS. ★ ★ ★ ★ ★ ★ ★ ★ ★ ★ ★ ★

HORATIO SEYMOUR

*"Grant has been drunk in the street
since the first of January."*

—Democrat attack on Ulysses S. Grant

SLEAZE-O-METER

10
9
8
7
6
5
4
3
2
1

Democrats described Ulysses S. Grant as a raging alcoholic, but voters didn't really care.

Some vice presidents—like Harry Truman and Lyndon Johnson—take a tragedy like the death of a sitting president and make the most of it. Others—like Andrew Johnson—well, they get impeached.

Not that it was all Johnson's fault. Abraham Lincoln was assassinated on April 14, 1865—among the most tumultuous and confusing times in American history. General Lee had surrendered to Ulysses Grant at the Appomattox Courthouse and the war was over—good news indeed—but now what to do? Many Radical Republicans, who had felt Lincoln was going to be too kind to the South, thought that Johnson should put down the hammer on the defeated rebels.

But Johnson quickly announced that he would follow the path laid down by Lincoln. He set the steps for Reconstruction by calling a general amnesty for all Confederate combatants, accepting back into the Union the "restored loyal governments" of Tennessee, Louisiana, Arkansas, and

Virginia, and moved to restore the civil governments of the other seven Southern states once they rewrote state constitutions to revoke slavery.

Johnson also put into place the so-called Black Codes—a very limited form of freedom for ex-slaves, which did not allow them to vote or acquire property. The Radicals wanted full civil rights for former slaves, including the right to vote.

Since Radicals controlled Congress after midterm elections, they set about voting down every one of Johnson's Reconstruction bills. When the president vetoed Congress, they overrode his veto. The battling got so intense that the Republicans finally assembled enough votes to impeach Johnson in the spring of 1868. They failed to convict by just one vote, but the president was effectively finished.

The Republican Party's new standard-bearer was Ulysses S. Grant, the plain-spoken hard-drinking former general whose dogged tactics and brilliant strategizing had won the war for the Union. His stature in America at the time is comparable to that of Dwight D. Eisenhower after the Second World War—the man was an icon. On May 20, four days after Johnson's impeachment trial, Grant was nominated for president at the Republican convention in Chicago. The vice-presidential nod went to Speaker of the House Schuyler Colfax.

But now the Radicals in the Republican Party, facing a national election, waffled on the "Negro question": full suffrage for freed blacks was supported, but it was declared that each state should be in charge of voting it in—an iffy process at best.

The Democrats—a party many now equated with the Confederacy—met in New York on July 4 in blazing hot weather. After twenty-one ballots, no candidate could be agreed on, and a dark-horse nominee was engineered by Samuel Tilden, the aggressive head of the New York delegation: New York Governor Horatio Seymour.

The reluctant Seymour became overwhelmed, first mounting the platform to decline the nomination in inadvertent rhyming couplet ("May God bless you for your kindness to me, but your candidate I cannot be."), then bursting into tears backstage ("Pity me . . . pity me!") before finally accepting the job. His running mate was Francis Blair.

The Democrats stood on a platform opposing the harsh

Reconstruction plans formulated by the Radical Republican Congress, wherein Southern states were organized into five military districts and corrupt legislatures, and the state governments were set up, which soon swarmed with carpetbaggers.

★ ★ ★ THE CANDIDATES ★ ★ ★

REPUBLICAN: ULYSSES S. GRANT The forty-six-year-old Grant, was of course, a legend—his career the stuff of American dreams. After graduating from West Point and serving in the Mexican War, he went through a period of obscurity in his father's Galena, Illinois, leather store before rejoining the army at the beginning of the Civil War and rising to commander-in-chief. He was the general Lincoln and the country had longed for. That he smoked, drank, and gambled to excess made things even better. In many people's eyes, he was, indeed, "United States" Grant.

DEMOCRAT: HORATIO SEYMOUR "The fault, dear Brutus, is not in our stars, but in ourselves." This line from *Julius Caesar* might well be applied to Horatio Seymour, one of the most obscure presidential candidates ever. Seymour was in desperate need of a good PR man and made a number of blunders. Aside from becoming weepy when drafted as the Democratic Party's presidential nominee, he also addressed a mob of draft rioters in New York in 1863 as "My friends," an opening gambit that calmed the crowd but didn't bring Horatio terribly good press.

★ ★ ★ THE CAMPAIGN ★ ★ ★

Republicans gleefully seized on Seymour's tentative acceptance of the Democratic nomination by mocking "The Great Decliner" in what became a famous little ditty:

There's a queer sort of chap they call Seymour,
A strange composition called Seymour,
Who stoutly declines,
Then happiness finds
In accepting, does Horatio Seymour.

Certain Republicans hinted that hereditary insanity ran in his family. And, of course, he was a Democrat—"Scratch a Democrat," the line ran, "and you'll find a rebel under his skin."

Republicans also went after VP nominee Francis Blair—a war hero from a distinguished political family. A private investigator discovered that Blair had spent two days in a Hartford hotel, where his room came to only ten dollars, but he spent sixty-five bucks on whiskey and lemons!

The Democrats were not idle, of course, and Grant presented an inviting target. Despite his many pluses, Grant's drinking became an issue. Even though many people, including reporters, had downplayed his bouts of blind drunkenness during the Civil War, stories abounded and his enemies called him a soak (slang for an alcoholic). One popular ditty went:

I am Captain Grant of the Black Marines,
The stupidest man that ever was seen.
I smoke my weed and drink my gin,
Paying with the people's tin.

The "Black Marine" slur was about Grant's supposed support for Negro suffrage, although Grant (and Seymour) tried to downplay this volatile issue.

★ ★ ★ THE WINNER: ULYSSES S. GRANT ★ ★ ★

It was closer than expected. Grant had refused to make speeches or really say much of anything (when cornered by a reporter at a train station in New Jersey and asked what he thought about his presidential prospects, he replied, "I don't think of it at all right this time. My principal object just now is to catch the train"). Grant had taken a trip to Indian Territory so that he could be seen with former Civil War heroes Sherman and Sheridan, but even then he refused to make speeches.

Meanwhile, three weeks before the election, Seymour hit the speechmaking circuit, in part because many Democrats feared a humiliating defeat and wanted to replace him with another candidate. These efforts may have helped, but they didn't help enough. Grant won 3,013,650 votes to Seymour's 2,708,744. For the first time in history, half a million blacks had voted—and it's safe to assume that the overwhelming majority went for Grant.

The Republicans finally saw self-serving benefit in the black vote; they pushed through the Fifteenth Amendment, ratified in 1870, which said that the right to vote should not be denied because of "race, color, or previous condition of servitude." Not until the Voting Rights Act of 1965, however, would many blacks vote freely in Southern states.

★ ★

GENERAL ORDER NO. 11 Grant was branded an anti-Semite, and the accusation has some basis in truth. His infamous "General Order No. 11" of 1862 began: "The Jews, as a class violating every regulation of trade established by the Treasury Department . . . are hereby expelled." The order was quickly revoked by Lincoln, but it became campaign fodder anyway. One might add that since anti-Semitism was so widespread in Grant's day, the people who were accusing him were probably guilty of it themselves.

THE NORTH'S DIRTY LITTLE SECRET In 1868, even though an entire war had just been fought over slavery, black votes were counted in only sixteen of the thirty-seven states. Eight of these states were in the former Confederacy. (Blacks were registered to vote in Mississippi, Texas, and Virginia, but the electoral votes in these states did not count because they had not yet been readmitted to the union.) Connecticut did not allow blacks to vote, and New York made ownership of $250 worth of property a requirement before allowing a black to cast his ballot.

1872
AT A GLANCE

ULYSSES S. GRANT
vs. HORACE GREELEY

Most historians agree that Ulysses S. Grant was an honest guy. They also concur that he had a lot of dishonest acquaintances. Among them were Jay Gould and Jim Fisk, a pair of financiers determined to corner the gold market. Gould and Fisk managed to befriend Grant's brother-in-law Abel Corbin and assistant secretary of the treasury Daniel Butterfield, who gave them access to the president. The resulting "Gold Ring" scandal reached into all corners of Grant's administration, as did affairs of the Whiskey Ring and Indian Ring. ("Ring," connoting a cabal of plotters, was the all-purpose scandal descriptive in the Grant years, much like "-gate" became the suffix of choice after the Nixon years and Watergate.)

Many Republicans—tired of the corruption and fed up with Grant's failure to reform the civil service and have any serviceable Reconstruction policy—wanted somebody else in his job. These so-called Liberal Republicans broke from the main Republican herd and sought an uprising of "honest citizens" to sweep Grant from office. They were a little like the reforming Democrats of the 1960s; but instead of trying to empower the common man they felt the "intellectually well-endowed" should rule government.

Holding their own table-thumping convention in Cincinnati in May, they nominated famous newspaper editor Horace Greeley for president and Missouri Governor Benjamin Gratz Brown as vice president. The Democrats, meeting a month later, decided to throw in their lot with the Liberal Republicans; Greeley became their candidate as well.

Greeley is one of the oddest candidates for president in the history of the country. He was a powerful newspaperman, the editor of the *New York Tribune*, and a crusading journalist—he had famously advised young men to "Go West." He was a balding, rotund vegetarian with tiny spectacles and big white sideburns—imagine a cross between a Dickens character, Truman Capote, and the musician David Crosby. And on top of all that, he was an atheist.

In the meantime, the regular Republicans, if you will, held their convention and renominated Grant. Knowing that smart positioning for his campaign would be Ordinary Guys Against Stuck-Up Snobs, Grant chose Henry Wilson of Massachusetts, a former shoemaker turned factory owner. Almost immediately, posters billing the two as "The Galena Tanner" (Grant's father had been a tanner) and "The Natick Shoemaker" started rolling off the presses.

THE CAMPAIGN With a legendary war hero running against an atheist vegetarian newspaperman, you can probably imagine how things went. New York Republican boss Thurlow Weed wrote to a friend, "Six weeks ago I did not suppose that any considerable number of men, outside of a Lunatic Asylum, would nominate Greeley for President." William Cullen Bryant echoed this sentiment, deciding that the only reason for Greeley's nomination was that "bodies of men as individuals sometimes lose their wits." For once, though, politicians weren't accused of being sots. A reporter wrote sardonically that Greeley's nomination had to be the result of "too much brains and not enough whiskey" at the Cincinnati convention.

THE WINNER: ULYSSES S. GRANT Grant won 3,598,235 votes to Greeley's 2,834,761. All thirty-seven states voted; thirty-one went for Grant.

"I was the worst beaten man who ever ran for high office," Greeley declared. And to make matters worse, his wife died just a week before Election Day. Soon after the election, Greeley began to suffer from hallucinations and was taken to a private sanitarium. "Utterly ruined beyond hope," as he wrote, he waited for "the night [to close] its jaws on me forever." He died November 29. Grant attended his funeral.

"Never in American history," wrote historian Eugene Roseboom, "have two more unfit men been offered to the country for the highest office. . . . The man of no ideas was running against the man of too many."

1876

RUTHERFORD HAYES

★ ★ ★ ★ ★ ★ ★ ★ ★ ★ ★ VS. ★ ★ ★ ★ ★ ★ ★ ★ ★ ★ ★

SAMUEL TILDEN

*" . . . it seemed as if the dead
had been raised."*

—Zachariah Chandler, Republican National Chairman, 1876

America's centennial year, 1876, was a time of glorious celebration across the country. From May through November, people flocked to Philadelphia's Centennial Exposition, especially to the vast Machinery Hall, which held thirteen acres of the engineering wonders of the age, including electric lights and elevators, as well as the typewriter, telegraph, and telephone. The visiting Emperor Dom Pedro of Brazil held Alexander Graham Bell's device to his ear and then immediately dropped it, exclaiming, "My God, it talks!"

The voice that shocked the good emperor signified American might and modernity—not to mention a century's worth of the grand triumph of American ideals and democracy. It is, therefore, quite ironic that one of the dirtiest and most brutal elections in nineteenth-century American history was about to occur. It is a further irony that both candidates, Rutherford B. Hayes and Samuel J. Tilden, were so-called reform candidates whose stated goal was to wipe out corruption in government.

In 1876, Ulysses S. Grant hungered for a third term, but the stench of scandal and cronyism hung so heavily over his administration that Republicans finally said *no mas*. In their convention in Cincinnati in mid-June, they chose Rutherford B. Hayes, governor of Ohio, who would run on a platform holding elected officials to rigid standards of probity and responsibility. His running mate would be New York Congressman William Wheeler

The Democratic Party was desperate for a presidential victory— after all, they hadn't won in sixteen years—and they were certain that they could take advantage of a Republican Party weakened by the series of corruption scandals that had rocked the Grant administration. They picked as their nominee Samuel J. Tilden, governor of New York. Tilden was the Rudy Giuliani of his age; as a crusading Manhattan D.A., he had smashed Boss Tweed's powerful ring of corruption and sent the Boss himself to prison. His VP was the Indianan Thomas Hendricks.

★ ★ ★ THE CANDIDATES ★ ★ ★

REPUBLICAN: RUTHERFORD B. HAYES No one ever claimed that the fifty-three-year-old Hayes was the most fascinating guy in the world. But he was a former congressman and honest-to-goodness Civil War hero (four times wounded), the happily married father of seven, and just about as hardworking and sincere as a politician could be. Hayes would often write notes to himself, accusing himself of not being thrifty or "prudent" enough and of partaking in "too much light reading." He prayed with his family every morning and sang gospel hymns with them in the evening—no heavy partying for this guy.

DEMOCRAT: SAMUEL J. TILDEN Tilden had a brilliant mind, but you wouldn't want him kissing your baby. He was an icy, aloof bachelor whose penetrating intellect made even his friends uncomfortable, and he was prone to bouts of ill health. And when he wasn't really sick, he imagined he was. An intense hypochondriac, he once visited his doctor every day for a month. One of his biggest political liabilities was that Tilden had taken no part in the Civil War—in fact, he had amassed millions from his railroad and iron mines during the conflict.

★ ★ ★ THE CAMPAIGN ★ ★ ★

Although the candidates were still not making public appearances, their political machines were percolating. Tilden began a public relations campaign to overcome his cold-fish image. Hiring editors, writers, and artists, he set up a "Newspaper Popularity Bureau," whose sole purpose was to manufacture the image of a warm and loveable Samuel J. Tilden; they issued press releases to newspapers all over the country. As the election heated up, Tilden created a so-called Literary Bureau in which teams of writers churned out anti-Hayes material, including a 750-page book that attacked Hayes for supposedly being party to Grantian scandals—"wicked schemes for speculation"—and for stealing $400 dollars from a Union

According to certain Democrats, Rutherford B. Hayes shot his own mother in a fit of rage.

deserter about to be executed. (Strangely enough, Hayes actually did take the money before the man was shot, but he passed it on to the man's family—a fact Hayes was unable to prove until after the election.)

But Tilden's dirty tricks couldn't hold a candle to those of Zachariah Chandler, the bewhiskered, bejeweled, and often besotted Republican National Chairman who was also Hayes's campaign manager. He kicked off the campaign with a fund-raising letter sent to every Republican appointee holding office: "We look to you as one of the Federal beneficiaries to help bear the burden. Two percent of your salary is __. Please remit promptly. At the close of the campaign, we shall place a list of those who have not paid in the hands of the head of the department you are now in."

Unfortunately, none of this bad behavior comes anywhere close to the dirty tricks perpetrated by both parties in the South. The Republicans—the party of the Great Emancipator, Abraham Lincoln—wanted freed blacks to vote and thus prodded many of them to the ballot boxes at gunpoint. Democrats in South Carolina and elsewhere started violent race riots, in some cases shooting and killing blacks who attempted to exercise their franchise. On both sides, men voted ten or twenty times, and local party bosses stood by ballot boxes, tearing up any votes for the "wrong" candidate.

★ ★ THE WINNER: SAMUEL J. TILDEN?!? ★ ★

By the time the polls closed on Election Day, Samuel J. Tilden was ahead 250,000 in the popular vote (out of a total of 8,320,000 votes cast) and had 184 electoral votes to Hayes's 165. (Nearly 82 percent of eligible Americans voted, the most in the nation's history.) One more electoral vote would put Tilden over the top, and since there were twenty more out there (divided among Florida, Louisiana, South Carolina, and Oregon), he seemed assured of victory.

In New York City, Hayes went to bed certain he had lost; his party chairman, Zachariah Chandler, went out and got drunk.

But then came one of those curious moments upon which history pivots. Prominent Republican General Daniel E. Sickles, on his way home from the theater, stopped into the deserted Republican National Headquarters to check the election returns. Sickles was a notorious figure at the time and remains so today—hero to some, villain to others. (In 1859, he killed Philip Barton Key, son of Francis Scott Key, and then was acquitted of murder using the first-ever-in-American-history "not guilty by reason of temporary insanity" plea. Sickles rose to the rank of general in the Civil War, lost a leg at Gettysburg, and was awarded the Congressional Medal of Honor—but many felt that his actions on the field nearly cost the Union the battle.)

Whatever historians might think of him, Sickles was a man of action. Deciding that Hayes could win if he somehow regained control of Florida, Louisiana, and South Carolina, Sickles, pretending to be Zachariah Chandler, wired leading Republicans in these states, saying: "With your state sure for Hayes, he is elected. Hold your state."

By the time Chandler was roused from a whiskey-induced stupor, the race to win was on. The struggle over the twenty remaining electoral votes lasted from November 8, 1876, to March 2, 1877. Republican-controlled "returning boards" (groups in each state who tallied electoral votes) simply threw out enough Democratic votes to swing Florida, Louisiana, and South Carolina to Hayes. Democrats cried foul, officials of both parties flocked to the South, and President Grant sent federal troops, just in case. In the end, an Election Commission was established, consisting of five U.S. senators, five congressmen, and five Supreme Court justices, all of whom split evenly along party lines. With the commission tied at 7-7, the Supreme Court justice who had the deciding vote resigned—and a Republican justice took his place. Hayes was voted into office with 185 electoral votes to Tilden's 184.

★ ★

WHO REALLY WON? Had it been a totally fair election, would Tilden have won? Probably. Most historians believe that, at the very least, he carried Louisiana and Florida. In the end, fittingly enough, this dirtiest of all nineteenth-century elections finished with a secret dirty deal. Southern Democrats promised not to contest the

Election Commission's results if Hayes, once in office, would pull federal troops out of the South and appoint at least one Southerner to his cabinet. Reconstruction collapsed—and the future of civil rights was set back for decades—but Hayes was awarded the presidency.

March 5, 1877, was Rutherford Hayes's Inauguration Day, but things had become so heated—someone had already fired a shot through the window of Hayes's home—that he had to be secretly sworn in.

TAKING AIM AT MOTHER Desperate to discredit Hayes, the Democrats spread the rumor that he once shot and wounded his own mother "in a fit of insanity." Anonymous letters written to newspapers claimed that Hayes, in Ohio before the war, returned home from a night of drinking, pulled a gun, and shot Sophia Birchard Hayes in the arm.

Since Sophia Hayes died in 1866, she wasn't around to deny the reports, but there is no record of any gunshot wound to Hayes's mother. And we certainly know that Hayes and his wife, Lucy, were not what you'd call heavy drinkers; once in the White House, they banned all alcoholic beverages and served only water at state dinners. International visitors were horrified.

TILDEN'S WOMEN? Since Samuel Tilden was a bachelor—and a New York City bachelor, at that—Republicans went to town claiming that he had had numerous affairs with women, some married. But the nastiest smear was contained in pamphlets published in the early fall of 1876; they claimed that Tilden had contracted syphilis some years earlier from an Irish whore on the Bowery, and that this venereal disease not only affected his actions, but made him susceptible to blackmail.

Tilden died of pneumonia in 1886, at age seventy-two. There is no medical record of his having any STD.

MOST VICIOUSLY HYPERBOLIC POLITICAL SPEECH Stumping for the Republican Hayes, writer Robert G. Ingersoll attacked the Democrats by claiming they were all Confederates at heart: "Every man that tried to destroy this nation was a Democrat. . . . The man that assassinated Abraham Lincoln was a Democrat. . . . Soldiers, every scar you have on your heroic bodies was given you by a Democrat."

1880

JAMES GARFIELD

★ ★ ★ ★ ★ ★ ★ ★ ★ ★ VS. ★ ★ ★ ★ ★ ★ ★ ★ ★ ★ ★ ★ ★

WINFIELD HANCOCK

"*[In 1880] the Republican Party
existed [only] to oppose
the Democratic Party.*"

—John D. Hicks, author of *The American Nation*

SLEAZE-O-METER

10
9
8
7
6
5
4
3
2
1

Under Rutherford Hayes, America entered the very heart of what Mark Twain dubbed the Gilded Age. A huge economic expansion was led by a few robber barons—er, industrialists—like Andrew Carnegie, John Rockefeller, John Jacob Astor, Jay Gould, and Cyrus W. Field. The rich got richer, the poor got poorer, and the disenfranchised were more disenfranchised.

Although contemporary historian Henry Adams called him "a third-rate nonentity," Hayes had not been a bad president. He was relatively honest and had attempted (albeit with little success) to reform the highly corrupt, patronage-ridden civil service. But he was hamstrung by the promises he'd made to Democrats to win in 1876. Hayes's fellow Republicans saw their president withdrawing troops from the South (troops that supported corrupt Republican carpetbag state governments), giving important positions to Southern Democrats, and approving money for Southern pork barrels. And they didn't like it.

Hayes wisely decided not to run for a second term—setting the stage for an internal Republican Party battle that has seldom been equaled in American political history. The party was divided into two wings. One was called the Stalwarts, made up of those loyal to the old-line party of General Ulysses S. Grant, who was fishing for a third term as president. The other was dubbed the Half-Breeds—moderates who wanted reform within the party and abhorred the thought of another four years of "Grantism," that is, the general's corrupt cronies dipping into the public trough at will.

As the Republican Convention met in Chicago's brand-new glass and iron Exposition Building on June 2, 1880, Roscoe Conkling, the powerful and vain U.S. senator from New York, thought he had votes locked up for Grant. The famous general had been out of the country on a two-and-a-half-year world tour, long enough for people to forget the scandals of his administration and look upon Grant with nostalgic fondness. The Half-Breeds were led by Maine Senator James G. Blaine, Conkling's sworn enemy (who had once called Conkling "a majestic, supereminent, overpowering, turkey-gobbler strut").

At stake was the fate of the party as well as that of the nation since most assumed the Republicans would win the White House, as they had since 1860 (one reason the editorial cartoonist Thomas Nast had just caricaturized the Republican Party as a stolid, dependable elephant—an image that stuck). Thousands crammed the convention halls as ballot after ballot was cast. Spontaneous demonstrations arose during the alphabetized roll calls, either for Grant or for Blaine himself for president. One woman spectator even climbed a "Goddess of Liberty Statue" on the convention stage and began ripping off her clothes.

After all was said and done, Conkling put Grant in nomination with a fiery speech culminating in a sappy poem:

> *Do you ask what State he hails from?*
> *Our sole reply shall be:*
> *He hails from Appomattox*
> *And its famous apple tree.*

But a new senator from Ohio, James A. Garfield, arose and nominated fellow Ohioan Treasury Secretary John Sherman, brother of William Tecumseh Sherman. John Sherman was a favorite of the Half-Breeds, although not of the public at large, for reasons that are evident in his nickname: the Ohio Icicle. But as ballots were taken, an extraordinary thing began to happen: More and more delegates voted for Garfield, swayed by the idea of him as a moderating force between the two sharply divided factions. After thirty-six ballots—the most ever cast at a Republican convention, before or since—the forty-eight-year-old Garfield became the dark horse Republican candidate for president. Chester Arthur, Stalwart machine politician from New York, was chosen as the vice-presidential candidate.

After this uproar, the Democratic convention seemed like a minor afterthought: On only the second ballot, they nominated General Winfield Scott Hancock, former Civil War hero and military governor. His runningmate was William H. English, a banker from Indiana, a state both parties desperately needed because of its large number of electoral votes.

★ ★ ★ THE CANDIDATES ★ ★ ★

REPUBLICAN: JAMES A. GARFIELD The low-key and likeable Garfield was the last American presidential candidate to be born in a log cabin. During the summer of his seventeenth year, he drove mules on the towpaths of the Ohio Canal (hence his nicknames "Towpath Jim" and "Canal Boy"). He rose to become president of Hiram College, then volunteered for the Civil War. He distinguished himself in numerous battles and became a major general, then was elected to Congress in the post–Civil War years.

DEMOCRAT: WINFIELD SCOTT HANCOCK Since nothing came between General Hancock and his feedbag, he was described sarcastically by Republicans as "a good man weighing two hundred and forty pounds." But in truth he *was* a good man, with such a strong military record during the Civil War that he had been known as "Hancock the Superb." However, he had never held public office or even dabbled in politics, and Republican machine politicians were ready to make mincemeat out of him.

★ ★ ★ THE CAMPAIGN ★ ★ ★

As America surged toward the twentieth century, the country faced pressing issues: the need for child labor laws and an eight-hour workday, the plight of blacks, the rights of women, and a graduated federal income tax, just to name a few. Democrat and Republican platforms did not address any of these concerns. Instead, they emphasized civil service reform, opposed aid to parochial schools, and called for curtailing Chinese immigration—"an evil of great magnitude," claimed the Republicans. (With nothing to lose, the Republicans also came out firmly against polygamy—the "gay marriage" red herring of its day.)

Like punch-drunk fighters who don't know the bell has rung, the two major parties were still fighting the Civil War, a decade-and-a-half after it ended, running two heroic generals against each other. Trying to smear Garfield with Grantian scandals, the Democrats claimed that he had taken $329 in bribes from a holding company for the Union Pacific Railroad during the Credit Mobilier scandal. After Garfield provided an innocent explanation, Democrats switched tactics and assailed him for having an unpaid tailor's bill in Troy, New York.

Ulysses S. Grant, stumping for Garfield, apparently forgot that he had called Hancock a "glorious soldier" during the Civil War and told a journalist that Hancock was "crazy to be president. He is ambitious, vain, and weak." Nominating Hancock, a Republican newspaper wrote, "no more changes the character [of the Democrats] than a figurehead of the Virgin on Kidd's pirate ship."

★ ★ ★ THE WINNER: JAMES GARFIELD ★ ★ ★

In a surprisingly close election in which 78.4 percent of eligible voters went to the polls, James Garfield won 4,446,158 votes to Hancock's 4,444,260. But Garfield's Electoral College margin was 214 to 155. The modest and capable Half-Breed from Ohio was going to Washington— although within a few short months of his inaugural address, he would become the second American president to be assassinated.

★ ★

SOAPY SAM "Soap" and "Soapy Sam" were 1880s slang for cash passed out to voters to encourage them to vote for a candidate. Soaping palms had been the custom in American elections for years, but money exchanged hands in an unprecedented fashion during the Garfield-Hancock contest.

Indiana was one of the states that had still not coordinated its local and congressional elections with the national Election Day in early November. Instead, Indiana held its elections on October 12; consequently, many looked to that state as a bellwether of the country-wide election. Since Democratic vice-presidential candidate William English was a Hoosier, Republicans were terrified that the state would go for Hancock, so they quickly sprang into action.

One Republican operative reported that, in his opinion, there were "30,000 merchantable votes in the State." James Garfield and Chester Arthur urgently requested cash from their Wall Street connections, and a silver-tongued bagman named Stephen Dorsey was sent to Indiana carrying, by some accounts, as much as $400,000 in two-dollar bills. Soapy Sam had come to the rescue.

To be fair, the Democrats also attempted to buy votes, but since they lacked Republican access to Wall Street dough, they were mostly unsuccessful. Their biggest dirty trick consisted of sending in "repeaters" or "floaters" from outside Indiana to vote repeatedly in different precincts. In the end, Soapy Sam helped carry the state for Republicans and Garfield.

SURPRISE! On October 20, 1880, James Garfield fell victim to what is probably the first October Surprise in U.S. presidential election history. A newspaper improbably named the *New York Truth* printed a letter purportedly written by Garfield to an H. L. Morey of the Employers Union of Lynn, Massachusetts. In it Garfield wrote that the "Chinese problem" (the fears of whites in the West that Chinese immigrants would take jobs from them) was not a problem at all, and that employers had the right "to buy labor where they can get it the cheapest."

This struck terror into those who had been trying to keep the Chinese out of America, particularly Californians. Garfield certainly did not write the Morey letter and was able to refute it. Investigation showed that there was no Morey and no Employers Union in Lynn, Massachusetts, either. The letter was traced to the hand of one Kenward Philp, a *Truth* journalist who was later arrested and indicted for fraud.

Despite the fact that Garfield was able to prove his innocence, the Morey letter hurt him. It caused him to lose California, which almost caused him to lose the close election of 1880.

THE THREE-PERCENT SOLUTION Chester "Chet" Arthur, the Stalwart from New York, may have been picked as vice president to placate party boss Roscoe Conkling, but he sure knew his job. New York was home to thousands of state and federal civil-service workers, all of whom held their jobs at the sufferance of the big bosses. The going rate to keep their livelihood? In 1876, the Republicans had set the mandatory campaign contribution at 2 percent of annual salary, but Arthur upped it to 3 percent, delivering hundreds of thousands of dollars to the Republican treasure chest.

James Garfield and Chester Arthur bribed voters in Indiana with as much as $400,000 in two-dollar bills.

1884

GROVER CLEVELAND

★ ★ ★ ★ ★ ★ ★ ★ ★ ★ ★ VS. ★ ★ ★ ★ ★ ★ ★ ★ ★ ★ ★

JAMES G. BLAINE

"Kind regards to Mrs. Fisher.
Burn this letter."

—James G. Blaine, Republican candidate for president

U nder the category of famous last words comes this utterance by James Garfield just before his inauguration: "Assassination can no more be guarded against than death by lightning, and it is not best to worry about either."

During his first four months in office, Towpath Jim had done quite well, making inroads in his battle to dismantle the patronage system that had a stranglehold on the country's civil service. But on July 2, 1881, he was shot and seriously wounded by Charles Guiteau, a deranged man who is usually described by historians as a "disappointed office seeker." (Guiteau had haunted Garfield for months, desperate to earn a position as consul to Paris, even though he was supremely unqualified.)

Guiteau was also a Stalwart. His goal in the assassination was to bring Vice President Chester Arthur the presidency. "I am a Stalwart," he proclaimed after his arrest, "and Arthur shall be President!" When Garfield died on September 19 (helped along to eternity by the unwashed and constantly probing fingers of his doctors), Guiteau's vision was realized: "Chet" Arthur was sworn in as the twenty-first president of the United States.

As president, the dapper and corpulent Arthur was well-liked but not terribly energetic—his emerging Republican rival for the 1884 presidential nomination, James G. Blaine, called him a stalled ox. So his party failed to nominate him for a second term, which left the field wide open for a deliciously scandal-ridden presidential race. It can be likened in some ways to Bill Clinton's 1992 race against George H. W. Bush, when the whole Gennifer Flowers affair reared its pretty blonde head.

★ ★ ★ THE CANDIDATES ★ ★ ★

DEMOCRAT: GROVER CLEVELAND Grover Cleveland was the picture of a Gilded Age politician—he had the well-fed look, the striped pants, the balding pate, the whole nine yards—with one critical exception: He was honest—so honest that he was known in the telling slang of the day as "ugly honest." A former reform mayor of Buffalo and governor of New York State, Cleveland was picked on the second round of balloting at the Democratic convention. For VP, Cleveland chose Hoosier Thomas Hendricks, Samuel Tilden's 1876 running mate, who could assure the pivotal votes of the state of Indiana.

REPUBLICAN: JAMES G. BLAINE

At last it was James G. Blaine's turn. This eloquent Maine-born former Speaker of the House, senator, and secretary of state under Garfield inspired deliriums of passion in his rabid supporters (known as Blainiacs). They had dubbed him the "Plumed Knight" for his courage and integrity, but many in the know thought that the good Maine man was on the take. It was, perhaps, a bad sign that the man he picked for his vice president, Illinois Senator John Logan, was suspected of corruption and known far and wide as "Black Jack."

★ ★ ★ THE CAMPAIGN ★ ★ ★

Talk about wishful thinking: The chaplain giving the opening invocation for the Republican convention in June of 1884 prayed that "the coming political campaign be conducted with the decency, intelligence, patriotism and dignity of temper which becomes a free and intelligent people."

Politicians nodded reverentially and then immediately went at it tooth and nail. A large portion of the Republican Party bolted to the Democrats immediately after Blaine's nomination, including such leading luminaries as Reverend Henry Ward Beecher, Charles Francis Adams, and Mark Twain. These men, sarcastically called Mugwumps (an Algonquin Indian word meaning "big chief") by their enemies, reviled Blaine for corruption and for being under the thumb of Republican party bosses. He had, as one editorialist put it, "wallowed in spoils like a rhinoceros in an African pool."

Blaine's dealings with the burgeoning railroads—who pushed as much money into Washington as defense contractors do today—were particularly suspect. An especially damning moment occurred when Democrats uncovered a letter written by Blaine to Warren Fisher, a

Boston railroad attorney. In the letter, Blaine appeared complicit in shady business dealings. It didn't help that Blaine signed off "My regards to Mrs. Fisher. Burn this letter!"

The Democrats impaled the Plumed Knight on his own lance, gleefully chanting "Burn this letter! Burn this letter!" and "Blaine, Blaine, James. G. Blaine, the Continental liar from the state of Maine!"

They thought they had a lock on the sleaze issue, since their "ugly honest" candidate—a.k.a. Grover the Good—was known to have unimpeachable morals. But then on July 21, Cleveland's hometown paper, the *Buffalo Evening Telegraph*, published a sordid story with a real grabber of a headline: "A Terrible Tale: A Dark Chapter in a Public Man's History—The Pitiful Story of Maria Halpin and Governor Cleveland's Son."

It turned out that in 1874, when he was bachelor about town, Cleveland had embarked on an "illicit" affair with a thirty-six-year-old widow named Maria Halpin. She later gave birth to a boy, whom Cleveland gallantly supported, even though he privately acknowledged doubts about the child's real paternity.

The Republicans went wild over this story (much as they did in 1992 when Bill Clinton's alleged dalliance with torch singer Gennifer Flowers made headlines). One Buffalo minister proclaimed: "The issue is evidently not between the two great parties, but between the brothel and the family, . . . between lust and law." Editorialists cried: "We do not believe that the American people will knowingly elect to the Presidency a coarse debaucher who will bring his harlots with him to Washington." Cleveland was called a "lecherous beast" and "moral leper" and, for good measure, "an obese nincompoop." (Cleveland tipped the hay scales at about 250 pounds.)

Republicans now had their own derisive chant: "Ma! Ma! Where's my pa?" (Cartoons pictured Halpin plaintively searching for Cleveland while holding a baby—a trifle ridiculous since, by this time, the child was ten years old.)

And so the 1884 presidential contest degenerated, as one foreign observer drolly noted, into a contest between "the copulative habits of one candidate and the prevaricative habits of the other." In other words, was it worse to be a fornicator or a liar and thief? It was the first time this conundrum crystallized so clearly in an American presidential race, but by no means was it the last.

Cleveland's response to the situation should have set an example for Bill Clinton. When Democrats rushed to Cleveland, begging him to defend himself, he simply said: "Above all, tell the truth."

And that is what they did. Cleveland acknowledged he was supporting the child (who had been adopted by others) and refused to say anything else about the issue. Cleveland had a few advantages over Clinton, of course—he wasn't married, and Maria Halpin stayed in seclusion and refused to give statements—but his honesty helped him weather the crisis. It also happened early in the campaign, leaving Cleveland time before Election Day to shift the focus to other issues.

Most Americans then—as now—were more forgiving of lechery than hypocrisy.

★ ★ THE WINNER: GROVER CLEVELAND ★ ★

It was a close race. Grover Cleveland won 4,874,621 votes; Blaine came in with 4,848,936. It was the first time since the 1856 administration of James Buchanan that a Democrat sat in the White House. And gleeful supporters of Grover Cleveland were able to chant: "Ma! Ma! Where's my pa?" "Gone to the White House! Ha! Ha! Ha!"

★ ★

BLACK WEDNESDAY October 29, 1884, is among the worst days that a presidential candidate has ever had—worse than Nixon during that first 1960 debate, worse than Edmund Muskie weeping at a news conference in 1972, worse than the Howard Dean Scream in the 2004 primaries. If not for that day's events, James G. Blaine would have won the 1884 election.

Just as Cleveland weathered the Maria Halpin crisis, Blaine was overcoming charges that he was on the take. His stumping and passionate speech-making seemed to be winning over voters. He arrived in New York with a slim lead in the

When Republicans learned of Grover Cleveland's illegitimate child, they called their opponent "a lecherous beast" and "a moral leper."

state and—on that fateful Wednesday morning—sat down to a breakfast meeting at just another whistle stop on the campaign trail for the weary Blaine.

Unfortunately, during the seemingly unending meeting, a local Presbyterian minister by the name of S. D. Burchard got carried away in attacking the Democrats; Burchard called them the party of "rum, Romanism, and rebellion," essentially slurring them as Irish Catholic drunks. Even more unfortunately, Blaine apparently wasn't listening and did not denounce Burchard's intemperance when he got up to speak.

A Democrat attending the meeting took down Burchard's words and raced to local party headquarters. Campaign operatives immediately set to work printing thousands of handbills describing Blaine as a "Catholic-hater." In a city full of Irish Catholic working-class immigrants, this would not sit well.

In the evening of October 29, Blaine—who still had no idea what was happening—attended an entirely different sort of event: a dinner at the stylish Delmonico's restaurant in the company of Republican tycoons the likes of Jay Gould, John Jacob Astor, and Cyrus W. Field. The following day, just as the "Rum, Romanism and Rebellion" handbills were hitting the streets, newspaper headlines described "The Royal Feast of Belshazzar Blaine and the Money Kings."

This was a brutal one-two publicity punch, and it cost Blaine the election. He lost New York State by a mere 1,149 votes. Had it not been (as he later put it) for "an ass in the shape of a preacher," he would have won New York and become president of the United States.

MARK TWAIN AND LADIES OF THE NIGHT Mark Twain, a Republican, left his party over the nomination of James G. Blaine, whom he considered hopelessly corrupt. When the whole Cleveland–Maria Halpin affair news broke, he couldn't believe the hypocrisy of those who criticized the Democratic candidate: "To see grown men, apparently in their right mind, seriously arguing against a bachelor's fitness for President because he has had private intercourse with a consenting widow! These grown men know what the bachelor's other alternative was—& tacitly they seem to prefer that to the widow. Isn't human nature the most consummate sham & lie that was ever invented?"

1888

BENJAMIN HARRISON
vs. GROVER CLEVELAND

The election of 1888 was close and dirty. In one corner was Grover Cleveland, the Democratic president who had for four years labored stubbornly to continue civil service reform and put an end to high import tariffs. (Along with many Democrats, he thought the protective barriers lined the pockets of tycoons while making the cost of goods prohibitive for working people.)

In the other corner was Republican nominee Benjamin Harrison, a distinguished Civil War veteran and Indiana senator. The aloof fifty-four-year-old Harrison was a second choice for many Republicans (1884 nominee James G. Blaine still had plenty of supporters), but Harrison had good bloodlines. He was the grandson of President William "Old Tippecanoe" Harrison, who had died in 1840 after only a month in office. He also supported the high tariffs that made the Republican tycoons so rich.

THE CAMPAIGN No one talked much about the Maria Halpin affair anymore because President Cleveland had married during his first term as president (the first such ceremony ever performed in the White House). Nevertheless, Republicans seized on the fact that Cleveland had wed his former ward, Frances Folsom, the daughter of his late law partner—she was twenty-one years old, and some twenty-eight years younger than the man she once referred to as Uncle Cleve. Many Republicans were titillated by the incestuous nature of their union; they referred to Cleveland as the "Beast of Buffalo" and even spread rumors that he beat Frances. In one of the most extraordinary official utterances made by a first lady in the nineteenth century, Frances issued a statement calling the charges "a foolish campaign ploy without a shadow of foundation."

Democrats nicknamed the difficult and aristocratic Harrison "Kid Glove," but in truth, they had a hard time laying a glove on this smart, veteran campaigner. Harrison had learned from Blaine's Black Wednesday mistake that too much campaigning could leave one vulnerable to the Reverend Burchards of the world.

And so he began the nation's first front-porch campaign, allowing crowds to gather at his Indianapolis home for a brief address once a day, and then sending out a carefully worded version of his remarks to the Associated Press for nationwide dissemination. This early form of spin control kept his message out in the public while letting him rest comfortably in his own bed at night. (Cleveland chose not to campaign, even from his front porch, and relied instead upon his inept running mate, seventy-five-year-old Allen G. Thurman, who, during speeches, would forget what he was supposed to be talking about and start complaining about his rheumatism.)

Of course, Benjamin Harrison also had the benefit of Republican money. Lots of it. The Republican national campaign manager, Matthew S. Quay, remarked that he would "fry the fat" out of Republican businessmen who benefited from the protective tariffs—and he did, collecting more than $3 million, much of it from the American Iron and Steel Association. At the same time, mill workers received slips tucked into their pay envelopes threatening them with the loss of their jobs if tariffs were abolished and cheap foreign goods were to flood the country.

THE WINNER: BENJAMIN HARRISON
It took a lot of dirty tricks—including more vote buying in Indiana, where Republican "floaters" were now paid as much as fifteen dollars a head and literally marched to the polls by party operatives before they got too drunk to vote—but Benjamin Harrison became president in 1888. Even though he lost the popular vote by 90,000 votes, garnering 5,443,892 to Cleveland's 5,534,488, Harrison won in the Electoral College 233 to 168. One big victory was in New York State, where thirty-six electoral votes went to Harrison after the Democratic candidate for governor there made a deal with Harrison's people: In return for enough Republican votes to give him the gubernatorial victory, he would deliver New York to Harrison.

The dirty tricks in this campaign were such that Republican bigwig Matthew Quay remarked pointedly, Harrison would never know how many Republicans "were compelled to approach the gates of the penitentiary to make him president."

1892

AT A GLANCE

GROVER CLEVELAND
vs. BENJAMIN HARRISON

The election of 1892 was a transitional one—not the most exciting presidential battle in history. But the country was experiencing major changes. The U.S. population had risen to more than sixty-two million; even more significantly, the population center had shifted westward. Six western states had been admitted to the Union in 1889 and 1890—North Dakota, South Dakota, Montana, Washington, Idaho, and Wyoming. A telephone line now stretched between New York City and Chicago. Thomas Edison had invented the kinetoscope, the first moving picture camera. And a new portable Kodak camera was put on the market in 1888. Instead of using dry plate negatives, it employed a spool of flexible film with one hundred exposures that could be developed at a dealer or sent directly to Kodak headquarters in Rochester, New York.

Suddenly, everybody was a shutterbug. Unfortunately, there wasn't much to be photographed in the election of 1892. Benjamin Harrison spent most of his White House tenure controlled by the corrupt Republican bosses who had helped him win in 1888. The bosses couldn't stand the prickly, born-again Christian president, claiming that Harrison was "as glacial as a Siberian stripped of his furs" and that talking to him even in warm weather made a person feel like putting on "winter flannels, galoshes, overcoat, mitts, and earlap."

Cleveland, on the other hand, was still popular with millions of Americans—after all, this was the man whose baby daughter, Ruth, had a candy bar named after her. He hungered for a third nomination and second term, and so the race against frosty Ben Harrison was on.

THE CAMPAIGN Cleveland still did not take to the stump, although he broke with tradition to become the first presidential nominee to make a public speech in acceptance of his nomination, rather than simply sending out a letter of acceptance.

And Harrison, preoccupied with his ill wife (who died two weeks before Election Day) did not repeat his front-porch PR coup of the previous election. With running mate Whitelaw Reid, he spent most of his time emphasizing his support of high tariffs and protectionism. Unfortunately, a violent Homestead, Pennsylvania, strike in July 1892—during which Andrew Carnegie's general manager, Henry Clay Frick, cut steel mill workers wages 20 percent and then hired armed Pinkerton agents to battle them when they struck—was a PR disaster and may have cost Harrison the election.

Homestead helped Cleveland (running with veep nominee Adlai E. Stevenson, grandfather of the future Democratic presidential candidate) immensely with labor, demonstrating in action that high tariff barriers did not translate to high wages for workers.

THE WINNER: GROVER CLEVELAND Cleveland won convincingly with 5,551,883 votes to Harrison's 5,179,244. He carried seven Northern states as well as the usual Democratic Southern voting bloc, and he entered the record books as the first and only president to serve two nonconsecutive terms.

But change was in the wind. The new Populist Party, a grassroots amalgam of farmers and factory workers whose platform called for fair wages, public ownership of railroads, telegraph and telephones, and a restoration of government "to the hands of plain people" had garnered more than one million votes for its candidate, James B. Weaver. Weaver had stumped throughout the country with a truly charismatic American orator, the little-known Mary Elizabeth Lease, a woman who decried a "government of Wall Street, for Wall Street, and by Wall Street" and who told farmers in rallies that resembled religious revivals "to raise less corn and more hell."

This western groundswell was heading East. And party bosses, both Republican and Democrat, were about to see the beginning of the end of their storied power.

1896

WILLIAM MCKINLEY

★ ★ ★ ★ ★ ★ ★ ★ ★ ★ VS. ★ ★ ★ ★ ★ ★ ★ ★ ★ ★ ★

WILLIAM JENNINGS BRYAN

"[Bryan] is an irresponsible, unregulated, ignorant, prejudiced, pathetically honest and enthusiastic crank."

—*New York Times*

SLEAZE-O-METER

10
9
8
7
6
5
4
3
2
1

Republicans warned that William Jennings Bryan was literally insane.

Poor Grover the Good. No sooner had he begun his second term when much of the world slid into a horrific economic depression that would last from 1893 to 1897. In America, within just a year of Cleveland's second inauguration, fifteen thousand businesses went under and four million workers lost their jobs. A half-million laborers went on strike against substandard wages and working conditions. Most of the strikes were broken by the police and the military. Bands of homeless people wandered the country in search of shelter and employment. An army of poor people marched on Washington. A more dismal picture would not be seen in the land until the Great Depression of the 1930s.

America was changing, and the political parties were changing with it. What many historians call the great realignment of 1896 was about to occur. In it, the Republican Party would finally reach out to blue-collar workers, in much the same way it did when Richard Nixon ran on his "Silent Majority" theme in the 1960s. In another foreshadowing of 1968, the Democrats embraced a young, passionate, and extraordinarily charismatic candidate.

The campaign was all about currency standards and precious metal—gold clashing with silver—and the sparks were about to fly.

★ ★ ★ THE CANDIDATES ★ ★ ★

REPUBLICAN: WILLIAM MCKINLEY The fifty-three-year-old McKinley—of the starched shirt, double-breasted coat, red carnation, and mainstream American Methodism—had a long political record as a congressman and then governor of Ohio. He was smart, dependable, and upstanding. If you were a certain class of American, you felt reassured just by looking at the guy and hearing his stentorian tones. His campaign was run by Mark Hanna, a powerfully astute political operator who pioneered many of the techniques used in modern campaigning.

DEMOCRAT: WILLIAM JENNINGS BRYAN At the age of thirty-six, Bryan was (and still is) the youngest man ever to receive a major party's nomination for president. He was known as "The Great

Commoner"—a Nebraska native, evangelical Christian, and passionate speaker who traveled 18,000 miles (all by train, of course) through twenty-seven states, making up to thirty-six speeches a day on behalf of a new currency standard and the down-trodden farmers. The lean, handsome Bryan ate six meals a day just to keep up his strength during the grueling campaign. He also enjoyed relaxing rubdowns with gin, leading many people he met to believe he was a drunk.

★ ★ ★ THE CAMPAIGN ★ ★ ★

William McKinley and Mark Hanna remembered the lessons of Benjamin Harrison's presidential campaign in 1888: Harrison had promised so many favors to eastern party bosses to get elected, he could hardly accomplish anything once he arrived in the White House.

They realized that the times were changing. The decisive moment came in the months before the Republican convention, when party bosses Matthew Quay of Pennsylvania and Senator Thomas Platt of New York demanded that McKinley make Platt secretary of the treasury. And they wanted McKinley to put the promise in writing.

McKinley simply told Hanna: "There are some things in the world that come too high. If I cannot be president without promising to make Tom Platt Secretary of the Treasury, I will never be president."

It was the tipping point. In a time of deep depression, the ordinary people were sick of party fat cats. They supported McKinley as the candidate against what was even then being called the machine—the grinding apparatus of party corruption. As Charles Dawes, one of McKinley's young campaign aides put it, McKinley's men would "make the machine sick before we get through with them."

Once nominated, however, McKinley's real enemy was William Jennings Bryan. The charismatic Nebraskan had stolen his party's nomination with his famous "Cross of Gold" speech, in which he advocated an expanded supply of money and silver coinage to alleviate the woes of working people. Bryan argued that "tight money"—money in which each dollar was backed by its equivalent in gold—was keeping farmers and those deeply in debt from being able to make a decent living, while those bankers who controlled the gold wallowed like Scrooges in chambers of wealth.

"You shall not press down upon the brow of labor this crown of thorns, you shall not crucify mankind upon a cross of gold," Bryan thundered, and he was joined by not only Democrats but also the Populist Party, who later nominated him for president and became known as Popocrats.

The Republicans who feared Bryan's western populism branded him as an anarchist who would bring economic ruin to the country. During the summer of 1896, attacks on Bryan in GOP newspapers mounted in hysteria. Bryan, the *New York Tribune* snarled, "was a wretched, rattle-pated boy, posing in vapid vanity and mouthing resounding rottenness." Theodore Roosevelt, stumping for McKinley, compared Bryan to "the leaders of the Terror in France in mental and moral attitude." (Some Republicans also likened him to Charles Guiteau, Garfield's assassin.) Bryan's followers were labeled by one Philadelphia paper as "hideous and repulsive vipers." Anti-Semitic caricatures abounded in editorial cartoons—silver-loving Shylocks who would be "Sure Winners if Bryan Is Elected."

Like most political campaigns, however, the Republican efforts worked on many levels. Cheap shots in newspapers were all to the good, but party organization and discipline were just as important. Mark Hanna, the Karl Rove of his day, came up with a brilliant strategy. Instead of trying to beat the peripatetic Bryan by stumping all over the country (not McKinley's style, in any event), Hanna had his candidate stay home in Canton, Ohio, and arranged for people to visit him. These front-porch meetings surpassed those of Benjamin Harrison's and were as orchestrated as any "town hall" meeting in today's electronic village. Hanna's railroad connections provided free excursion passes to Canton for carefully chosen groups of students, workers, farmers, merchants, ex-soldiers, and others. The night before each event, the audience could submit questions in writing, and McKinley would respond the next day in short, carefully scripted speeches.

Leaflets extolling McKinley were printed in the millions (in seven or eight languages) and distributed nationwide. McKinley buttons were manufactured by the thousands. Billboards with McKinley's picture were planted alongside miles of roads. Fourteen hundred speakers were enlisted, ready to be sent into action if an area seemed to be going Democrat. McKinley's men aimed right at the breadbasket in these hard times—they boasted that McKinley was the man with the "Full Dinner Pail." He was "The Advance Agent of Prosperity." He was solid and dependable.

Democrats tried to fight back. They attacked Mark Hanna as "the most vicious, carnal, and unrelenting oppressor of labor . . . in existence" and hinted that he was capable of murder to achieve his ends. Bryan stumped so hard that he lost his voice. But in the end, as is almost always the story in American politics, money talked. Bryan's campaign purse was, at most, a million dollars; McKinley had three times that amount, maybe more.

★ ★ THE WINNER: WILLIAM MCKINLEY ★ ★

McKinley beat Bryan handily, 7,108,480 votes to 6,511,495, with an electoral margin of 271 to 176. McKinley had managed the stupendous feat of keeping the upper middle class in his corner and garnering the votes of urban blue-collar workers, who would now form the core of the revised Republican Party.

Bryan had polled well in the West and, in fact, later estimated that appearances were deceiving. Had 18,000 votes in key states gone his way, he would have been president. Bryan's brand of Populist politics would change the Democratic Party forever (even though Bryan himself, intimidated by the Southern voting base, would never do much for African Americans). Regardless, the Great Commoner began calling 1896 the "first" battle. He knew he would be back.

★ ★

THE MADMAN IN THE WHITE HOUSE In September, just as the election was heating up to a fever pitch, the McKinley-supporting *New York Times* published an interesting little article entitled "Is Mr. Bryan Crazy?" The story examined a number of the Democratic candidate's utterances and claimed that they were not the workings of a rational mind. The *Times* editors also included a letter from a distinguished alienist stating that if Bryan won the election, "there would be a madman in the White House."

Not content with this, the paper interviewed several more alienists and published the results two days later. These eminent medical geniuses said that Bryan suffered from megalomania (delusions of grandeur), paranoia querulent (complaining too much), and querulent logorrhea (talking about complaining too much). One other "expert" simply said, "I don't think Bryan is ordinarily crazy. . . . But I should like to examine him as a degenerate."

MARK HANNA—LIKE A VIRGIN In describing the canny, ahead-of-his-time political operator Mark Hanna, Theodore Roosevelt once remarked, "He has advertised McKinley as if he were a patent medicine!" Hanna was an Ohio political broker who spotted the young McKinley as early as 1884, when he was an Ohio congressman, and proceeded to groom him to become president.

At the time, many observers thought that Hanna called the shots and could "shuffle [McKinley] and deal him like a deck of cards." But friends who knew both men disagreed. One contemporary said that Hanna, the hardened politician, felt about the pure-as-the-driven-snow McKinley as "a bashful boy [feels] towards the girl he loves." And McKinley's biographer, Margaret Leech, wrote: "Hanna was drawn to McKinley's idealistic standards like a hardened man of the world who becomes infatuated with virgin innocence."

BIG MONEY AND POOR WEDNESDAY Eastern tycoons didn't particularly like the independent-minded McKinley, but they disliked Bryan and his silver standard even more. They began spending big money to keep the Boy Orator out of the White House. Led by James G. Hill, the powerful New York railway mogul, Wall Street pushed Republican businesses into line. In those days, political contributions were not left to chance. Banks were assessed one quarter of one percent of their capital. Most big businesses, especially life insurance companies, contributed in a similar fashion. Standard Oil—becoming very big business indeed in an increasingly machine-dependent age—put $250,000 into the Republican war chest. All told, the party collected some three million dollars, although some estimates range even higher.

1900
AT A GLANCE

WILLIAM MCKINLEY
vs. WILLIAM JENNINGS BRYAN

T he year 1900 announced a new American century in which things were looking far rosier than they had four years earlier. McKinley had gotten lucky. The Depression ended soon after he took office, with the advent of good harvests, rising prices, and new gold discoveries in Alaska, Australia, and South Africa (these doubled the world's supply of gold and allowed the Treasury Department to issue more banknotes). Arguments for a new silver currency standard were suddenly a lot less persuasive. McKinley could also take credit for the blossoming of American imperialism. In 1898, the United States fought the Spanish-American War, ostensibly to liberate Cuba. The U.S. victory resulted in the acquisition of the Philippines and Puerto Rico.

THE CAMPAIGN It was a foregone conclusion that McKinley was the Republican candidate for 1900—the only suspense was identifying his running mate. The main contender appeared to be Theodore "Teddy" Roosevelt, the "Rough Rider" hero of Cuba and governor of New York, but party architect Mark Hanna hated Roosevelt's manic energy and impulsiveness. During the Republican Convention in Philadelphia, Hanna screamed to delegates, "Don't any of you realize that there is only one life between that madman [Roosevelt] and the presidency?"

Roosevelt, for his part, pretended that he wasn't interested in the veep nod but showed up at the convention wearing a hat that looked suspiciously like his old broad-brimmed Rough Rider hat (leading one observer to smile and say, "Gentleman, that's an acceptance hat"). The prediction turned out to be true: McKinley and Roosevelt stood together on the podium when the convention was done.

The Democrats nominated William Jennings Bryan again, dooming their candidate to another hopeless fight. The silver issue was dead, yet Bryan would not give it up, leading Republican Speaker of the House Thomas B. Reed to quip that Bryan would "rather be wrong than be president." Bryan went after McKinley on imperialism and the stranglehold of trusts and monopolies on American business, but people just didn't care. "Let well enough alone" was the Republican slogan, and that about summed it up. McKinley didn't even bother to make his front-porch appearances; instead, the fiery Roosevelt traveled 21,000 miles and rivaled Bryan in passionate speech-making (although Roosevelt chagrined Mark Hanna and the Republican faithful by referring to Bryan as "my opponent," as if Roosevelt himself were running for president).

THE WINNER: WILLIAM MCKINLEY McKinley smashed Bryan 7,218,039 votes to 6,358,345, this time winning many of the agricultural states in the West. Bryan's career in politics wasn't over—he still had one more presidential campaign left in him—but his popularity was clearly trending downward.

Interesting footnote: In the summer of 1899, William McKinley posed for a photo with his first-term vice president, rich New Jersey businessman Garret A. Hobart, who died in office later that year. The photograph was so admired that another one was issued in the summer of 1900, with McKinley sitting in an identical pose with VP candidate Theodore Roosevelt.

Strangely, no one can remember McKinley and Roosevelt posing for the photograph together. Even stranger, the photo shows McKinley wearing the exact same clothes and sitting in the exact same chair as the McKinley/Hobart photo from a year before. Additionally, there is a faint, barely discernable line running down the middle of the McKinley/Roosevelt photograph, which has led some historians to speculate that the photograph was a composite assembled by the McKinley campaign—no doubt for the innocent reason that McKinley and Roosevelt didn't have time to sit down together. If so, it's most likely the first-ever doctored photograph employed in a presidential campaign.

There would be plenty more.

1904

AT A GLANCE

THEODORE ROOSEVELT
vs. ALTON PARKER

On September 6, 1901, President William McKinley attended Buffalo's Pan-American Exposition, afterward shaking hands with the public at a reception on a very hot day in which men and women alike pulled out huge handkerchiefs to wipe their brows.

One of these handkerchiefs concealed a .32 caliber Iver-Johnson revolver belonging to Leon Czolgosz, a young man who had been stalking McKinley all day. Czolgosz, who believed himself to be an anarchist, went by the name Fred Nieman, which means Fred Nobody. He is easily the most pathetic of all presidential assassins and so lamebrained that real anarchists refused to hang out with him, thinking he was either insane or a police spy. When Czolgosz reached McKinley in the reception line, he shot the president twice. In a week, McKinley was dead—the third president killed by an assassin in thirty-five years.

Czolgosz would fry in the electric chair, only the fiftieth person to be so afforded the honor; the new American century had begun with a bang and a sizzle. When forty-two-year-old Theodore Roosevelt was sworn in as president, he remarked: "It's a dreadful thing to come into the presidency this way, but it would be a far worse thing to be morbid about it."

Morbid Roosevelt certainly was not. With his high-pitched, braying voice, his obsession with exercise, and an abundance of natural energy, he was, in the words of historian Henry Adams, "pure act." The writer Henry James, who didn't like Roosevelt at all, called him "a monstrous embodiment of unprecedented and resounding noise."

THE CAMPAIGN In his first term as McKinley's successor, Roosevelt showed a political subtlety that many people thought he did not possess (this is, after all, the man who called the president of Venezuela a "villainous little monkey"). Understanding the deepening voter dissatisfaction with big business, Roosevelt very publicly went after "the malefactors of great wealth" in antitrust suits while at the same time maintaining generally cordial relations with the Wall Street capitalists who would fund his 1904 campaign. He was nominated to great acclaim on the first ballot at the Republican convention in Chicago.

Roosevelt's Democratic opponent was the extremely colorless Alton B. Parker, chief justice of the New York Court of Appeals and probably one of the most obscure presidential candidates of all time. Parker—whom Roosevelt referred to as "the neutral-tinted individual"— was chosen to appeal not only to Democrats but also to crossover Republicans sick of Roosevelt's progressive labor policies. Unfortunately, Parker had very little skill when it came to campaigning and speaking, so he spent much of his time alone on his Hudson Valley farm. The best the Democrats could claim for their man was that, if elected, Parker would "set his face sternly against Executive usurpation of legislative and judicial functions."

Not exactly stirring stuff. There was a brief flurry of activity in the fall when Roosevelt thought he might actually lose in New York; he made a personal appeal to his Wall Street connections, which resulted in hundreds of thousands of dollars being bestowed upon him practically overnight. These enormous sums amassed so quickly embarrassed Roosevelt, who worried that tycoons like J. P. Morgan and Henry Clay Frick thought they were buying him. (In fact, after the election, Frick claimed, "We bought the son of a bitch and then he did not stay bought.")

Roosevelt could, and did, win without owing anybody anything. The election of 1904 was a Republican landslide, with the president garnering 7,626,593 votes to Parker's 5,082,898. The electoral vote margin was even more lopsided at 336 to 140.

1908

WILLIAM TAFT

★ ★ ★ ★ ★ ★ ★ ★ ★ ★ ★ ★ VS. ★ ★ ★ ★ ★ ★ ★ ★ ★ ★ ★ ★

WILLIAM JENNINGS BRYAN

"What does Taft stand for, by the way?
Why, T.A.F.T. means 'Take Advice
from Theodore!'"

—Democratic joke

SLEAZE-O-METER

10
9
8
7
6
5
4
3
2
1

In his great exuberance upon winning the 1904 election by such a gratifying margin, Theodore Roosevelt did something he would always regret. Accepting his country's nod for another term on election night, he stated: "Under no circumstances will I be a candidate for or accept another nomination" for a second elective term.

In other words, the forty-six-year-old president had declared himself a lame duck at the moment of his greatest victory. It was perhaps one of the most foolish statements in president-elect history. Roosevelt's second term certainly had major successes—he won a Nobel Peace Prize for helping end the Russo-Japanese War, watched work on the Panama Canal begin, helped pass a Pure Food and Drug Act, and further curbed big business excess—but he was less effective than he might have been if he hadn't ruled out the possibility of a second full term.

At least he had the satisfaction of handpicking his successor—his good friend and secretary of war, William Howard Taft. At first, Taft was reluctant, but Roosevelt convinced him and Taft was quite touched: "I must go over and thank Theodore," he said. To which the convivial president replied, patting Taft on the back: "Yes, Will, it's the thing to do."

Republicans were sorry to see Roosevelt go. When the party faithful met at their convention in Chicago, the mere mention of Roosevelt's name by the convention chairman led to a forty-nine-minute chanting demonstration of "Four, four, four more years!" But as per Roosevelt's wishes, Taft was nominated on the first ballot. His opponent would be the Great Commoner, William Jennings Bryan, a little older and a great deal balder, running for the third time on a very tired Democratic ticket.

★ ★ ★ THE CANDIDATES ★ ★ ★

REPUBLICAN: WILLIAM HOWARD TAFT Taft was a well-liked, jovial politico who had risen high in the ranks of the party, in large part due to his friendship with Theodore Roosevelt. Roosevelt had used the affable Taft as a sort of ambassador-at-large to smooth out difficulties all over the world—from the Vatican's claim to properties in the newly acquired Philippines to troubles getting the Panama Canal under way. Taft weighed 330 pounds, and his vice-presidential running mate—a conservative New York congressman named James "Sunny Jim" Sherman—tipped the scales at more than 200 pounds. Pound for pound, they offered the most political tonnage of any presidential ticket in history.

DEMOCRAT: WILLIAM JENNINGS BRYAN There was something both glorious and sad about seeing the old warrior running again for a third try. Even though the odds weighed heavily against him, Bryan hit the stump swinging, along with his running mate, an Indiana state senator named John Kern.

★ ★ ★ THE CAMPAIGN ★ ★ ★

In retrospect, it is difficult to see how Bryan could have beaten any candidate backed by Roosevelt, but the Republicans weren't taking any chances. They immediately launched a vicious personal attack, with Teddy himself describing Bryan as "a kindly man and well-meaning in a weak way . . . but he is the cheapest faker we have ever proposed for president." Even First Lady Edith Roosevelt opined that Bryan was "a trifle too fat and oily for the fastidious."

Bryan struck back. His main campaign theme was "Shall the people rule?" and he hammered an argument that many Americans were beginning to support: that far too many politicians were still in the pockets of big business. Bryan was aided by publisher William Randolph Hearst, founder of the new Independent Party and Roosevelt's enemy. In September, Hearst published secret letters from Standard Oil Company files proving that prominent Republican Senator Joseph Benson Foraker had received sums as high as fifty thousand dollars for what were vaguely labeled as legal fees. (Ironically, these same secret letters implicated the treasurer of the Democratic campaign, Charles Haskell, who was forced to resign.)

The Democrats repeatedly made the argument that Taft was merely

At a combined 530-plus pounds, William Taft and James Sherman were the heaviest presidential ticket in U.S. history.

a proxy for Roosevelt. There was plenty of truth to this. The president sent a steady stream of instructional letters to Taft, including one in which he urged the good-natured candidate to get out on the stump and "hit [Bryan] hard . . . attack him!" (Taft, tactful as always, replied to this note of Roosevelt's by writing, "I have your letter . . . and if any [strategy] can elect me, I believe this letter can.")

For the most part, voters liked and trusted Taft. Although never a good orator and prone to gaffes (speaking to some old Union Army veterans, Taft kept harping on the fact that their hero, Ulysses S. Grant, drank too much), he had a childlike good humor. In speeches, he would proudly announce that he was "an honorary locomotive fireman" and boast that he was good friends with everyone in the International Brotherhood of Steam Shovel and Dredge Men. Taft would find that he had plenty of good friends among voters, too.

★ ★ THE WINNER: WILLIAM HOWARD TAFT ★ ★

Taft's 7,676,258 votes outnumbered Bryan's 6,406,801 by a margin of 1,269,000 votes—not as big as Roosevelt's win in 1904, but still pretty impressive. "We beat them to a frazzle!" exclaimed not Taft but a giddy Roosevelt; the new president-elect headed straight to Hot Springs to play golf. His first public statement? "I really did some great work at sleeping last night."

The election was William Bryan's last presidential hurrah, but he would go on to influence the country in other ways—first serving a stint as Woodrow Wilson's secretary of state and later crusading against Darwinism (and Clarence Darrow) in the Scopes Monkey Trial.

★ ★

TEDDY KNOWS BEST Theodore Roosevelt closely stage-managed William Howard Taft's run for president, including giving him sage advice in numerous letters: "I hope that your people will do everything they can to prevent one word being sent out about either your fishing or playing golf," he said in one missive. "The American people regard the campaign as serious business." He went on: "Let the audience see you smile always, because I feel your nature shines out so transparently when you smile. . . . You big, generous, high-minded fellow." He also remonstrated with Taft's advisors not to let the outsized presidential candidate be allowed on horses: "Dangerous for him and cruelty to the horse."

JOBS FOR TAFT Businesses, as usual, were in the Republican corner during the 1908 election, and they made no secret about their loyalty. The vice president of the New York Central Railroad instructed that 2,500 freight and passenger cars be repaired—whether they needed it or not—to give jobs to numerous employees and make the economy appear healthier. The president of a midwestern fire insurance company sent out 2,000 of his door-to-door salesmen with instructions to always slip in a word for Taft while making a sale. A Missouri steel company added 400 men to its payroll just before Election Day in order, the chairman said, to pick up votes for Taft.

THE PERILS OF BEING UNITARIAN As a Unitarian—considered barely a religion by many Americans—Taft was attacked by Democratic and Republican religious newspapers. "Think of the United States with a President who does not believe that Jesus Christ was the Son of God, but looks upon our immaculate Savior as common bastard and low, cunning impostor," cried one midwestern editor.

This became such an issue that Theodore Roosevelt made a point of publicly attending Unitarian church with Taft—in the hope, Roosevelt explained, "that it would attract the attention of the sincere but rather ignorant Protestants who support me."

Taft, to his credit, made no apologies for his mode of worship: "If the American public is so narrow as not to elect a Unitarian, well and good. I can stand it."

1912

WOODROW WILSON

★ ★ ★ ★ ★ ★ ★ ★ ★ ★ VS. ★ ★ ★ ★ ★ ★ ★ ★ ★ ★

THEODORE ROOSEVELT

★ ★ ★ ★ ★ ★ ★ ★ ★ ★ VS. ★ ★ ★ ★ ★ ★ ★ ★ ★ ★

WILLIAM HOWARD TAFT

SLEAZE-O-METER

"Taft is a fathead . . . with the brains of a guinea pig!"

—Theodore Roosevelt

8
7
6
5
4
3
2
1

It's interesting to note that, with the exception of Grover Cleveland's two nonconsecutive terms, Republican Party candidates had occupied the White House since 1860—an astonishing 44 years. But things were about to change in an especially acrimonious election that saw the Republican Party literally tear itself apart.

After Taft's 1908 victory, Roosevelt headed off to Africa for big-game hunting—the ex-president was personally responsible for killing nine lions, eight elephants, twenty zebras, seven giraffes, and six buffalos.

Back at home, progressive Republicans had a different kind of big game in their sights: William Howard Taft. The new president was more conservative than his predecessor and soon found himself under the sway of big business. Progressives complained that Taft was selling out, and Taft whined in a letter to Roosevelt, "It is now a year and three months since I assumed office and I have had a hard time."

His former mentor was not an ideal confidant. As soon as Roosevelt returned home in 1910, he was besieged by progressive Republicans trying to convince him to run for a second full term. It didn't take much persuasion. Roosevelt began to criticize Taft's policies, claiming that he was a pawn of "the bosses and . . . the great privileged interests." Taft was stunned to hear such vehement attacks coming from a man he considered a personal friend (not to mention a man that Taft still referred to as "the President"). "If only I knew what the President wanted," he told an aide, "I would do it."

What Roosevelt wanted became very clear in February of 1912, when he declared his candidacy for his party's nomination for president. "My hat is in the ring!" he roared (unwittingly coining a phrase in the process). "The fight is on and I am stripped to the buff!"

Taft picked up on the boxing metaphor when he issued his own statement: "I do not want to fight Theodore Roosevelt, but sometimes a man in a corner comes out swinging. . . . I was a man of straw but I have been a man of straw long enough. Every man who has blood in his body . . . is forced to fight."

At this point in American history, some states had already begun holding primary elections to pick their delegates, a fairly pro forma procedure wherein delegates simply voted for the choice of their party bosses. All that changed during the election of 1912. In what can probably be considered the first-ever contested presidential party primaries, Roosevelt used his clout and charisma to beat Taft nine states to one. Roosevelt even won in Taft's home state of Ohio. Arriving at the Republican Convention in June, Roosevelt was on a roll, featured in newspapers all over the country, far better public fodder than Taft, who remained quietly in the White House.

It may be hard for us today, in an age of carefully orchestrated national political conventions, to understand the mayhem that occurred in 1912. But when you consider that Roosevelt showed up on the first day wearing a sombrero, smoking a cigar, and referring to the sitting president as "a rat in a corner," it's clear that a lot has changed in the last 100 years.

There was even more action happening behind the scenes. The delegates Roosevelt won in the primary elections were in the minority— Taft's conservative political bosses controlled the Republican National Committee and made a point of lining up Taft delegates from the states in the majority, which did not hold primaries. In back-room wheeling and dealing, they also purchased the support of as many as 200 to 300 delegates from southern states—these states would vote Democratic in a national election, but they did have Republican delegates they were willing to trade for favors or cold cash.

Roosevelt and his men made challenge after challenge when Taft's men tried to seat these delegates; but their challenges were denied, so much so that progressives began to cry that they were being "steamrolled" (another expression coined in 1912). Tensions ran so high that police squads were brought in and barbed wire put around the stage. Finally, when Taft ended up with a commanding lead in delegates, 561 to Roosevelt's 107, Roosevelt and his supporters stormed out of the convention. They formed their own independent party made up of everyone from social workers, reformers, and feminists to unhappy mainstream Republicans. They called themselves the Progressive Party but were known popularly as the Bull Moose Party because Roosevelt had proclaimed: "I am fit as a bull moose!"

Thus, the most successful political party of the last half-century had managed to split itself in two—hardly a recipe for victory, since simple arithmetic showed that Democrats had about forty-five percent of the national vote locked up. As one onlooker said, referring to Taft and Roosevelt, "The only question is, which corpse gets the flowers?"

★ ★ ★ THE CANDIDATES ★ ★ ★

REPUBLICAN: WILLIAM HOWARD TAFT William Howard Taft reacted poorly to hostility. Although he tried to rally, calling Roosevelt a "destructive radical" and even (in what was becoming fashionable alienist-speak) "neurotic," he wrote sadly to his wife: "Sometimes I think I might as well give up as far as being a candidate is concerned. There are so many people in the country who don't like me."

Taft's running mate was his vice president, James Sherman, who unfortunately died just days before the election. Columbia University President Nicholas Murray Butler agreed to replace him—but only, he told Taft, on the condition that Taft not win.

PROGRESSIVE-BULL MOOSE: THEODORE ROOSEVELT Since Roosevelt had made the infamous 1904 blunder of declaring that he would never seek another term, he now had to do a little backpeddling. He told voters that what he really meant was that he wouldn't run for three consecutive terms. In spite of this lame explanation, Roosevelt remained enormously popular in America. Had he wrested the nomination from Taft, it's likely he would have gone on to take the national election. For his running mate, Roosevelt chose Hiram Johnson, the governor of California.

DEMOCRAT: WOODROW WILSON The Democratic Convention, held in Baltimore shortly after the Republican slugfest, featured a battle between Missouri Congressman "Champ" Clark, Speaker of the House, and a new type of Democrat entirely: Woodrow Wilson, former president of Princeton University, current governor of New Jersey, a diffident but extremely smart and ambitious man. He was a product of William Jennings Bryan—not a Populist, but the model of a liberal, progressive Democrat.

Wilson eventually got the nod on the forty-sixth ballot, partly because Champ Clark had made himself a figure of ridicule by doing testimonials for a patent medicine company ("It seemed that all the organs in my body were out of order, but three bottles of Electric Bitters made me all right!").

Ever the scholar, Wilson refused to be too joyous about his nomination: "I can't effervesce in the face of responsibility," he said. His vice-presidential candidate was Thomas Marshall, governor of Indiana, who is now known in history for having said: "What this country needs is a really good five-cent cigar." A statement as true today as it was then.

★ ★ ★ **THE CAMPAIGN** ★ ★ ★

Three evenly matched candidates squared off for the presidency—a scenario unlike any other in American history. Personalities began to dominate the election. Taft was honest but passive, Roosevelt explosive but full of energy, Wilson coherent but perhaps cold.

Taft, while admitting it was hard to "keep myself in the headlines," tried anyway. He attacked Roosevelt by saying he "is to be classed with the leaders of religious cults who promote things over their followers by . . . any sort of manipulation and deception."

This was not as far-fetched as it might sound since Roosevelt's ringing cry was: "We stand at Armageddon and we battle for the Lord!" and his progressive followers had an almost religious fervor. He developed a program he called the New Nationalism, in which he claimed the government would play a strong role in regulating the economy and overseeing greedy and corrupt corporations.

While Woodrow Wilson attacked Taft and Roosevelt as "Tweedledum and Tweedledee," two sides of the same Republican coin, he knew that the latter posed a real threat because Roosevelt's progressivism was so close to his own. So Wilson developed his own program, the New Freedom, which placed more emphasis on oversight of

Teddy Roosevelt was shot before delivering a campaign speech—then addressed the crowd, bleeding from the chest, and blamed the attack on his opponents.

monopolies but far less of a powerful role for federal government. The plan would also seek more cooperation with labor unions.

In his public appearances, Wilson didn't come off as a traditional politician—he was a bit stiff, hated kissing babies, and whenever a speech called for him to sound forceful, the results were unconvincing. But Wilson was able to laugh at himself ("It is a fine system when some remote, severe, academic schoolmaster may become President of the United States"), and people warmed up to him. He seemed like a good alternative to Roosevelt's increasing bombast, which had begun to strike many as strident and unnecessarily violent. In the last week of the campaign, gamblers set five-to-one odds in Wilson's favor.

★ ★ ★ THE WINNER: WOODROW WILSON ★ ★ ★

Divided, the Republicans fell. Wilson pulled 6,293,152 votes to Roosevelt's 4,119,207 and Taft's 3,483,922. Although Wilson had won only 41 percent of the popular vote, he performed strongly in the electoral college, with 435 votes (compared to 88 for Roosevelt and only 8 for Taft). Roosevelt was the first and only third-party presidential candidate in American history to pull more votes than a major party candidate. But while he remained a major force in Republican politics (having rejoined the party after 1912), he would never again run for president.

★ ★

ALBUMS AND MOTION PICTURES New forms of technology began to take hold in the election of 1912, not only among the electorate, but among the candidates. Woodrow Wilson spent hours closeted in a tiny, rudimentary recording studio making speeches that were pressed onto 78 RPM phonograph albums and made available for home listening. And Wilson was such a stickler for accuracy that he also brought along a primitive recording device while making campaign speeches so that he could correct any mistakes made by reporters who were hastily scribbling down his words.

Roosevelt hired a moving picture man, whom he nicknamed "Movie," to film some of his own whistlestops. If he didn't have a prepared speech, Roosevelt would sometimes just spout nonsense—"Barnes, Penrose, and Smoot! Recall of judicial decisions! *Alice in Wonderland* is a great book!"—while waving his arms around, in order to fake scenes for Movie to shoot. To silent-movie audiences of the day, the results were convincing enough.

A DANGEROUS PROFESSION Being a presidential candidate always has its risks, but 1912 was a particularly tough year. Wilson's Pullman car was hit by a freight train, which shaved off the little back porch from which the candidate usually spoke. On another occasion, Wilson's Model T overturned, and doctors had to stitch the candidate's scalp back together.

Roosevelt had his own share of train shenanigans: To the horror of reporters and politicians accompanying him, he once took the controls of a locomotive and drove it pell-mell down the tracks. But his worst moment came in Milwaukee on the night of October 14, when a man named John Shrank walked up to him before a speech and shot him in the chest. (Shrank claimed that the ghost of William McKinley had appeared to him and told him to shoot Roosevelt for running for a third term.)

Shrank was apprehended, and amazingly enough, Roosevelt insisted on carrying on with his speech. In one of the great dramatic moments in American politics, he ascended to the platform and said: "Friends, I shall ask you to be as quiet as possible. I don't know whether you fully understand that I have just been shot; but it takes more than that to kill a bull moose."

And then he pulled out his speech from his breast pocket. It was dripping with blood, and people gasped in horror. With a bullet inside him that had fractured a rib and come perilously close to piercing his lung, Roosevelt still had the presence of mind to blame the shooting on his opponents. "It is a natural thing that weak and violent minds should be inflamed . . . by the kind of artful mendacity and abuse that have been heaped upon me for the last three months."

He made his speech and then went to the hospital, where doctors said he was saved by the folded papers, a glasses case, and his thick chest muscles. Roosevelt rested for two weeks; in sympathy, the other candidates stopped campaigning during that time as well.

WILSON'S STOLEN VALISE The only hint of a romantic scandal in this campaign came when Woodrow Wilson's longtime friendship with a lovely divorcée named Mary Allen Peck was made public knowledge. Many Democrats suspected (but never proved) that Republican operatives stole a valise of Wilson's, hoping to find incriminating letters and concoct a scandal. No letters were ever produced, but Wilson (who was married) apparently thought they might be. He solemnly assured an aide that "we Southerners like to write mush" but explained that nothing had gone on between him and Peck.

This was probably true. As Theodore Roosevelt, who could be quite mean, said, "It wouldn't work. You can't cast a man as Romeo who looks and acts so much like an apothecary clerk."

1916

AT A GLANCE

WOODROW WILSON
vs. CHARLES HUGHES

During Woodrow Wilson's first term in office, Congress passed the Sixteenth Amendment, which provided for a federal income tax. Horrible as that was, the worst news in the world was that a massive, bloody war was going on in Europe. Most people in the United States, including Woodrow Wilson, wanted to stay out of that conflict, but it was becoming increasingly difficult, especially after a German submarine sank the British passenger liner *Lusitania* in 1915, killing 124 Americans. Wilson would manage to avoid the war for another two years, but he couldn't stop anti-German hysteria from escalating.

On other fronts, Wilson was an active, liberal president. During his first term, he backed several bills that helped ease the plight of workers in America, including the Child Labor Bill, which forbade children under the age of fourteen from working in factories. He was also responsible for federal laws allotting funds for new highways and schools. The economy boomed, although this was due in part to the high price American companies could demand for their goods in war-ravaged Europe. With Wilson swearing to keep Americans out of the war, he was nominated by deafening applause on the first ballot at the Democratic Convention in St. Louis in June. His vice president continued to be Thomas Marshall.

The Republicans sought their own "intellectual" in the White House and nominated Supreme Court Justice Charles Evans Hughes, with Theodore Roosevelt's former vice president Charles Fairbanks as his running mate. Roosevelt hemmed and hawed a bit before offering Hughes his backing—he called the former justice a "whiskered Wilson" and suggested that the only difference between the two was "a shave"—but in the end, he came around and supported Hughes.

THE CAMPAIGN Wilson chose the now-somewhat-old-fashioned route of refusing to campaign, and at first it seemed like he didn't need to. The Democratic slogan—one of the finest campaign slogans in all American presidential history—was "He kept us out of war." This played exceedingly well, particularly in western states where more and more women had received the right to vote. (The Nineteenth Amendment would give voting rights to all women in 1920.) Wilson supporters claimed "a vote for Hughes is a vote for war!" Although, in fact, Hughes wanted to keep the country at peace. He was, however, undermined at every turn by Theodore Roosevelt, who, while ostensibly stumping for his party's nominee, kept making bellicose anti-German statements.

Nevertheless, the GOP managed to hurt Wilson on a number of issues. Although Americans wanted peace, they wanted their country to be prepared and respected by the world. Republicans, led by Roosevelt, successfully suggested that Wilson had not done enough to respond to the *Lusitania* attack or build up American armed forces. Wilson's reputation was also sullied in the eyes of many religious Americans because of his personal life. His wife, Ellen, had died in 1914, and Wilson shocked the country by marrying again in December 1915—this time to a forty-something widow named Edith Bolling Galt. Republicans quickly spread rumors that the president had had an affair with Galt before Ellen's death. Some even argued that Ellen had died of a broken heart.

THE WINNER: WOODROW WILSON The race was surprisingly close. Election Day was November 7, and with much of the East reporting, by late in the evening Hughes had won almost all the electoral votes he was going to need—just one more state, California, would put him over the top. Democratic-leaning newspapers conceded defeat, while Republican ones carried huge headlines that read "THE PRESIDENT-ELECT—CHARLES EVANS HUGES." Wilson confessed to a friend a feeling of relief that he no longer had to shoulder the weighty responsibility of being president, yet, cautious as ever, he decided not to concede until the next morning, when returns from the West (notoriously slow in reporting) were in.

It was a good thing. It turned out that Wilson had won California by 3,800 votes and swept the West. Nationwide, he beat Hughes 9,126,300 votes to 8,546,789, an amazing instance of snatching victory out of the jaws of defeat.

1920

WARREN G. HARDING

★ ★ ★ ★ ★ ★ ★ ★ ★ ★ ★ VS. ★ ★ ★ ★ ★ ★ ★ ★ ★ ★ ★ ★

JAMES COX

*"[Harding] is a very respectable
Ohio politician of the second class."*

—*New York Times*

Wilson may have promised to keep the country out of war, but by the time of his inauguration in 1917, new circumstances forced him to break his word. The Germans had opened up unrestricted submarine warfare against merchant shipping, and several American vessels were sunk by U-boats. Even worse, Wilson discovered that Germany had proposed a secret alliance with Mexico. In return for joining the Axis powers, Mexico would be given most of the southwestern United States.

Wilson declared war on Germany in April of 1917, sending thousands of "doughboys" to France to join in the hostilities. America's role in the conflict lasted just eighteen months, but combat cost the lives of 53,000 American soldiers. When the armistice was signed in November of 1918, Wilson tried to get Senate ratification of the Treaty of Versailles, which included his cherished League of Nations, but the Republicans thwarted him at every turn. Worn out, Wilson suffered a stroke and spent the rest of his administration partially disabled.

The end of the war brought higher costs for goods and widespread unemployment. Worse, the recent Russian Revolution had left many Americans on edge. This was just the opportunity the Republicans hungered for—a chance to reposition themselves as the party of the full dinner pail and the good old uncomplicated prewar days.

★ ★ ★ THE CANDIDATES ★ ★ ★

REPUBLICAN: WARREN G. HARDING Warren G. Harding was the most libidinous candidate to run for president until Bill Clinton waltzed in from Arkansas seventy years later; the good-looking Harding was particularly popular among women voters, who were now casting their ballots in large numbers. When Republican operatives decided to nominate the fifty-five-year-old Ohio senator, they asked if he had anything hidden in his personal life that would "disqualify" him from winning the presidency. Harding asked for some time to reflect on the question, and he may have pondered that he chewed tobacco, played poker, loved to drink (Prohibition had just been voted in), and was having affairs with not only the wife of one of his friends but also a young woman thirty years his junior, with whom he had an illegitimate daughter.

Then he said, nope, nothing to hide, guys—it's all good.

Harding's vice-presidential running mate was almost his polar opposite; Calvin Coolidge was the hard-nosed and taciturn governor of Massachusetts. When Coolidge received word that he had received the vice-presidential nod, he told his wife, "I've been nominated for vice president." She said, "You aren't going to take it, are you?" To which Coolidge replied, "I suppose I'll have to."

DEMOCRAT: JAMES. M. COX The Democrats faced a serious disadvantage in 1920. They couldn't part company with the recently crippled Woodrow Wilson—it would seem like they were abandoning their man when he was down. So their nominee was James Cox, the liberal governor of Ohio and former newspaper editor, who promised to campaign for Wilson's pet project, the League of Nations. His running mate would be the young and charismatic assistant secretary of the navy, Franklin D. Roosevelt, distant cousin and nephew-in-law of Theodore.

★ ★ ★ THE CAMPAIGN ★ ★ ★

With a candidate like Harding, the Republicans knew they had to act quickly. The first thing they did was get rid of the evidence. They sent his married lover, Carrie Fulton Phillips, on an extended, all-expenses-paid tour of Asia, along with her entire family. And just to be completely safe, Republicans also sent Harding's brother-in-law to Europe because the guy had just married a Catholic (and Catholics didn't play well in the conservative Midwest.)

Now it was time for "a return to normalcy," as Harding had explained in one of his campaign speeches. His speechwriter had actually written "a return to normality," but Harding pronounced it "normalty." Benevolent journalists translated it as "normalcy," and the phrase became a popular Republican campaign slogan.

Normalcy apparently meant small-town, turn-of-the-century American values—Harding was never terribly clear about this—but the phrase played well in a country that was becoming increasingly conservative. James Cox worked incredibly hard, campaigning 22,000 miles in thirty-six states, giving 400 speeches before two million people, but he was handicapped by association with Woodrow Wilson and his anti-Prohibition stance. (Harding, of course, loved his booze, but he expressed public support for Prohibition, echoing popular sentiments throughout the country.)

Democrats furiously attacked Harding. They called him "weak, colorless, and mediocre." They called him "a dummy, an animated automaton, a marionette." They said he was part of a "Senatorial cabal" of "pygmies" and "white-livered and incompetent politicians." But nothing worked. Despite Harding's excesses, he knew what he was doing. An admiring biographer wrote of him that he was a brilliant politician, shrewd when it came to "vacuity"—giving people satisfying emptiness.

★ ★ # THE WINNER: WARREN G. HARDING ★ ★

In the fall of 1920, in the first-ever poll taken during a presidential campaign, *Literary Digest* magazine sent out millions of postcards to its readers, asking whom they would vote for. Harding won by a huge margin, especially among women. The same held true on Election Day. Harding and Coolidge won by a landslide, defeating the Democratic ticket 16,153,115 votes to 9,133,092, with a huge margin in the Electoral College of 404 to 127.

The Roaring Twenties were about to begin, with just the man for the job at the helm—a president who knew how to have a good time.

★ ★

THE ADVENT OF THE AD MAN When Albert Lasker signed on as a Harding campaign consultant, the playbook for presidential elections was rewritten forever. Lasker was the head of a Chicago advertising and public relations firm and a true innovator; he coordinated a PR blitz for Harding that included movies, radio, photography, newspapers, and magazines. Some sample Lasker ad headlines:

"America First!"

"Independence means Independence, now as in 1776."

"Let's be done with wiggle and wobble!"

"This country will remain American. Its next President will remain in our own country."

These utterances may strike us as inane, but in 1920 they spoke to an American public that was becoming more insular in an uncertain world.

Then, as now, people liked their movie stars, and Lasker helped Harding populate his front porch in Marion with Hollywood names. Long before Al Gore got chummy with Sean Penn and Susan Sarandon, newsreel cameras captured Harding

Warren G. Harding was the first candidate to hobnob with Hollywood stars on the campaign trail.

at home, hamming it up with the likes of Al Jolson, Lillian Russell, Douglas Fairbanks, and Mary Pickford. The same cameras caught James Cox doggedly, grimly stumping away. People had no trouble deciding which candidate was more fun.

JUMPING THE FENCE
Harding had so many skeletons in his closet, it's hard to imagine why any of his opponents would feel compelled to invent new ones. But that's what happened when William Chancellor, a racist professor from Wooster, Ohio, claimed that he had thoroughly researched Harding's past and discovered that the candidate had African American ancestors.

In a paper entitled "Genealogy of Warren G. Harding of Marion, Ohio," Chancellor claimed that Harding's great-grandfather and great-grandmother were black and that his father was a mulatto who had married a white woman. As part of his "evidence," Chancellor cited Amos Kling, Harding's father-in-law—an unbalanced man who hated Harding—saying that Harding was "colored."

Woodrow Wilson and James Cox forbade the use of this material against Harding (although it was rumored that the latter whispered the story on more than one occasion). Most newspapers refused to touch it, although the slurs did appear in Democratic handbills. Harding himself was unruffled. When one newspaper reporter finally asked him directly, "Do you have any Negro blood?" Harding answered, to the horror of his party operatives, "How do I know, Jim? One of my ancestors may have jumped the fence."

A STRING OF WET SPONGES
What's in a word? Warren G. Harding's long, meandering speeches, full of archaic nineteenth-century turns of phrase, satisfied his admirers but drove his opponents crazy. (A sample: "What is the greatest thing in life, my countrymen? Happiness. And there is more happiness in the American village today than in any other place on the face of the earth.") After listening to one such speech, the great American humorist H. L. Mencken wrote that it "reminds me of a string of wet sponges; it reminds me of tattered washing on a line; it reminds me of stale bean soup, of college yells, of dogs barking idiotically through endless nights. It is so bad that a sort of grandeur creeps into it. It drags itself out of a dark abysm. . . . "

CALVIN COOLIDGE
vs. JOHN DAVIS

Warren Harding worked and played hard—late-night poker games and his supposed trysts in White House closets with his young mistress, Nan Britton, were balanced by an attempt to keep the country moving into prosperity as the effects of the crisis after World War I wore off. But Harding was hit by a virulent flu in early 1923, and those symptoms may have hidden a heart attack. Doctors became concerned about the president, whose systolic blood pressure readings routinely topped 175.

Pressures on Harding's administration continued as scandals began to unfold, including one in which Charles Forbes, head of the new Veterans Bureau, was found to have stolen two million dollars from World War I veterans (a *New York Times* reporter came across Harding with his hands literally around Forbes's neck, shouting, "You double-crossing bastard!"). Returning from an Alaska vacation prescribed by his doctors, Harding collapsed and died in a San Francisco hotel room on August 2, 1923.

This left the country under the care of "Silent Cal" Coolidge. Coolidge inherited Harding's scandals—including the infamous Teapot Dome Affair, in which government oil fields were leased to private business in return for bribes. Not much of this rubbed off on Coolidge, who was the epitome of rectitude. He was easily nominated for president when Republicans convened in Cleveland in June 1924. His vice-presidential running mate was Charles Dawes, budget director and former bright young political operative for William McKinley.

The Democrats allowed their New York convention to be broadcast over the radio—the first time this had ever happened—and more than one million listeners were treated to endless days of squabbling from Ku Klux Klan members. The

KKK had made major inroads into southern and western Democratic circles and wanted a platform amenable to their racist agenda. But after an astonishing 103 ballots (the most ever cast in a presidential party convention, before or since), anti-Klan forces prevailed and nominated John W. Davis, former solicitor general under Woodrow Wilson. His running mate was Charles Bryan, governor of Nebraska and brother of William Jennings Bryan.

THE CAMPAIGN Say what you might about Calvin Coolidge, the man was smart enough to keep his mouth shut. "I don't recall any candidate for president who ever injured himself very much by not talking," he told reporters hungry for a quote. When it came to America, he was "for the economy. After that, I am for more economy." The Republican campaign slogan "Keep Cool with Coolidge" seemed to sum it up.

John Davis hit the campaign trail, but he was a lackluster speaker who didn't think he would really win ("I went all around the country telling people I was going to be elected," he later wrote, "and I knew I hadn't any more chance than a snowball in hell.") Democrats did discover that twenty-seven Republican ambassadors were AWOL from their duties in foreign countries while campaigning for Coolidge. And it was found that Silent Cal had quietly pocketed a $250 speaking fee when he was vice president. (But then so had Woodrow Wilson's veep, Charles Marshall, who claimed he was so poorly paid as the nation's second in command that "I had to do it, steal, or resign.")

Radio continued to play a growing role in the American electoral process. After Harding's death, the newly formed National Broadcast Association went to Coolidge and told him that both Woodrow Wilson and Harding had basically worn themselves into sickness and death by traveling too much. Perhaps Cal might like to avail himself of the radio?

Silent Cal got the message. On election night, he stayed home and broadcast over a national radio hookup, ending with a very folksy goodnight to the country: ". . . including my father, up on the Vermont farm, listening in."

THE WINNER: CALVIN COOLIDGE Americans ate it up. Calvin Coolidge became the country's thirtieth president by beating John Davis 15,719,921 votes to 8,386,704, an almost two-to-one margin. Supreme Court Chief Justice Oliver Wendell Holmes summed up everyone's feelings quite nicely: "While I don't expect anything very astonishing from [Coolidge], I don't want anything very astonishing."

1928

HERBERT HOOVER

★ ★ ★ ★ ★ ★ ★ ★ ★ ★ VS. ★ ★ ★ ★ ★ ★ ★ ★ ★ ★ ★

AL SMITH

*"ROME SUGGESTS THAT POPE
MOVE HERE!"*

—Headline in Republican newspaper

SLEAZE-O-METER

10
9
8
7
6
5
4
3
2
1

Republicans warned that Roman Catholic candidate Al Smith was secretly plotting with the pope—and that the Holland Tunnel had a secret passageway leading to the Vatican!

On August 2, 1927, while vacationing in his "Summer White House" in the Black Hills of South Dakota, Calvin Coolidge walked outside to waiting reporters and handed them a slip of paper that read: "I do not choose to run for President in nineteen-twenty-eight." Taking no questions, Silent Cal walked back inside his house—and out of the presidency.

No one could quite figure out why Coolidge had made this decision. The economy was booming, and the president, despite or because of his rock-bottom New England reticence and numerous eccentricities, was quite popular. Perhaps he still harbored grief from the death by blood poisoning of his sixteen-year-old son Calvin Jr. in 1924. Or perhaps it was because, as Mrs. Coolidge allegedly said, "Papa says there's going to be a depression."

Whatever the reason, Coolidge's choice not to run set the scene for an election that was, in the words of one historian, "one of the most revolting spectacles in the nation's history."

★ ★ ★ THE CANDIDATES ★ ★ ★

REPUBLICAN: HERBERT HOOVER Herbert Hoover would later gain a reputation as a man who twiddled his thumbs while America's greatest economic crisis set in—but in 1928, he was a formidable candidate. He was the secretary of commerce and a self-made millionaire who had become known for overseeing humanitarian aid to thousands of starving Europeans during and after World War I. Unfortunately, he was also was one of the stiffest, most stilted, most machinelike candidates ever to run for president—so much so that Republicans were forced to plant articles with such headlines as "That Man Hoover—He's Human."

DEMOCRATIC: AL SMITH Al Smith was the polar opposite of Hoover, a politician born and bred within New York's Tammany Hall system. Smith loved meeting people and pressing the flesh. Going into 1928, he was the four-time governor of New York strengthened by a national following and the support of up-and-coming political stars like Franklin Delano Roosevelt and his wife, Eleanor. Al had two problems, however, and they were big ones. He supported the repeal of Prohibition, and he was America's first Catholic presidential candidate.

★ ★ ★ THE CAMPAIGN ★ ★ ★

Neither party was hurting for money in the election of 1928, which may explain why things became so nasty. The Republicans would ultimately spend $9.4 million, the Democrats $7.1 million (the Democrats also ponied up $500,000 on radio time, at the rate of $10,000 an hour for a coast-to-coast hookup).

Republican ads underscored the prosperity Americans were feeling. "Hoover and Happiness or Smith and Soup Houses," or, even more effective, "A Chicken in Every Pot—Vote for Hoover." The message, as one Republican pamphlet put it, was "Your Vote Versus the Spectacle of Idleness and Ruin."

Hoover's handlers often filmed him romping with a large dog to loosen up his image a bit, but he was a man who always wore a full suit and stiff collar, who read his speeches in a perfunctory monotone. ("I can only make so many speeches," he once said. "I only have so much to say.") During interviews he would restrict himself to answering questions without elaborating, and when he was finished, he looked at the questioner blankly, "like a machine that has run down," as one startled reporter put it.

Hoover wisely stayed away from debating the more colorful Smith (he would not even mention his opponent's name) and presented himself as a smart businessman who would run the government like an efficient corporation.

But the election soon took a sickening turn. The Ku Klux Klan continued to be a powerful force in America, with a membership that historians now estimate as high as two to four million. When Smith's campaign train headed West, it was met by burning crosses on the hills and explosions from dynamite charges echoing across the prairies. Klansmen and other religious bigots swayed ignorant voters by telling them that the Catholic Smith, having supposedly sworn fealty to the pope, would turn the United States over to "Romanism and Ruin." Protestant ministers told their congregations that if Smith became president, all non-Catholic marriages would be annulled and all children of these marriages declared illegitimate. Preachers even warned their congregations that if they voted for Al Smith, they would go straight to hell.

Hoover officially proclaimed that his opponent's religion had no bearing on his ability to be president, but even Hoover's wife, Lou, whispered that people had a right to vote against Smith because of his faith. She and many other Republicans spread rumors of Smith's alcoholism, which were already rampant because he favored the repeal of Prohibition or, at least, the right of states to choose for themselves. Republicans sneeringly referred to him as "Alcoholic Smith," told of drunken public behavior, and claimed that he had already secretly promised to appoint a bootlegger as secretary of the treasury.

In truth, Smith was a moderate drinker who enjoyed a cocktail in the evening from legal, pre-Prohibition stock. But as we've seen, truth rarely factors into presidential campaigns.

★ ★ ★ THE WINNER: HERBERT HOOVER ★ ★ ★

Herbert Hoover won in a landslide that included five states from the usually Democratic South, beating Smith 21,437,227 votes to 15,007,698. A joke went around New York that on the day after the election, Smith wired the pope a one-word telegram: "Unpack!"

★ ★

HOW BAD WERE THE ANTI-CATHOLIC SLURS? Consider the following: At the time of the election, New York's Holland Tunnel was just being completed. Republicans circulated pictures of Al Smith at the mouth of the tunnel, declaring that it really led 3,500 miles under the Atlantic Ocean to Rome—to the basement of the Vatican.

In Daytona Beach, Florida, the school board instructed that a note be placed in every child's lunch pail that read: "We must prevent the election of Alfred E. Smith to the presidency. If he is chosen president, you will not be allowed to read or have a bible."

And this lovely poem spread in leaflets in upstate New York during the summer of 1928:

> When Catholics rule the United States
> And the Jew grows a Christian nose on his face
> When Pope Pius is head of the Ku Klux Klan
> In the land of Uncle Sam
> Then Al Smith will be our president
> And the country not worth a damn.

THE BABE Smith was lucky enough to have the endorsement of the country's biggest sports hero, Babe Ruth. After the Yankees' victory in the World Series of 1928, Babe Ruth stumped for Smith from the back of a train carrying the team home from St. Louis. Unfortunately, Ruth wasn't the most dependable spokesman. He would sometimes appear in his undershirt, holding a mug of beer in one hand and a sparerib in the other. Worse, if he met with any dissent while praising Smith, he would snarl, "If that's the way you feel, the hell with you!" and stagger back inside.

NUDE ART AND GREYHOUND RACING? THE HORROR! When people
got tired of attacking Smith for his religion, there were other fruitful areas for invective. One Protestant minister railed against Smith for dancing and accused him of doing the "bunny hug, turkey trot, hesitation, tango, Texas Tommy, the hug-me-tight, foxtrot, shimmy-dance . . . and skunk-waltz." Another minister claimed that Smith indulged in "card-playing, cocktail drinking, poodle dogs, divorces, novels, stuffy rooms, evolution . . . nude art, prize-fighting, actors, greyhound racing, and modernism."

MR. AND MRS. SMITH Al Smith met his wife, Kate, when they were both growing up in Tammany's impoverished Fourth Ward on New York City's Lower East Side. She and Smith shared a deep love, but Kate was anything but sophisticated. During the 1928 campaign, she was slammed with barely disguised anti-Irish bigotry by prominent Republican women. They claimed that with Kate as first lady, the White House would

smell of "corned beef, cabbage, and home brew." Mrs. Florence T. Griswold, Republican national committeewoman, made a speech in which she said, "Can you imagine an aristocratic foreign ambassador saying to her, 'What a charming gown,' and the reply, 'Youse said a mouthful!'" Her audience roared with laughter.

RADIOHEADS By 1928, radio networks like the National Broadcasting Company (NBC) and the Columbia Broadcasting System (CBS) extended nationwide—any major political address could expect to reach forty million listeners.

Although Herbert Hoover was a far worse stump speaker than Al Smith, he was much better at talking in a studio, where the speaker had to stand very still, exactly ten inches away from the large "pie" microphone, to reduce distortion and extraneous noise. (It was not something Hoover liked, however. When someone asked him if he got a thrill out of speaking over the radio, he snapped: "The same thrill I get when I rehearse an address to a doorknob!")

Smith, far better at campaigning in person, had a much worse time on the radio. No matter how much he tried, he could not refrain from moving around, which caused his voice to fade in and out. And his thick New York accent ("rad-deeo" for radio, "foist" for first) alienated many listeners in rural America. Campaign strategists in both parties would make a note for future elections.

1932
AT A GLANCE

FRANKLIN D. ROOSEVELT
vs. HERBERT HOOVER

W hat a difference four years can make. The stock market crash of 1929 sent America reeling into the hangover of the Great Depression, the worst economic crisis the country has ever faced. Twenty-three hundred banks collapsed in 1931 alone. By 1932, more than 300,000 children were forced out of bankrupt school systems. The Depression steadily worsened until millions of Americans were out of work. The name Hoover became synonymous with desperation and poverty—Hoovervilles were shantytowns, Hoover blankets were newspapers, and Hoover Pullmans were boxcars in which, by some counts, 200,000 starving Americans rode throughout the country seeking jobs.

You know things are bad when *Time* magazine calls you "President Reject," but the Republicans were stuck with Hoover, even though he had started making Marie Antoinette-ish statements, such as "Many people have left their jobs for the more profitable one of selling apples." Hoover ran partnered by his vice president, Charles Curtis, who was seventy-two years old and whose main claim to fame was having Native American blood. Before he gave a campaign speech, Curtis would always have an Indian "maiden" recite Longfellow's poem "Hiawatha."

The Democrats had far more exciting prospects with their nominee, fifty-year-old New York Governor Franklin Delano Roosevelt. Although he had been crippled by a bout of polio in 1921, he possessed indefatigable reserves of energy as well as the not inconsiderable political gift of being able to tell people exactly what they wanted to hear. Roosevelt's vice-presidential candidate was "Cactus Jack" Garner, hard-drinking Texan and Speaker of the House.

THE CAMPAIGN It's possible that almost any Democrat could have beaten Hoover in 1932, but Roosevelt's well-oiled political machine left nothing to chance. Through radio, pamphlets, speeches, and direct-mail campaigns, Roosevelt reminded people of empty Hoover promises, namely "prosperity is just around the corner" and "the worst has passed." Of course, most Americans hadn't forgotten these promises, and they were still holding a grudge. Hoover had become so unpopular in America that the Secret Service warned him not to leave the White House. At a campaign stop in Kansas, voters threw tomatoes at his train, and a few people were arrested for pulling up spikes from the tracks. Mounted riot police had to break up a demonstration against Hoover in Detroit (tone-deaf as always to the country's mood, Hoover was traveling in a limousine procession provided by Henry Ford). Marchers demanded that Hoover be lynched. At one point, he broke down and said to his aides, "I can't go on with it anymore." In his final campaign appearance in New York City, he was surrounded by crowds screaming, "We want bread!"

Roosevelt—who had broken with long tradition to become the first presidential candidate to accept his party's nomination in person at the convention—traveled the country, spoke of his "new deal for the American people," and was continuously upbeat.

THE WINNER: FRANKLIN ROOSEVELT In a triumph that was almost literally a reversal of 1928, Roosevelt beat Hoover 22,829,501 votes to 15,760,684 and destroyed him in the Electoral College, 472 to 59. In fact, Roosevelt took 42 out of 48 states. Hoover, even a sympathetic biographer has written, was not just beaten, "he was excommunicated." And a powerful new era in American history was about to begin.

1936

AT A GLANCE

FRANKLIN D. ROOSEVELT
vs. ALFRED "ALF" LANDON

After declaring in his inaugural address that the only thing Americans had to fear was "fear itself," Roosevelt sent his "brain trust" of advisors to Congress, desperate to stem the disastrous inroads of the depression. In record time, he had established the Works Projects Administration (WPA) to give work to jobless Americans, the Social Security Act to provide unemployment and old-age insurance, the Tennessee Valley Authority (TVA) to harness the power of the Tennessee River and provide electricity to seven southern states, and the Civilian Conservation Corps (CCC) to send young urban men into rural areas to plant trees and fight forest fires.

These measures had an immediate effect on the nation's recovery, but naturally Roosevelt's political enemies didn't like them. Conservatives thought the president was flirting with communism, while progressives claimed the New Deal didn't go far enough. Nevertheless, Roosevelt easily won his party's nomination in 1936. He was the most popular Democratic president in memory, holding twice-weekly, easygoing press conferences in his office and making national radio addresses in his satiny, reassuring voice.

Faced with Roosevelt's star power, the Republicans did the best they could. They nominated Kansas Governor Alf Landon, who presented himself as the everyday American. He embarked on a "holy crusade" against the excesses of the New Deal, which, according to Landon, had centralized government too radically in Washington and gave too much power to labor.

THE CAMPAIGN One of Alf Landon's problems was that he never seemed terribly presidential. Even his first name had a rumpled, doggy quality to it. Republicans hired a film director named Ted Bohn—a forerunner of modern political candidate-groomers—to teach Landon not to smile with his mouth hanging open, to walk slightly ahead when in a group in order to dominate pictures, and to shake hands with his chin up to give the impression of firmness. The training did little good.

Roosevelt—who privately referred to Landon as "the White Mouse who wants to live in the White House"— didn't have to do much campaigning. But when he did, he was met by vast throngs of Americans, as many as 100,000 during some speeches, who voiced their approval for his policies. Desperate, the Republicans tried to manipulate the media, asking the Associated Press to always identify Landon in its stories with the tag "budget-balancer." (The AP said it would, but only if it could tag Roosevelt as "humanity's savior.")

THE WINNER: FRANKLIN ROOSEVELT Despite the fact that the Republicans spent nearly nine million dollars on the campaign, Roosevelt kicked butt, big time. He beat Landon 27,757,333 votes to 16,684,231, the biggest voter plurality until 1964, with a stupendous 523 to 8 margin in the Electoral College.

The 1936 election brought a harbinger of dirty campaign tricks to come. Republicans had prepared a powerful radio ad called "Liberty at the Crossroads," which took the form of a short drama in which a marriage license clerk reminds a prospective bridegroom that he would, in the future, have to deal with a large national debt created by Roosevelt's New Deal programs.

"Someone's giving us a dirty deal," the bridegroom whines. "It's a low-down mean trick." And a dark voiceover (marked in the script as "The Voice of Doom") intones: "And the debts, like the sins of the fathers, shall be visited upon the children, aye, even unto the third and fourth generations."

Neither NBC nor CBS, the two largest radio networks, would air this ad—claiming that it was unethical to "dramatize" real-life politics—but plenty of smaller stations with unsold air time quickly snapped it up. They knew a good political soap opera when they saw it, and so did the more than sixty million people who now had access to radios. "Liberty at the Crossroads" was ahead of its time in its dramatizing (and manipulating) people's fears—you can trace a direct line from it to Lyndon Johnson's notorious "Daisy" ad in the presidential campaign of 1964.

1940

FRANKLIN D. ROOSEVELT

★ ★ ★ ★ ★ ★ ★ ★ ★ ★ ★ ★ VS. ★ ★ ★ ★ ★ ★ ★ ★ ★ ★ ★ ★

WENDELL WILLKIE

"We can't have any of our principal speakers refer to it, but the people way down the line can get it out. I mean the Congress speakers, and state speakers, and so forth. They can use the raw material. She's an extremely attractive little tart."

—President Franklin Roosevelt musing aloud on how to smear
Wendell Willkie by making news of his mistress public

D id Franklin Delano Roosevelt want a third term as president? Of course not. Who was he to break with powerful tradition and aspire to something even Washington and Jefferson never had? People would say he suffered from unreasonable ambition. It was time the country stood on its own two feet, with a new leader to guide the way. No, sir, Roosevelt told an aide, he was "violently and vividly" opposed to another term.

All of this meant—if you understood anything about Franklin Roosevelt—that he was almost certainly going to run for an unprecedented third term in 1940.

When members of his cabinet, including Postmaster General Jim Farley and Roosevelt's vice president, John Garner, lined up for Roosevelt's job, Roosevelt smiled but quietly sabotaged their plans. Farley was a brilliant ward politician, but he knew too little about the international scene. And Garner had turned virulently antilabor—perhaps the $200,000 dollars he "won at poker" from industrialists and coal mine owners had something to do with it—making him an embarrassment to Roosevelt's liberal administration.

America was emerging from the depression but seemed to be heading directly into another war. By the spring of 1940, the Nazis had sliced through France like butter and were poised to invade England. In private, FDR began to muse that perhaps his country still needed him. When the Democratic Convention started on July 15, he demonstrated his political brilliance by telling the chairman, "I have not had today and have never had any wish or purpose to remain in the office of president . . . after next January." At the same time, Roosevelt dispatched his close aide, Harry Hopkins, to Chicago with a private message to Democratic bosses, such as Chicago Mayor Ed Kelly: He would accept the nomination, but only on the first ballot and only if he won by more than 150 votes.

The next night, the convention chairman read Roosevelt's message declining the nomination to the assembled Democratic delegates, and they reacted with an uproarious, deafening demonstration in favor of Roosevelt (all secretly prepared in advance by Mayor Kelly). One evening later, Roosevelt was nominated for president in one ballot, beating both

Farley and Garner. Roosevelt then immediately ousted Garner, and made Agriculture Secretary Henry Wallace his running mate.

★ ★ ★ THE CANDIDATES ★ ★ ★

DEMOCRAT: FRANKLIN DELANO ROOSEVELT Franklin Roosevelt was the first American president to even consider running for a third term and probably the only one, short of George Washington, who could have pulled it off. He was at the height of his popularity—a dazzling yet wholly human figure whose "fireside chats" reached more than sixty million listeners and whose New Deal programs had begun to revive the economy.

REPUBLICAN: WENDELL WILLKIE Wendell Willkie was a forty-eight-year-old utilities executive who, until 1939, had been a Democrat and even a delegate at the 1932 Democratic National Convention. Although he had never held elective office, he was a maverick politician with a strong following of avid supporters who loved his crusading, aggressive style. Willkie was tall, shambling, folksy, and charismatic. Taking his grassroots organization into the Republican National Convention in June 1940, he beat out experienced campaigners, including District Attorney Thomas E. Dewey of New York and Senator Robert Taft of Ohio, son of the twenty-seventh president.

★ ★ ★ THE CAMPAIGN ★ ★ ★

Willkie literally rolled up his sleeves and launched a powerful whistle-stop campaign, traveling 19,000 miles in fifty-one days and making more than 500 speeches. His dramatic speaking manner—hair tousled, arms waving wildly—earned him plenty of favorable press, as did his populist stance against political bosses. "Bosses don't hurt me," he once said. "All I ask is a fair shake."

He attacked Roosevelt for being a "third-term candidate" in favor of "one-man rule." Although Willkie agreed with Roosevelt on the need to provide aid to Great Britain (currently being bombed by the Nazis), he preferred a more isolationist stance. "A vote for Roosevelt is a vote for war," he cried in impassioned speeches across America. An FDR victory meant "wooden crosses for sons and brothers and sweethearts." Like a reeling and weaving Rocky Balboa, he begged Roosevelt for a chance to debate. "Bring on the champ!" he cried.

Naturally, the Democratic machine was not prepared to allow Roosevelt to debate the underdog. In the early stages of the campaign, the president didn't even stump. Democrats sarcastically called Willkie "the simple, barefoot, Wall Street lawyer" whose utility company had used spies to bust up labor unions. It wasn't long before the smears became a whole lot worse. Democrats claimed that Willkie's hometown of Elwood, Indiana, had signs that read, "Nigger, don't let the sun go down on you." And numerous Democratic pamphlets featured a photograph of Willkie's father's grave to show that the man had been buried in a neglected potter's field.

But Willkie's fevered campaigning began to pay off. Early pollsters like the American Institute of Public Opinion showed Roosevelt leading by a surprisingly slim margin. Some newspaper surveys even put Willkie on top. Roosevelt, who had not taken Willkie seriously at first, now began to exaggerate his opponent's isolationist stance and told reporters that "anyone who is pro-Hitler in this country is also pro-Willkie." The Republican candidate stepped up his campaigning, even though his throat was so hoarse he had to be accompanied everywhere by a doctor. FDR finally took to the stump, giving five fiery speeches in the last week of campaigning, telling aides that Willkie "didn't know that he was up against a buzzsaw."

THE WINNER: FRANKLIN DELANO ROOSEVELT

Roosevelt, up against the strongest opponent he had ever faced, won the election 27,313,041 votes to Willkie's 22,348,480, a substantial margin but not quite as good as his previous victories. It was a sweet win for

Roosevelt, but he was about to face one of the biggest challenges an American president has ever faced.

★ ★

THE GREAT (UNTOLD) REPUBLICAN SMEAR Henry Wallace was Roosevelt's secretary of agriculture and a pretty good one, too—but this liberal politician had a dreamy, spiritual side. To the horror of President Roosevelt's men, just after Wallace accepted the VP nod, Republicans discovered photostats of letters written by Wallace to a strange Russian mystic named Nicholas Roerich. In one note, Wallace wrote: "I must read Agny Yoga and sit by myself once in a while. We are dealing with the first crude beginnings of a new age. May the peace of the Great One descend upon you."

Another letter to Roerich talked about current events in a weird code: "The rumor is the Monkeys are seeking friendship with the Rulers so as to divide the Land of the Masters between them. The Wandering One thinks this is very suspicious of the Monkeys." Translation: The Japanese (the Monkeys) wanted to divide Manchuria (the Land of the Masters, which the Japanese had invaded) with the British (the Rulers). And Roosevelt (the Wandering One) didn't like it.

The Republican national chairman, Joseph W. Martin, told the Democrats that the original copies of the letters were being held by the treasurer of the Republican National Committee in a bank vault. He threatened to make them public—did the Democrats want people to know that a lunatic like Wallace was only a heartbeat away from the presidency?

This alarmed the Democrats greatly, but oddly enough, at Wendell Willkie's personal order, these letters were never used.

Was this because he held his own "secret"?

THE GREAT (UNTOLD) DEMOCRATIC SMEAR Roosevelt knew that the married Wendell Willkie had a mistress in New York City, a writer and editor named Irita Van Doren. As it turned out, Irita used to be the mistress of Jimmy Walker, the flamboyant New York mayor. This liaison outraged Walker's wife so much that Jimmy was forced to pay her $10,000 each time she made a personal appearance with him.

Roosevelt wondered humorously to aides if Willkie's wife had to be hired in the same fashion to smile at the press during campaign stops. Perhaps, he suggested, the voters might be interested to learn about Willkie's girlfriend.

But voters never did, and they never learned about Henry Wallace's letters, either. There is no knowledge of direct communications between Roosevelt and Willkie, but it's only natural to suspect that some agreement was worked out. Russian mystics? Coded messages? New York mistresses? In a race this close, campaign managers would have been foolish to let such opportunities go to waste.

PLAYING THE RACE CARD

African Americans had been able to vote since the post–Civil War period, but often, especially in the South, they were discouraged from casting their ballots by white segregationists using poll taxes and other means of intimidation. But the rise of black labor leaders and the unionization of many black workers in the 1930s helped turn out blacks to vote for Roosevelt in record numbers. Roosevelt was considered a friend of the working man, and it didn't hurt that his wife, Eleanor, was an outspoken advocate of civil rights. But as the country geared up for war, black leaders were concerned that blacks would be segregated into jobs as cooks and support troops, as they had been in World War I, and not given a chance to prove their mettle on an equal basis with whites.

At Eleanor's suggestion, Roosevelt met with black leaders William White of the NAACP and A. Phillip Randolph of the Brotherhood of Sleeping Car Porters. Roosevelt gave them the impression that he was going to help end military segregation—in return for black votes, of course. But then Roosevelt's press secretary, Steve Early, later announced that blacks and whites would not be intermingled; worse, Early claimed that this policy had been approved by White, Randolph, and others who had met with the president.

White and Randolph were furious, and Roosevelt hastily tried to make amends. He met with Secretary of the Navy Frank Knox and made this suggestion: "Since we are training a certain amount of musicians on board ship—the ship's band—there's no reason why we shouldn't have a colored band on some of these ships, because they're darned good at it."

Race relations took another turn for the worse just a week before the election, when the president made a rousing speech at Madison Square Garden in New York City and then returned to Penn Station to board his train back to Washington. Press Secretary Steve Early attempted to get on the train, but a black New York City policeman named James Sloan didn't know who he was and prevented him from

Crowds hurled everything but the kitchen sink at Wendell Willkie, yet he kept coming back for more.

boarding. Whereupon Early, a Southerner, kicked Sloan in the groin, sending the cop—who had just returned to work after a hernia operation—straight back to the hospital.

The tussle made headlines, and Republicans distributed leaflets showing pictures of Sloan in his hospital bed, with a caption that read: "Negroes: If you want your President to be surrounded by Southern influences of this kind, vote for Roosevelt. If you want to be treated with respect, vote for Wendell Willkie."

Fortunately for Roosevelt, Early apologized, Sloan declared himself a tried-and-true Democrat, and the entire incident was defused.

SPECIAL DELIVERY BY AIR

When making appearances in factory towns and other democratic strongholds, Willkie found himself attacked consistently with flying vegetables and other projectiles. Commentators noted that never before had any candidate had so many objects hurled in his direction—they included, by one reporter's count, cantaloupes, potatoes, tomatoes, oranges, eggs, ashtrays, rocks, chairs, a phone book, and even a bedspread. Willkie usually took such attacks in stride, but outside Detroit, he lunged at one protestor who had spattered his wife with an egg.

IMAGE CONTROL

Stricken by polio in 1921, Franklin Roosevelt was partially paralyzed from the waist down and forced to use a wheelchair and heavy leg braces for the rest of his life. Yet the American public almost never saw him that way, thanks to a carefully orchestrated campaign to make Roosevelt seem as vital as anyone else. Roosevelt arrived at least an hour early for public speaking events, so people did not view him being lifted out of cars, and he used his Secret Service agents and his sons as supports when he stood to make speeches. At one point, when Roosevelt had to attend the funeral of a prominent congressman, the street outside the church was raised to the level of the church floor so that Roosevelt might appear to walk in under his own power. And one reason his wife, Eleanor, became so prominent in politics at a time when most first ladies kept to domestic White House matters was because she was his "eyes and ears," going out to give speeches and gather reaction from around the country.

Of course, none of this would have worked had the press not cooperated. They almost never took pictures of the president's wheelchairs and braces—but when they did, their cameras were quickly destroyed by the Secret Service.

1944
AT A GLANCE

FRANKLIN D. ROOSEVELT
vs. THOMAS DEWEY

B y the summer of 1944, Franklin Roosevelt had led America through the deadliest war in history, bringing the nation to the brink of a victory he would not live to see. At the age of sixty-two, the president suffered from heart disease and high blood pressure, and he was prone to bouts of bronchitis that further worsened his chronic insomnia. Nevertheless, he managed to keep his health problems under wraps, and his doctor, Vice Admiral Ross McIntire, issued reassuring public announcements that Roosevelt was in wonderful shape.

If the country had not been at war, it is almost certain that Roosevelt would not have sought a fourth term. But he told friends and advisors that he would not stand to see a Republican victory, which would mean a Republican president presiding over what promised to be a powerful post-war era for America. At the Democratic National Convention, Roosevelt was nominated on the first ballot. The only suspense came in the choice of a vice president since it was very likely that Roosevelt might not live out a full term. After some debate, Roosevelt ended up choosing Senator Harry Truman of Missouri, a well-liked politician who had received national attention for rooting out corruption in defense contracts.

Meanwhile, Republicans toyed with the possible candidacy of General Douglas MacArthur, hero of the Philippines, but the general's presidential boat was sunk when he was found to have criticized Roosevelt, his commander-in-chief, in letters written to a Nebraska congressmen. (Also working against him were some recently discovered letters of a very different sort, written by MacArthur to an ex-Singapore chorus girl who called him "Daddy.")

In search of safer waters, Republicans nominated forty-two-year-old

Thomas E. Dewey, governor of New York, with Ohio Governor John Bricker as his running mate. Dewey had a record as being an honest governor (and he had been an aggressive New York D.A. who prosecuted mobsters like Legs Diamond and Lucky Luciano). He was the first presidential candidate to be born in the twentieth century, and he had an air of efficiency that struck some people as drably modern, especially in comparison to Roosevelt.

THE CAMPAIGN This was America's first war-time general election since 1864, and the Democrats made the war the issue, praising Roosevelt's successful management of the conflict and his worldwide status as a leader to show the inadvisability of changing commanders at the current time. And the economy, buoyed by defense contracts, was booming.

As in 1940, FDR did little campaigning until the last weeks of the election, but Dewey stumped hard. Because of his pencil moustache, slim stature, and neatly combed black hair, Roosevelt called him "the little man on the wedding cake." This line has been attributed to everyone from actress Ethel Barrymore to Alice Roosevelt Longworth (Teddy Roosevelt's daughter), but FDR made full use of it.

Dewey returned fire, saying Roosevelt was a leftist who had become the darling of American communists. And though he rarely mentioned Roosevelt's health directly, he harped on the "tired old men" of Washington and how they needed to be replaced by young and energetic visionaries like himself.

Then Republicans made the mistake of repeating an apocryphal story about Roosevelt and his Scotch terrier Fala. According to the tale, Roosevelt was visiting the Aleutian islands and accidentally left Fala behind; he later sent a destroyer to pick up the animal. The Republicans tried to use the anecdote to illustrate the president's extravagance, but Roosevelt diffused the charges with gentle sarcasm in a national address: "I don't resent attacks and my family doesn't resent attacks, but Fala does resent them . . . he has not been the same dog since."

THE WINNER: FRANKLIN ROOSEVELT Roosevelt beat Thomas Dewey 25,612,610 votes to 22,117,617, winning in the Electoral College 432 to 99. On hearing the news, Roosevelt quipped: "The first twelve years are the hardest." And perhaps he was right. On April 12, 1945, he died suddenly of a cerebral hemorrhage at the presidential retreat in Warm Springs, Georgia.

1948

HARRY TRUMAN

★ ★ ★ ★ ★ ★ ★ ★ ★ ★ ★ VS. ★ ★ ★ ★ ★ ★ ★ ★ ★ ★ ★

THOMAS DEWEY

*" I know every one of these [reporters].
There isn't one of them has enough sense
to pound sand into a rat hole."*

—Harry Truman, on the journalists who predicted he would lose

SLEAZE-O-METER

10
9
8
7
6
5
4
3
2
1

The presidential election of 1948 is, to date, the most amazing political upset in American history. It contains one of the best campaigns ever run by anyone—President Harry Truman's give-'em-hell extravaganza—as well as one of the worst—that of New York Governor Thomas Dewey. But throughout 1948 and right up to Election Day, November 2, there was not a reporter, pollster, or political expert in the country who thought Truman had any chance of winning at all.

Why was Truman held in such low esteem? After all, he had presided over victory in World War II and the hopeful beginnings of the United Nations, and he had faithfully carried on FDR's New Deal policies. But, with the artificial wartime price controls rescinded, inflation had driven up prices by nearly 40 percent, war with the Soviets was close to breaking out over Stalin's blockade of Berlin, the southern wing of the Democratic Party was upset by Truman's support of civil rights, and a Republican-dominated Congress blocked Truman's every move.

The Gallup poll gave Truman a 36 percent approval rating—the kind of rating that takes you deep into Nixon-Watergate, Carter–Iran Hostages, and George W. Bush–Iraq War territory. Jokes were spread across the country: "I wonder what Truman would do if he were alive." Democratic-leaning newspapers posed rhetorical headline questions like, "Must It Be Truman?" *Life* magazine published admiring profiles of Dewey with speculation on which worthies would make up the Dewey administration. And Truman's own party made overtures to Dwight D. Eisenhower, the immensely popular supreme commander of allied forces during the war, since Eisenhower had not committed to being a member of any political party.

The Republicans were delighted to see Truman in such dire straits. At their national convention, Congresswoman Clare Boothe Luce called Truman "a gone goose" and suggested (in a nod to a popular Coca-Cola ad) that his time in office had not been "the pause that refreshes." The Republicans happily renominated their 1944 candidate, Thomas E. Dewey, along with the liberal Earl Warren, governor of California and future Supreme Court justice, to balance the ticket.

All these insults simmered inside Truman. By the time he was nominated by his dejected party in July of 1948, with Kentucky Senator Alben Barkley as his running mate, he was ready, in the most famous sound bite from 1948, to "Give 'em hell!"

★ ★ ★ THE CANDIDATES ★ ★ ★

DEMOCRAT: HARRY TRUMAN Early in the campaign, the sixty-four-year-old Truman had occasional moments when his confidence vanished (meeting up with Dewey in New York, he whispered, "Tom, when you get to the White House, for God's sakes do something about the plumbing!"), but he was fired by an almost superhuman confidence. He was determined to win this election, even though his own mother-in-law had told him he should quit.

REPUBLICAN: THOMAS DEWEY Dewey had a lot going for him. At the young age of forty-six, he had already established a national reputation as both a crime-buster in New York and a respectable presidential candidate from 1944. This time around, Dewey assembled a team of young political experts to help put him over the top. Their chief (and fatal) advice to him: The presidency is yours. Say nothing that will get you in trouble, and you will win the election in a walkover.

★ ★ ★ THE CAMPAIGN ★ ★ ★

Truman had more to worry about than Thomas Dewey—he also had to fend off challenges from splinter groups within his own party. Henry Wallace, former Roosevelt vice president, was the candidate of the Progressive Party, which ran on a world peace platform and attracted quite a few liberal Democrats, students, unionists, and American Communists. On the other side of the spectrum, anti–civil rights Southerners, led by South Carolina Governor Strom Thurmond, formed the so-called Dixiecrat Party.

With the Democrats so divided, Dewey didn't think he could lose. He ran a very careful campaign on what he called a unity platform, speaking vaguely of America's greatness and portraying himself as a meticulous, upstanding, honest administrator. Elmo Roper, a pollster as famous in his day as George Gallup, had Dewey 44 to 31 percent and announced that he was going to stop polling: "My whole inclination is to predict the election of Thomas E. Dewey by a heavy margin and devote my time and energy to other things." *Newsweek* published its own poll of fifty respected political reporters. Who would win the election? Dewey, said the pundits, fifty to zero.

Truman refused to let his opponent get away with vagueness, and he started out on an incredible whistle-stop train tour of more than 31,000 miles and 350 speeches. He attacked Republicans as "gluttons of privilege," "bloodsuckers with Wall Street offices," and "economic tape-worms." His main target, interestingly, was not Dewey but the Republican-dominated eightieth Congress, which he called "the do-nothing Congress" and which he castigated for not helping to stop rising food and housing prices. Truman spoke to crowds of thousands in towns big and small all across America. He had one thing going for him that Dewey didn't: He struck people as authentic. He used words like "damn" and "hell" while Dewey uttered "good gracious" and "oh, Lord."

Truman introduced his wife, Bess, as "the Boss" (at least until she told him not to do it anymore) and sometimes blurted out incredibly dumb things. Carried away by enthusiasm at one rally, Truman said of Stalin, "I like old Joe. He is a decent fellow." But when Republicans tried to use this against him to prove he was sympathetic to Communists, they found they couldn't get much mileage out of it. Truman was not the Teflon president that Ronald Reagan would be, all smooth with shiny surfaces. Instead, as he campaigned to more and more enthusiastic crowds, he seemed like granite. Anything coming his way simply bounced off.

★ ★ ★ THE WINNER: HARRY TRUMAN ★ ★ ★

The press had Truman measured for his loser's suit right up to and including Election Day, which, in 1948, was November 2, two days after Halloween. On November 1, Gallup gave the election to Dewey by five points. The *Wall Street Journal* published an article listing who Dewey's chief advisors would be. One writer wrote, "We're going to miss lil' ole Harry." Columnist Stewart Alsop wondered in the *New York Times* "how the government can get through the next ten weeks" with Truman as a lame-duck president. Overseas in Great Britain, Alistair Cooke wrote an article about Truman entitled "A Study in Failure."

On November 2, Truman went to bed a loser, and on November 3 he woke up a winner. He beat Dewey 24,179,345 votes to 21,991,291 and was pictured in a photo that immortalized forever the foolish confidence of a press swayed by polls rather than the true desires of ordinary people—a grinning Truman holding the *Chicago Tribune* with a front-page headline reading, in big, bold letters, "DEWEY DEFEATS TRUMAN."

Why did Truman win? Perhaps, as Dewey later claimed, it was because voter turnout was light for that era—only about 51 percent, which indicates that many Republicans were convinced by the polls and stayed home on Election Day, too confident of victory. Or maybe he won because Wallace's Progressives made Truman appear less liberal, while Thurmond's Dixiecrats made the president's civil rights record look even better than it was, especially to blacks.

Or maybe he won because, as the underdog in the fight of his life, he simply went out, threw caution to the wind, and "gave 'em hell." It was a lesson that future Democratic campaigners like Al Gore and John Kerry failed to learn, to their peril.

★ ★

THE FEDERAL BUREAU OF DEWEY FBI Director J. Edgar Hoover was no fan of Harry Truman, and—as he would do later with members of the Kennedy family—

he attempted to find incriminating confidential information to use against the president to influence the outcome of the election. Hoover secretly put agents to work to find stuff that would be detrimental to Truman because, being a longtime friend of Thomas Dewey, he hoped that "President Dewey" would name him as attorney general. One FBI agent remembered that they didn't find much, but the agency actually had the nerve to prepare position papers for Dewey on Truman's supposed "softness" on Communism, which Dewey then released to the press as if they were written by his staff.

DEWEY TO TRUMAN: DON'T TOUCH THAT WHEEL! In the weeks leading up to Election Day, Dewey became so sure of his victory that he began to act like the presidency was already his. He became enraged when Truman announced that he was going to send a personal emissary to Stalin to try to mediate with the Soviet leader. Dewey fumed to reporters: "If Harry Truman would just keep his hands off things for another few weeks! Particularly, if he will keep his hands off foreign policy, about which he knows considerably less than nothing."

TRUMAN TO DEWEY: BITE ME! Well, maybe those weren't his exact words—but Truman went after Dewey with a vengeance. During his stump speeches, he loved to act out both sides of an imaginary dialogue between a doctor (Dewey) who diagnoses his patient (America) as having a great deal of troublesome but not-quite-specified "issues."

"I feel really good, Doc," America would say. "I've never been stronger. What could be wrong with me?"

"I never discuss issues with a patient," Dr. Dewey said, "but what you need is a major operation."

Here Truman made a moustache-twirling motion.

"Is it serious, doc?" the patient asked.

"Not very," Dr. Dewey said, "it just means taking out your entire brains and replacing them with Republican ones."

FOR THE BIRDS In 1946, only about 7,000 homes in America had televisions. By 1948, technology had made televisions both better and cheaper, and 148,000 people had shelled out for the big black boxes. Presidential candidates on both sides were quick to take advantage of technology. Both Truman and Dewey bought air

At the first televised Democratic Convention, the release of a flock of pigeons didn't go as planned.

time, but the honor for the first presidential candidate to do a paid political ad goes to Harry Truman, who gave a televised speech on October 5, 1948, from Jersey City, New Jersey.

Both 1948 political conventions were televised on the East Coast. In order to facilitate this, Republicans and Democrats agreed to hold their events in Convention Hall in Philadelphia—the Republicans in June, the Democrats a month later. For the first time in history, television cables ran over the convention floor, with batteries of hot lights arched over the stage (in the non-air-conditioned hall, the temperature at the podium was ninety-three degrees). Speakers wandered around wearing thick pancake makeup (women were told that brown lipstick showed up better on black-and-white television sets, so most female orators looked like they'd just bitten into a big piece of chocolate).

But people seemed to understand the medium—TV was theater, TV was spectacle. When India Edwards, executive director of the Women's Division of the Democratic National Committee, reached the podium to speak, she waved a steak in the air to emphasize the high price of meat.

But the biggest spectacle did not come off the way it was intended. At two o'clock in the morning, when Harry Truman was about to go on stage to accept his party's nomination, a flock of pigeons was released from underneath a huge floral Liberty Bell. The birds, who had been trapped all night in the hot and humid bell, went berserk. In a scene straight out of Alfred Hitchcock's *The Birds*, the pigeons began dive-bombing delegates, smashing into the rafters of the hall and flying straight into the television lights.

After a moment of stunned silence, Truman and everyone in the hall broke into uproarious laughter. The few people awake and still watching were privileged to see one of the most wonderful moments of live television ever recorded.

1952

DWIGHT EISENHOWER

★ ★ ★ ★ ★ ★ ★ ★ ★ ★ VS. ★ ★ ★ ★ ★ ★ ★ ★ ★ ★

ADLAI STEVENSON

*"General Eisenhower exemplifies
what the fair sex looks for
in a man—a combination of
husband, father, and son!"*

—Clare Boothe Luce

SLEAZE-O-METER

10
9
8
7
6
5
4
3
2
1

The 1950s are often remembered as a time of peace, security, and a big car with tail fins in every driveway, but they were also shaped by pervasive national fear and paranoia.

During Truman's administration, America became embroiled in the Korean War, a so-called police action fought to keep the Chinese Communists and Russians out of the Korean Peninsula but that proved to be a highly unpopular and costly war for the Americans.

Then there was Joe McCarthy. The junior senator from Wisconsin began inspecting the activities of "subversive Americans" and ruined countless careers and lives in a Communist witch hunt. He was a vocal opponent of the Truman administration and constantly repeated his charge that the Democrats were responsible for "twenty years of treason."

At the age of sixty-eight, Truman had decided that seven years of being president was quite long enough, thank you, and so he passed on another term. Because of his stunning upset victory in 1948, Truman was certain that anyone he anointed to follow in his shoes could beat the Republicans (who, after all, had not been in power for two decades, their longest period without a president since the inception of the party in 1856). Truman decided that Governor Adlai Stevenson of Illinois would be his man. A Truman supporter, Stevenson was a strong liberal with a good record and a man of charm and intelligence.

Have you ever offered someone something you are positive they will thank you for profusely, only to have them say, "Um, gee, can I think about it?"

That's how Stevenson responded to Truman's offer—partly because he knew that Dwight Eisenhower was going to be the formidable Republican candidate. He also knew that if he accepted too eagerly, he might be perceived as Truman's lapdog—and, despite the president's high opinion of his own powers, he wasn't all that popular in the country anymore. But Stevenson finally accepted the nomination in a powerful speech at the Democratic Convention in July. The first presidential election dominated by television was about to begin.

★ ★ ★ THE CANDIDATES ★ ★ ★

REPUBLICAN: DWIGHT EISENHOWER Dwight Eisenhower, known popularly as Ike, had been a brilliant commander-in-chief during World War II and later served as Columbia University's president and a NATO commander. He had spent most of his adult life surrounded by a staff that met virtually all his needs—in the morning, he was literally dressed from head to toe by a valet. Eisenhower didn't even know how to use a rotary telephone. Yet, somehow, the average man on the street could relate to the general. Eisenhower radiated confidence and sincerity and a certain homely Americanism. His most famous campaign slogan—"I Like Ike"—just about said it all. Eisenhower's running mate was a young California senator named Richard M. Nixon.

DEMOCRAT: ADLAI E. STEVENSON Stevenson had a wonderful Democratic pedigree. His namesake grandfather had been vice president under Grover Cleveland in 1892 and William Jennings Bryan's running mate in 1900. Stevenson himself had been an assistant secretary of the navy during the war and was now the liberal Democratic governor of a populous and important state. But two significant characteristics were working against him. First, he spoke in elegant compound sentences. Second, he was divorced, and Americans had never voted a divorced man into the White House. (That would have to wait until Ronald Reagan in 1980). Stevenson's veep nominee was John Sparkman, a ticket-balancing senator from Alabama.

★ ★ ★ THE CAMPAIGN ★ ★ ★

It's difficult to run against "the most admired of all living Americans" (as one Roper Poll found Eisenhower to be in 1952), and, even given his underdog status, Stevenson conducted a poor campaign. Part of the problem was his vacillating over whether or not to accept the Democratic nomination; people saw him as weak and indecisive—like

John Quincy Adams before him, a brooding Hamlet—not the person to fight Communism and bring the country out of a nasty war.

Another problem for Stevenson was television. Simply put, Eisenhower's people understood the new medium and Stevenson's didn't. In 1952, 40 percent of American homes, 18 million in all, owned a television. And Americans were buying them at an amazing rate of twenty thousand sets a day.

Stevenson, an eloquent campaign speaker, would become the first American presidential candidate to be truly reduced—made less than he actually was—by television. To begin with, Stevenson's people always bought thirty-minute segments during which Stevenson gave set political speeches on various topics of interest. A half-hour is a very long time to look at one talking head, as we have since discovered, and Americans literally tuned him out. It didn't help that Stevenson hated cue cards and teleprompters and would often digress from his set speech, almost always running over the allotted time. The networks were draconian about time, never granting one second more than what was purchased. Those still watching Stevenson got used to seeing him cut off in midsentence.

Eisenhower's television ad men, who included the legendary Ben Duffy, knew that simpler and shorter was much better. They prepared a series of twenty-second spots entitled "Eisenhower Answers the Nation." The camera would first go to a person or a married couple who had a concerned question: "Mr. Eisenhower, what about the high cost of living?" And it would pan back to Eisenhower: "My wife, Mamie, worries about the same thing!"

Eisenhower shot all these segments in the studio. Shorn of his glasses, which tended to glare and hide his eyes, he had to read from cue cards written in giant letters. Eisenhower hated doing the spots—"To think that an old soldier has come to this," he said—but they were brilliantly effective. When George Ball, a disgusted Stevenson aide, griped that soon "presidential campaigns would have professional actors as candidates," he actually predicted the future.

It wasn't that Ike didn't make mistakes. He was photographed shaking hands with Senator Joseph McCarthy, whom many people of both parties now considered to be a national disgrace. And McCarthy probably did not help Ike by doing a televised endorsement speech for the general in which he repeatedly referred to Adlai Stevenson as "Alger"; this was a smarmy reference to the supposed State Department spy Alger Hiss, whom veep candidate Richard Nixon had helped to convict while a member of the House Committee on Un-American Activities.

But with the world looking more and more like a dangerous place—America had just tested the first hydrogen bomb and the Soviet Union had atomic weapons of its own—the American people were forced to choose between a plain-spoken modern man of action or a long-winded "egghead" who couldn't end a speech on time.

★ ★ THE WINNER: DWIGHT EISENHOWER ★ ★

At 10:30 on Election Night, CBS's powerful UNIVAC computer called the election for Eisenhower. The Democrats kept hope alive as Stevenson made gains in Pennsylvania and Ohio, but then the Republican "streamroller" headed West, completely flattening its opponents. Stevenson took only nine states. Eisenhower beat him in the popular vote 34,936,234 to 27,314,992.

Stevenson conceded graciously, quoting Abraham Lincoln, who said after a losing election that he was too old to cry but it hurt too much to laugh. He didn't abandon his dreams of the presidency—but for the next four years, the beaming face of Ike Eisenhower would come to symbolize a secure, happy, and ordinary America.

★ ★

ADLAI STEVENSON, HOMOSEXUAL Since Eisenhower had a very boring and unassailable personal life—few people at the time knew that his valet John Moaney pulled up the candidate's underwear every morning—the divorced Stevenson was the main target of smears. Stevenson loved women and dated any number of them, but that didn't stop Republicans from spreading rumors that he was gay—especially since, as the campaign began, a friend and aide named Bill Blair had arrived to live in the Illinois governor's mansion. Truman was so alarmed by these rumors that he sent an aide to Illinois to investigate the matter. The man returned to assure the president that Stevenson was straight.

The rumors did not stop as the campaign wore on. A strange man pretending to be an FBI agent called on a friend of a member of Stevenson's staff in order to "officially" investigate Stevenson's supposed homosexuality. No one ever found out who he was. But new rumors spread that Stevenson's former wife, Ellen, had left him because he was gay (Ellen didn't help matters any when she threatened to write a tell-all memoir entitled *The Egghead and I*. Their divorce had mainly been engendered by Stevenson's devotion to his career and Ellen's impatience with his lack of attention to her.)

ADLAI STEVENSON, MURDERER One of the worst rumors that circulated in 1952 appeared in leaflets distributed in the Midwest claiming that Stevenson

Republicans warned voters that Adlai Stevenson was a closet homosexual.

had killed a young girl "in a jealous rage." The jealous rage part wasn't true, but much of the rest was surprisingly accurate. The incident occurred around Christmas of 1912, when the almost thirteen-year-old Stevenson and some friends were playing with a .22 rifle they thought was unloaded. The official story at the time was that, as Stevenson went to put the gun away, it discharged and killed a girl named Ruth Merwin. But children who were there said that in fact Stevenson, fooling around, had pointed the gun right at Merwin and pulled the trigger; the bullet hit her dead center in the forehead.

In either version, the death was accidental, but Stevenson carried around the guilt of the incident for the rest of his life, so much so that he never even told his wife or any of those closest to him about it. It is unknown how the Republicans discovered the secret, but fortunately their leaflets were not widely circulated, and America as a whole was unaware of the episode.

YOU'RE MAKING ME ILL. Saved for posterity were the notes Adlai Stevenson jotted down to himself one night in 1952 as he tried to figure out whether or not he should accept his party's nomination for the presidency. They provide a fascinating (and slightly scary) look into the mind of a politician:

I would not accept the nomination if offered to me.

I [illegible] that the Presidency is a duty from which no American should shrink in fear ... but even if I had the self-confidence to aspire to [crossed out] for that dread office, I could not accept the Democratic nomination.

I have repeatedly said, my only amb. is to be Gover. of Ill. I have a lot of unfinished business here in Ill. . . . that is the limit of my ambitions and probably the full measure of my competence too.

I do not wish to be nominated for the Presidency. I am a candidate for reelection as Gov. of Ill. That is my only ambition.

Would I accept the nomination of the Dem. Party? Yes, I would. I don't suppose one can refuse except in the most extenuating of circumstances. And I suppose the friendly people of Ill. would release me from my commitments in that event.

1956

DWIGHT EISENHOWER
vs. ADLAI E. STEVENSON

By 1956, tensions in America had simmered down a little. President Eisenhower's Big Four summit conference in Geneva, in which America, France, England, and Russia made some accords, lessened fears on the Cold War front. On the home front, Joseph McCarthy had been completely discredited (and would die of cirrhosis in 1957).

But all the work took a toll on the president's health. In September of 1955, Eisenhower suffered a heart attack. Although he recovered, people began to wonder if he was up to the strains of the office. Less than a year later, Eisenhower went back to the hospital for more surgery—this time, for an intestinal disorder. Nevertheless, the Republicans nominated Ike on the first ballot at their convention. Eisenhower had tried to get rid of Richard Nixon by offering him a cabinet post, but the vice president refused. To avoid an unseemly public battle, Eisenhower agreed to keep him on as a running mate.

Adlai Stevenson, who had worked diligently for the Democratic Party in the previous four years, wanted another shot at the presidency. Despite a primary challenge from Senator Estes Kefauver of Tennessee, Stevenson won—and picked Kefauver as his running mate.

THE CAMPAIGN Stevenson, gallant as ever, had his work cut out for him. One sign of Eisenhower's enduring popularity was a 1955 Gallup Poll, in which six out of ten Democrats said that if by some far-fetched chance the Republicans did not nominate Ike in 1956, the Democrats should. It's hard to fight that kind of deep emotional feeling, and Stevenson's task was made harder still when his men tried to find an advertising agency to handle the campaign. Twenty major ad agencies in New York said no thanks to the lucrative deal—they were afraid of being dumped by their main clients, a bunch of Republican-supporting businesses.

Eisenhower, running on his "four more years of prosperity" theme, was almost unassailable. The Democrats hammered away at what they called his part-time presidency (doctors had prescribed plenty of rest and exercise for Ike) but had to be careful not to be seen as attacking a sick man. Their best ad line was "Defeat part-time Eisenhower and full-time Nixon," which raised the specter of Nixon as the power behind the throne. In fact, 1956 marks the true beginning of that favorite Democratic sport: Nixon bashing. A series of radio and TV ads asked, "Nervous about Nixon? President Nixon?" In one, shopkeepers from Nixon's hometown claimed that they had to choose between displaying Nixon campaign posters or being evicted.

The nervous-about-Nixon campaign never ran. Stevenson, ever the gentleman, would not allow the attack ads to air.

THE WINNER: DWIGHT EISENHOWER Eisenhower beat Stevenson 35,590,472 votes to 26,022,752, thus ending the eloquent Illinoisan's career as presidential wannabe, although he did go on to become an effective and distinguished ambassador to the United Nations. When Stevenson was a little late conceding on the election night of 1956, Eisenhower's arrogance showed through: "What in the name of God is the monkey waiting for?" he snapped. "Polishing his prose?"

But the Democrats—with ambitious senators like Lyndon Johnson, John F. Kennedy, and Hubert Humphrey currently jockeying for national prominence— would soon have their revenge.

1960

JOHN F. KENNEDY

★ ★ ★ ★ ★ ★ ★ ★ ★ ★ VS. ★ ★ ★ ★ ★ ★ ★ ★ ★ ★ ★

RICHARD NIXON

"Nobody knows to this day who the American people really elected in 1960."

—Tom Wicker

SLEAZE-O-METER

10
9
8
7
6
5
4
3
2
1

The year 1960 represented a powerful changing of the guard in American politics—oldsters like Eisenhower and Truman were out, youngsters like John F. Kennedy, with his "New Frontier," and Richard Nixon, running as the "New Nixon," were in.

And it was about time. Eisenhower, with his cabinetful of Republican millionaires (eight of them) and his penchant for smoothing things over without really fixing them, had left the country with more than a little hard work to do. The Russians had beaten the Americans to space with *Sputnik I*, and their belligerent premier, Nikita Khrushchev, was making threatening noises. Eisenhower sent federal troops to enforce school integration in Little Rock, Arkansas, but this action did nothing to address the roots of the issue of civil rights. And American advisors were gradually becoming a presence in a distant country called Vietnam.

The most explosive decade in the twentieth century was about to begin with an election that many feel remains, to this day, too close to call.

★ ★ ★ THE CANDIDATES ★ ★ ★

DEMOCRAT: JOHN F. KENNEDY Scion of the fabled Massachusetts family, forty-three-year-old John F. Kennedy was a war hero who was first a congressman, then a senator, and was now running for president, all in the short span of fourteen years. It was a meteoric rise—helped in good measure by his family's money, his movie-star good looks, and his lovely wife, Jackie. But Kennedy had a big strike against him—he was Catholic. The last Catholic to run for president, Al Smith, had been practically burned at the stake.

Senator Lyndon B. Johnson, senate majority leader, was Kennedy's running mate. Kennedy and Johnson hated each other, but JFK needed the Texan as a Southern ticket-balancer. So why did Johnson take the job? As he told a woman friend at the Democratic Convention, "One out of every four presidents has died in office. I'm a gamblin' man, darlin', and this is the only chance I got."

REPUBLICAN: RICHARD M. NIXON The forty-seven-year-old Nixon's rise had been just as meteoric as Kennedy's, in exactly the same span of time, with two terms as Eisenhower's vice president to boot. His star had risen in the eyes of the American public after his so-called Kitchen Debate with Russian premier Nikita Khrushchev at a trade show in Moscow in 1959. Standing in the mocked-up kitchen of a "typical American home," Nixon deftly parried Khrushchev's bullying sallies and came across as a hero for American ideals and democracy.

This did not necessarily help him with his boss, who had distrusted his vice president ever since the Checkers Speech. When asked if Nixon had participated in any major decisions in his administration, Eisenhower replied, "If you give me a week, I might think of one."

Nixon's running mate was Republican UN Ambassador Henry Cabot Lodge.

★ ★ ★ THE CAMPAIGN ★ ★ ★

The battle of 1960 was hard hitting and fast moving. Instead of traveling by rail, candidates flew in chartered planes all over the country, visiting cities and towns selected by modern statistical analysis.

To combat his reputation for being devious and underhanded, Nixon created his New Nixon persona: mellow, mild, and reasonable. Democrats weren't buying it, particularly former president Harry Truman, who once remarked, "If you vote for Nixon, you might go to hell."

Of course, Kennedy had his own share of image problems. His promise of a New Frontier had little meaning for most people, and his speeches played much better in large urban centers than in the heartland. Most of America's farmers were not impressed with his rich-boy charm. (After talking to an unsympathetic audience at a South Dakota state fair, Kennedy muttered to aides: "Well, that's over. Fuck the farmers.")

And then, of course, there was the problem of his Catholicism. The level of anti-Catholic bias in the country had sunk since the days of Al Smith, and Kennedy was able to skillfully defuse the issue. He went to Houston to address a prominent group of Protestant ministers and convincingly denied that he had any allegiance to the pope. To his credit, Nixon refused to make Kennedy's religion an issue; the Democratic forces under campaign manager Bobby Kennedy kept bringing it up, however. At one point, Bobby teared up during a speech and said, "Did they ask my brother Joe whether he was a Catholic before he was shot down?" (Joe Kennedy, eldest of the brothers, had been killed by the Nazis during the war.) And Democrat campaign workers continued to make cynical use of the issue, asking voters (in a technique that today would be called push-polling): "Do you think they're going to keep Kennedy from being president just because he is Catholic?"

"Tricky Dick" Nixon actually ran a far cleaner campaign than Kennedy. Faced with attack ads, such as the glowering picture of Nixon over the headline "Would You Buy a Used Car from This Man?" Nixon hammered away at his opponent's "inexperience" in foreign affairs and his lack of a really viable agenda for the country. The election was being rated by pollsters as too close to call by September, when Nixon foolishly agreed to a series of four debates with Kennedy. The first one was broadcast from Chicago on September 26.

Sixty million Americans watched the debate, and millions more listened to the radio broadcast. Most of those listening to (and not viewing) the debate thought that Nixon had won. But those who tuned into their televisions saw a poised, cool, and confident Kennedy and a strained, tired-looking Nixon whose makeup seemed to be streaking with sweat over his five o'clock shadow. Afterward, Nixon's mother called to ask if he was ill; in fact, he was fighting off the effect of a debilitating infection that occurred after he had banged his knee on a car door earlier in the campaign.

Although there were three more debates to go—debates in which Nixon looked much more refreshed and confident—it is the first debate in Chicago that voters, and American history, remembered.

The first televised presidential debate ushered in a whole new era of dirty tricks.

★ ★ ★ THE WINNER: JOHN F. KENNEDY ★ ★ ★

Going into election night, many commentators were predicting a Kennedy victory, although by no means a landslide. An engaged American public went to the polls—this was one of the last elections to date where more than 60 percent of eligible voters cast their ballots. The final outcome was Kennedy 34,226,731 votes and Nixon 34,108,157 votes, a difference of 119,450 votes, or less than one-tenth of one percent (although Kennedy won in the Electoral College 303 to 219). It was the closest election since the Benjamin Harrison–Grover Cleveland contest in 1888. (By contrast, in 2000, Al Gore would win the popular vote by more than a half-million votes over George Bush, although he lost in the Electoral College.)

After a nearly sleepless night, Richard Nixon conceded to John F. Kennedy, and Camelot was ready to have its brief, shining moment on stage. But behind the glittering myth remains the question, Who really won in 1960?

★ ★

"NO ONE STEALS THE PRESIDENCY OF THE UNITED STATES." Many Republican bigwigs could not understand why Nixon refused to contest the election results of 1960. He certainly had good reason to be suspicious. Immediately after the election, Earl Mazo, an investigative reporter for the *New York Herald Tribune*, began a series of highly convincing articles detailing voter fraud in two key states, Texas (Lyndon Johnson's home state) and Illinois (home to the powerful Democratic machine run by Chicago Mayor Richard Daley).

In Texas, there was widespread evidence of stolen ballot paper, dead men voting, and phony registering. "A minimum of ten thousand votes for the Kennedy-Johnson ticket were simply nonexistent," Mazo wrote, with certain polling stations reporting thousands more votes than they had registered voters.

In Chicago, Mayor Daley held back on releasing statewide election returns, probably to see just how many votes Kennedy would need. It would later become apparent that Nixon had actually taken 93 of the state's 102 counties, yet somehow he managed to lose in Daley-controlled Cook County by 450,000 votes. (Nixon would end up losing the state and its twenty-seven electoral votes by just over eight thousand votes, out of 4.7 million cast.) In the early morning hours, Daley called up John Kennedy and said: "Mr. President, with a bit of luck and a few close friends, you're going to carry Illinois." In Illinois, Mazo found evidence of cash payments for votes by precinct captains, dead voters, duplicate voting, and "pre-primed" ballot machines, which would automatically record three votes for every one cast.

Had the election gone the other way in both of these states, fifty-one electoral votes would have found their way to Nixon's total, making him the president.

Mazo had published only four parts of his proposed twelve-part series in the *Herald Tribune* and was about to examine possible Democratic fraud in other states such as Alabama and California, when Richard Nixon asked him to visit him in the vice president's office. When Mazo showed up, Nixon implored him to stop writing the series in the interest of national unity. "No one steals the presidency of the United States," Nixon told him.

In an age when the press was far more cooperative with politicians than it is now, Mazo agreed to discontinue his articles. But did Nixon really believe that Kennedy had not stolen the presidency? Probably not, but faced with the difficulty of proving these charges, faced with the uproar asking for a recount would have caused, Nixon made the wise choice not to contest.

The Democrats had out-tricked Tricky Dick. And Nixon would not forget.

HOW TO PREPARE FOR A NATIONALLY TELEVISED HISTORIC PRESIDENTIAL DEBATE As your teachers in school undoubtedly told you, there is a right way and a wrong way to prepare for the big test.

The "wrong" way: Richard Nixon shows up in Chicago at midnight on the day before the debate, exhausted from barnstorming through eleven states and plagued by a recurrent fever. The next morning, instead of resting, he gives a major speech and then spends six hours in his hotel room by himself, studying policy reports and refusing to see anyone. Then he heads for the television studio, on the way banging his already infected knee once again. His temperature is over 100 degrees. Instead of wearing regular makeup for television, he insists on smearing on something called Lazy Shave, a kind of talcum powder that casts his face in a ghostly pallor. And he agrees that the debate can take place with both candidates standing—something the Democrats, aware of his hurt knee, insist on.

The "right" way: Kennedy shows up in Chicago a day and a half before the debate and asks an aide, "Any girls lined up?" On the day of the debate, he gets a suntan on the roof the Palmer House Hotel, has lunch with some friends, and then "studies" in his hotel room by doing Q&A sessions with staff while lying on the bed in his underwear. Ninety minutes before the debate starts, Kennedy slips into a room where a call girl awaits him and emerges fifteen minutes later, according to an aide, "with a big grin on his face." Then he dashes to the television studio, arriving only moments before the debate begins.

JUMPERS, RUNNERS, CLUTCHERS, AND SCREAMERS It's hard to think of a presidential candidate with more sex appeal than John F. Kennedy—and his appearances on national television just underscored the phenomenon. Journalists accompanying Kennedy on his campaign would divide the women into categories—"jumpers," who would try to leap on his campaign car, "runners," who would chase after him everywhere, "clutchers" who, given the chance, would grab his arms and not let go, and "screamers," who would let out loud wails of, "Oh, Jack, I love you! I love you!"

Kennedy, of course, was never averse to taking advantage of adoring groupies. One day, after his voice gave out from too much campaigning, Kennedy wrote down a few notes on an envelope for a staffer, who preserved them for posterity. "I got into the blonde," one said. Another plaintively read: "I suppose if I win—my poon days are over?"

He would win—but they were far from over.

1964

LYNDON JOHNSON

★ ★ ★ ★ ★ ★ ★ ★ VS. ★ ★ ★ ★ ★ ★ ★ ★ ★

BARRY GOLDWATER

"We can't let Goldwater and the Red Chinese both get the bomb at the same time. Then the shit will really hit the fan!"

—Lyndon Johnson

SLEAZE-O-METER

10
9
8
7
6
5
4
3
2
1

After the tragic events of November 22, 1963, when President John Fitzgerald Kennedy was shot down by assassin Lee Harvey Oswald, many thought that his mainly ignored vice president didn't have the strength or savvy to unite the country. Among these people were plenty of East Coast liberals who—in Lyndon Baines Johnson's own bitter words—thought he was "corn pone," an uncouth West Texan hillbilly who lifted up his beagles by the ears. The disdain was mutual. Johnson loved to tell "liberal" jokes along the lines of: "What's the difference between a liberal and a cannibal? A cannibal doesn't eat his friends."

Johnson was not interested in reform as an intellectual exercise. He was a tried-and-true New Deal Democrat, which meant, as a friend said, that he was an old-fashioned, roll-up-his-sleeves do-gooder. Johnson continued policies begun by Kennedy, declared war on poverty with numerous government-assistance programs, and helped pass a strong Civil Rights Act. The mood of the country was positive. America was more secure than it had been in a decade because of the Nuclear Test Ban Treaty. Johnson was gradually committing more troops to Vietnam, but most Americans, for the time being, were indifferent to this fact. The liberals may not have liked Johnson, but he still had plenty of support from the nation at large.

He also deeply wanted another term, and he was prepared to wage one of the dirtiest campaigns of the twentieth century to get one.

★ ★ ★ THE CANDIDATES ★ ★ ★

DEMOCRAT: LYNDON BAINES JOHNSON The man known as LBJ—the last of the midcentury Democratic three-initial presidents— was a garrulous Texan whose folksy, back-slapping manner hid an extraordinary desire for power and an intimate knowledge of how to get it, honed in twenty years in the United States House of Representatives and Senate. His vice-presidential running mate was Hubert Humphrey, a true liberal and civil rights activist whom Johnson treated as shabbily as possible. When he chose Humphrey for veep, he said to him: "If you didn't know you were going to be vice president a month ago, you're too damn dumb to have the office."

REPUBLICAN: BARRY M. GOLDWATER The fifty-five-year-old
Goldwater was born in Arizona to a Jewish father and Presbyterian mother. He worked in the family's successful department-store business, served as an air force pilot, and became a U.S. senator in 1952. Goldwater was an ultra-conservative who favored giving army field commanders the right to use tactical nuclear weapons and liked to say very provocative things, such as, "Sometimes I think this country would be better off if we could just saw off the Eastern seaboard and let it float out to sea."

These were not the beliefs of Republicans like Eisenhower or even Nixon, but in 1964, the Republicans were controlled by ultra-conservatives—and Goldwater was the result. His running mate was a complete unknown, William E. Miller, a conservative ideologue and upstate New York congressman.

★ ★ ★ **THE CAMPAIGN** ★ ★ ★

When Barry Goldwater was nominated at a Republican Convention that saw moderates and conservatives fighting tooth and nail, the Democrats were gleeful—one Democratic politician laughed that the Republicans were on a "kamikaze mission."

Johnson knew he was going to beat Goldwater, but a simple victory wasn't enough—he wanted to destroy his opponent and thereby gain a huge mandate for his first elective term. At the outset of the campaign, Johnson received a report from his media advisors that the way to really cremate Goldwater was to portray him as "ridiculous and a little scary: trigger-happy, a bomb-thrower . . . to keep fear of Goldwater as unstable, impulsive, [and] reckless in the public's mind."

The president didn't lose any time. At campaign stops, he would point to the sky and say that John F. Kennedy's spirit was "there in heaven watching us!" Who would the martyred JFK, and this audience, like to see in the White House—Johnson or Goldwater? "Which man's thumb do you want to be close to the button . . . which man do you want to reach over and pick up that hotline when they say, 'Moscow calling'?"

This might seem like alarmist rhetoric, but Goldwater only encouraged the remarks when he said things like, "Let's lob one into the Kremlin and put it right into the men's room." He also played to the racial tensions that were increasingly present in America, particularly in urban areas. "All men are created equal at the instant of birth . . . but from then on, that's the end of equality," he said. Goldwater struck at white Americans' fears of black criminals: "I don't have to quote the statistics to you. You know. Every wife and mother—yes, every woman and girl knows what I mean."

Since Goldwater would often couple these announcements with statements like, "You know, I haven't got a really first-class brain," many Americans were terrified of him. *Newsweek* called him "the fastest gun" and *Life* said he was a man of "one-sentence solutions." A nationwide survey of American psychiatrists found that a sizable percentage thought Goldwater was unfit to serve as president because he suffered from clinical paranoia.

As the campaign heated up, Johnson instructed his staff to influence the press in whatever way they could ("reporters are puppets," he told them). When Goldwater attacked vice-presidential candidate Hubert Humphrey as a draft dodger (Humphrey had actually registered for the draft in World War II but received a deferment), top Johnson staffer Walter Jenkins and press secretary Bill Moyers influenced editors at the *Washington Post* and *New York Times* to report on how degrading the Republican charges were. White House aide Walter Heller wrote a secret memo to Johnson in which he suggested that "it might be healthy to get some respected columnist to give wider circulation to adverse Goldwater impact on the stock market." The person he picked was syndicated financial columnist Sylvia Porter, who wrote two columns about how a Goldwater victory would be bad for America's economy.

Goldwater fought back. His campaign produced a scurrilous book entitled *A Texan Looks at Lyndon: A Study in Illegitimate Power*, which brought together all the nasty stories about Johnson and harkened back to nineteenth-century campaign pamphlets in its free-swinging slurs. Johnson, according to author J. Evetts Haley, was guilty of all types of vote buying and sleazy politicking; even worse, he was responsible for the murder of several business associates and even the assassination of John F. Kennedy. In the first year of its publication, the book supposedly outsold the Bible in the state of Texas.

Two conflicting bumper sticker slogans of the time say it all.

Goldwater Supporter:
IN YOUR HEART YOU KNOW HE'S RIGHT.

Johnson Supporter:
IN YOUR GUT YOU KNOW HE'S NUTS.

★ ★ ★ THE WINNER: LYNDON JOHNSON ★ ★ ★

In the end, the American people were suitably frightened. On November 3, NBC News called the race for Johnson in a landslide by 6:30 P.M., well before the polls closed. Sixty-two percent of voters showed up at the polls and Johnson received the biggest percentage of the popular vote in U.S. history (61.1). His 16,000,000 vote margin (43,129,566 to 27,178,188) was the largest until that time (though it was later eclipsed by Richard Nixon's 1972 margin of victory and Ronald Reagan's 1984 totals). Republicans were horrified, Democrats joyful. It looked like a long reign for the corn-pone president.

But in the 1960s, things had a way of changing very quickly.

★ ★

"DAISY" What may well be the most famous and effective campaign commercial of all time debuted in the 1964 election.

On September 7, during NBC's top-rated "Monday Night at the Movies," viewers were treated to a lovely shot of a little blonde girl walking through a field. She stops to pick up a daisy and begins pulling off the petals and counting in a high, innocent voice, "1 . . . 2 . . . 3 . . . 4." As she finishes, a military voice begins a count-down: "10 . . . 9 . . . 8 . . . 7 . . . 6." As the counting reaches zero, the little girl looks up, startled. You stare into her frozen face and . . . a huge mushroom cloud explodes, filling the screen. Over the mushroom cloud, Lyndon Johnson's voice says, "These are the stakes. To make a world in which all of God's children can live, or to go into the dark. We must love each other, or we must die."

Johnson's team paid to air the ad only once—but to the delight of the Democrats, newscasts continuously replayed the spot in its entirety, driving home the message and offering free exposure. The more the Republicans screamed, the worse it was. Perhaps the ad was overkill. Yet no one who saw it could ever forget its stark simplicity.

IF IT'S FIVE O'CLOCK, IT MUST BE DIRTY TRICKS TIME

It is amazing that Lyndon Johnson wasn't impeached for some of the dirty tricks he pulled on Barry Goldwater—they were as bad as the unethical tactics that got Richard Nixon thrown out of office ten years later.

In order to smear his opponent, Johnson set up a top-secret sixteen-man com-mittee, which was dubbed the "anti-campaign" or the "five o'clock club" because of its after-business-hours nature. Johnson directly controlled this committee through two of his aides, who chaired each meeting. Among their activities were:

- Developing books to smear Goldwater, with such titles as: *Barry Goldwater: Extremist of the Right; The Case Against Barry Goldwater*; a Goldwater joke book enti-tled *You Can Die Laughing*; and even a children's coloring book, in which the wee ones could color pictures of Goldwater dressed in Ku Klux Klan robes.

- Writing letters to columnist Ann Landers under the guise of ordinary people who were terrified of Goldwater becoming president.

- Secretly feeding hostile questions to reporters on the Goldwater campaign.

- Sending CIA agent E. Howard Hunt (later infamous for his role in the Watergate break-in) to infiltrate Goldwater campaign headquarters. Hunt got access to advance texts of Goldwater speeches and fed the information to the White House staff, who undercut Goldwater initiatives on a number of occasions.

THE REPUBLICANS FIGHT BACK The Republicans didn't just sit on their hands, of course. They fought back with plenty of dirty tricks of their own:

- The Republican National Committee planted numerous newspaper articles wondering how Johnson had amassed a personal fortune of ten to fourteen million dollars during a lifetime in public service. One innocent answer was that his wife, Lady Bird, owned a radio station, but Johnson was also not above taking advantage of sweet real estate deals offered by admiring Texan friends.

- A Republican congressional aide spread the probably false story that Johnson had been given a large sum by the State Department for his personal use while visiting in Hong Kong as vice president in 1961.

- Republican ads in Western newspapers spread rumors that Johnson had kidney cancer and speculated on how long he had to live.

- A poll published in October showed Goldwater making gains in numerous states. The group taking the poll was called Opinion Research. When suspicious Democrats questioned these results, other pollsters proved that Opinion Research worked for the Goldwater campaign and appeared to be falsifying its results.

CHOICES A group calling itself Mothers for a Moral America made an extremely controversial pro-Goldwater film called *Choices*, which showed Americans that they had a "choice between good and evil."

On the positive side, the film portrayed conservative young people having good clean fun, the American flag flying high, the Statue of Liberty gleaming in the sun, and Barry Goldwater giving impassioned speeches.

The bad side included pornographic books with such names as *Jazz Me Baby* and *Men for Sale*, dances like the Twist, women in topless bathing suits, black kids dancing and throwing rocks while rioting, and a speeding Lincoln Continental from the windows of which beer cans are hurled (this last bit was a knock at LBJ, who loved to drive at high speeds on his Texas ranch while tossing down a few cold ones).

Which side would you choose? Tough call. Mothers for a Moral America

Democrats encouraged children to color pictures of Barry Goldwater dressed in the robes of the Ku Klux Klan.

turned out, in the later words of a Goldwater aide, to be a "front group" for the Goldwater campaign. The film was scheduled to air on television late in the campaign, but Democrats found out about it and raised such a fuss about its racist content that Goldwater was forced to pull it.

JOHNSON'S GAYDAR In early October, the Goldwater campaign received an unexpected gift—the arrest of Walter Jenkins, Lyndon Johnson's top staffer, on a public morals charge for soliciting sex in the men's room of a Washington, D.C., YMCA.

The forty-six-year-old Jenkins had worked for Johnson for years. He was married with six children but mainly seemed to live for his work. On October 7, 1964, he went to a Washington party, drank about five martinis, and then went around the corner to the YMCA, where he encountered another man in a basement men's room. Just as things were getting hot and heavy, they found themselves surprised by three undercover cops.

Johnson was horrified—he later told a biographer, "I couldn't have been more shocked about Walter Jenkins if I'd heard that Lady Bird had killed the pope." The president was certain that the Republicans had framed Jenkins, although it was soon revealed that Jenkins had another arrest for soliciting sex in the same bathroom five years earlier.

Despite LBJ's best efforts to suppress the story, it hit the wire services. Jenkins resigned, and Goldwater, who had served in the air force reserve with Jenkins, publicly claimed that Republicans should make no use of this personal tragedy. Privately, he gleefully said to reporters: "What a way to win an election, communists and cocksuckers!" But before his operatives could use the Jenkins arrest to push home the message of immorality in the White House, larger events, including the explosion of China's first atomic bomb, took over the news.

There is one tragicomic footnote to the affair: Some weeks after the incident, LBJ was talking to FBI Director J. Edgar Hoover about what had happened, a conversation that was captured on routine White House tape recordings and later released under the Freedom of Information Act. "I guess you're gonna have to teach me about this stuff," Johnson said, "I swear I can never recognize [gay people.]"

And Hoover—long rumored to be gay himself, as LBJ must certainly have known—reassured his commander-in-chief: "There are some people who walk kind of funny that you might think may be queer. But there was no indication of that in Jenkins's case."

1968

RICHARD NIXON

★ ★ ★ ★ ★ ★ ★ ★ ★ ★ ★ ★ VS. ★ ★ ★ ★ ★ ★ ★ ★ ★ ★ ★ ★

HUBERT HUMPHREY

"*I say categorically that I have no contemplation at all of being the candidate for anything in 1964, 1966, 1968, or 1972. . . . Anybody who thinks that I could be a candidate for anything in any year is off his rocker.*"

—Richard Nixon, after losing the California gubernatorial race in 1962

SLEAZE-O-METER

10
9
8
7
6
5
4
3
2
1

B y early 1968, Lyndon Johnson had become a prisoner of Vietnam. More than 500,000 American troops were caught up in the quagmire of a savage war that cost American taxpayers $80 million a day. The human price was far worse. Sixteen thousand Americans had died in combat in Vietnam as 1968 began. A thousand a month would die before the year was over.

Protestors disrupted almost every public appearance Johnson made, chanting: "Hey, hey, LBJ. How many kids did you kill today?" They demanded that he bring the troops home. And it seemed that Johnson's "Great Society" was crumbling around him. In the past two years, blacks had rioted in almost every major city in the country, and Richard Nixon, the Republican Party's main hope for the presidency after the Goldwater debacle, had called the "War on Poverty" a cruel hoax.

It was too much for Johnson. On March 31, 1968, he made the surprise announcement that he would not seek another term as president.

★ ★ ★ THE CANDIDATES ★ ★ ★

REPUBLICAN: RICHARD M. NIXON He was back. After running for California governor in 1962 and being soundly beaten, he had famously told reporters, "You won't have Nixon to kick around anymore because, gentlemen, this is my last press conference." ABC responded with a half-hour news show called "The Political Obituary of Richard Nixon." Nixon went off to practice law in New York.

Except he couldn't stay away. After Johnson pulverized Goldwater, Nixon started to look quite attractive to moderate Republicans who wanted their party back. Nixon began fund-raising; put together a loyal staff, which included H. R. Haldeman, John Ehrlichman, and John Mitchell; and found media advisors who would make over his image. He entered several Republican primaries and won the Republican nomination in August of 1968 on the first ballot.

His only miscue was to pick as his running mate Maryland Governor Spiro Agnew, a handsome but not very bright politician who had far too big a mouth.

DEMOCRATIC: HUBERT HUMPHREY Johnson's refusal to run for another term left the Democrats scrambling. Humphrey, Johnson's vice president, was the anointed successor. Humphrey was smart and committed to civil rights, but he projected a soft, avuncular image. He was seen as such a lackey to LBJ that at one point in the campaign, he was forced to declare: "The president has not made me his slave, and I am not his humble servant."

To make matters even more difficult, Humphrey had two powerful antiwar opponents in Senator Eugene McCarthy of Minnesota and Senator Robert Kennedy of Massachusetts (the latter would almost certainly have captured the Democratic nomination for president had he not been shot down in Los Angeles in June of 1968). During a tumultuous Chicago convention in August, while protestors rioted in the streets, the Democrats nominated Humphrey as their candidate, with Senator Edmund Muskie of Maine as his running mate.

★ ★ ★ THE CAMPAIGN ★ ★ ★

As Joe McGinniss famously described in his book *The Selling of the President*, Richard Nixon surrounded himself with a team of media advisors who groomed him for success. No more relentless campaigning—Nixon would take frequent breaks for rest. No more debating—despite the fact that Humphrey taunted him as "Richard the chicken-hearted." No more open press conferences in which Nixon might put his foot in his mouth. Now Nixon's handlers scripted television "panel shows" on which "ordinary citizens" (all Nixon supporters) lobbed him leading questions.

According to the polls, Nixon started the campaign with a good twenty-point lead over Humphrey, with especially strong support from blue-collar voters. Nixon became the law-and-order candidate of the "Silent Majority"—the country's long-suffering working people who were fed up with hippies and rioting students and blacks and bra-burning feminists.

Humphrey was in a tough position. Blue-collar voters didn't like him, but the antiwar protestors didn't like him either. His campaign was chronically short on cash because Democratic fat cats didn't want to contribute to a losing cause. At one point, nearly in tears, Humphrey cried, "Why me? What about Nixon?" But Nixon was much harder to reach, isolated in television studios and traveling the country in his private Boeing 727 named *Tricia*, after his youngest daughter. He had perfected the art of the modern candidacy, the sound bite, whereas Humphrey just couldn't stop talking. "I watched Humphrey give an eleven-minute answer to a question once," said a Nixon advisor. "Even the host was looking off-camera saying, 'What the hell did I ask this guy, I forgot.'"

Finally by September, the race began to tighten. Nixon's vague pronouncements on ending the war—in fact, the vagueness of most of his stances—began to wear badly on a public desperately seeking answers. At the same time, racist third-party candidate Alabama Governor George Wallace began making inroads with conservative Republicans.

Then President Johnson dropped a huge October surprise. On Halloween night 1968, he went on television to announce that Hanoi had agreed to begin peace negotiations in Paris in return for the cessation of bombing of North Vietnam. Suddenly, Humphrey shot ahead in the polls—with the Democrats actively involved in peace negotiations, who would want to break the line of succession?

Nixon bitterly (and cleverly) announced: "I am told that this spurt of activity is a last-minute attempt by President Johnson to salvage the candidacy of Mr. Humphrey. This I do not believe." In the last week of the election, some polls showed the Democratic candidate ahead for the first time in the contest—that is, until South Vietnam President Nguyen Van Thieu said that his country would not participate in the peace talks, and negotiations broke down.

★ ★ ★ THE WINNER: RICHARD NIXON ★ ★ ★

In a close election, Richard Nixon beat Hubert Humphrey 31,785,480 to 31,275,166, a margin of about a half-million votes, although Nixon's

Republicans were quick to accuse Hubert Humphrey of putting voters to sleep.

electoral vote lead was 301 to 191. The fifty-five-year-old Nixon had made one of the most extraordinary political comebacks in American history. In his victory speech, he said that the theme of his administration would be one he had seen printed on a teenage supporter's sign during a campaign stop: "Bring Us Together."

It was typical of the era that this comforting story of unity was not quite what it seemed. The teenager was a girl named Vicki Cole, the daughter of a Methodist minister in a small Ohio town. She had first held a much more partisan sign that read, "LBJ Taught Us, Vote Republican," but after losing it, she found the "Bring Us Together Again" sign lying on the ground. It was a serendipitous occurrence that would win her a trip to the White House and a personal visit with Richard Nixon after the election.

In fact, when reporters interviewed Cole, she explained that her true pick for president was the slain Democrat Robert F. Kennedy.

★ ★

OCTOBER SURPRISE? It is generally believed that if Lyndon Johnson had successfully announced peace talks with North Vietnam in the last week of the 1968 election, Hubert Humphrey might very well have won the election. But South Vietnam President Nguyen Van Thieu refused, and negotiations broke down.

There were many, LBJ among them, who believed that Nixon had conspired with Thieu to break off the deal by convincing him that a President Nixon would give better terms to South Vietnam. Despite some circumstantial evidence—Nixon's top advisor and later Attorney General John Mitchell had made contact with a Thieu intermediary—the charges were never proved. Contemporary observers, including Hubert Humphrey, felt that Nixon would not have taken the risk of being seen as obstructing the peace talks; others emphasized that Thieu did not need any help in understanding that Johnson's announcement was indeed a political one, timed to meet the November elections and not necessarily in South Vietnam's best interest.

THE SHAPE OF THINGS TO COME After losing his California gubernatorial bid against Governor Pat Brown in 1962, Nixon pulled off some truly dirty tricks with the help of H. R. Haldeman, who would later become his chief of staff.

They set up a phony organization called the Committee for the Preservation of the Democratic Party, which mailed a half million postcards to registered Democrats, expressing concern over the "capture" of the party by a "left-wing minority" that included Brown. The Democrats discovered the ruse during the campaign, got a court order forcing Nixon to cease sending out the postcards, and then sued the Republicans for damages, winning an out-of-court settlement.

Another ploy was stunning in its crudity. After finding a photograph of Brown kneeling to speak to a Laotian refugee girl, Nixon and Haldeman cropped out the refugee and put a picture of Russian Premier Nikita Khrushchev in her place, so that it looked as if Brown was kneeling in supplication to America's worst enemy.

SPIRO "MOUTH" AGNEW

In Richard Nixon's carefully scripted campaign, VP candidate Spiro Agnew was the only one who ad-libbed—to disastrous effect. Agnew, the first Greek American candidate for vice president, had been picked for his staunch law-and-order stance as governor of Maryland, but Nixon soon realized that the man was a bit of a loose cannon. While on a flight to Hawaii, he saw a Japanese American reporter sleeping on the plane and shouted to a friend, "What's wrong with that fat Jap?"

Agnew, at least, was an equal-opportunity offender. He referred to Polish Americans as "Polacks" and commented, while visiting a ghetto, "when you've seen one city slum, you've seen 'em all."

Democratic ad men capitalized on this with a television commercial that simply showed the words "SPIRO AGNEW FOR VICE PRESIDENT," followed by thirty seconds of raucous laughter.

1972

RICHARD NIXON

★ ★ ★ ★ ★ ★ ★ ★ ★ ★ VS. ★ ★ ★ ★ ★ ★ ★ ★ ★ ★ ★ ★

GEORGE MCGOVERN

"I could not muster much moral outrage over a political bugging."

—Richard Nixon

SLEAZE-O-METER

10
9
8
7
6
5
4
3
2
1

In 1972, the Vietnam War was still raging despite Richard Nixon's campaign vows to bring it to a halt. In America, four student war protesters had died at Kent State College, in Ohio, shot by National Guardsmen. Some 200,000 people marched on Washington in 1971, demanding an end to the hostilities. The 1972 election was pivotal. Americans, reeling from the unparalleled recent upheavals, sought a president with competence, integrity, and compassion. What they got was an election in which it seemed that all the smear tactics and nasty politics of the previous decade seemed to coalesce into a political campaign that would be forever synonymous with the words "dirty tricks."

★ ★ ★ THE CANDIDATES ★ ★ ★

REPUBLICAN: RICHARD NIXON Nixon's triumphs during his presidency had largely been on the foreign affairs front, with historical summit trips to China and Russia. At home, faced with growing opposition to his policies and an economy shored up by wage and price controls, he had walled himself inside his presidency, sticking close to the White House and relying on the same group of advisors and rich friends for comfort and advice.

DEMOCRAT: GEORGE McGOVERN McGovern was a history and political-science teacher turned senator from South Dakota. He was affable and low-key, and he could be tough-minded. Unlike Nixon, McGovern was a World War II hero who had won the Distinguished Flying Cross for piloting his bomber over North Africa and Italy.

But like Humphrey before him, McGovern was not terribly exciting. His nomination and acceptance speech at the Democratic Convention in Miami took place at 2:48 A.M.—prime time, as one observer said, "in Guam." The nod for VP went to Senator Thomas Eagleton of Missouri.

★ ★ ★ THE CAMPAIGN ★ ★ ★

The Republicans received a surprise early in the campaign when they learned that Thomas Eagleton had been hospitalized for clinical depression three times between 1960 and 1966—indeed, he had been given electroshock therapy. There were also rumors that he had been treated for alcoholism. At first, McGovern said he was behind Eagleton "one thousand percent," but eventually he succumbed to party pressures and replaced him with R. Sargent Shriver, Kennedy intimate and former ambassador to France. It was easy for Republicans to paint McGovern as indecisive and a man who did not stand by his friends.

Nixon had decided to run as President Nixon, not as candidate Nixon; he made appearances only in the Rose Garden and at carefully controlled campaign events. Behind the scenes, however, his campaign swarmed with dirty tricks. When the *New York Times* opposed Nixon's mining of Haiphong Harbor in North Vietnam, a full-page ad appeared in the paper the next day, from fourteen concerned "citizens" supporting Nixon. The only problem was that the ad had been secretly placed by the Committee to Re-Elect the President (its true acronym is CRP, but it's so much more fun to call it CREEP). The names signed to the ad were those of relatives of CREEP team members. CREEP also sent thousands of pro-Nixon postcards to a Washington, D.C.–based television station that was taking a public-opinon poll on the mining of Haiphong, resulting in an outcome of three to one in support of the president's actions.

And these were only the more public actions. Nixon had also ordered a special team of the Internal Revenue Service (the ominously named Special Services Staff, or SSS) to conduct field audits on his enemies, who included Larry O'Brien, head of the Democratic National Committee. How did Nixon know who his enemies were? Because, of course, he had an "Enemies List," compiled by staffers John Dean and Chuck Colson. The list swelled to some 200 names—including Paul Newman (involved in "Radic-Lib causes"), black Congressman John Conyers ("known weakness for white females"), and

Maxwell Dane, one of the partners in the advertising agency that had produced Johnson's famous "Daisy" spot.

And we haven't even mentioned the most famous group of dirty tricksters in American history, men whose actions far outsleazed LBJ's Five O'Clock Club: the Special Investigations Unit, a group known more informally as the "Plumbers." Nixon had told top advisor John Ehrlichman to "set up a little group right here in the White House" to fix leaks, and so Ehrlichman assembled a task force that included ex-CIA agents E. Howard Hunt and G. Gordon Liddy as well as numerous others.

A night watchman would discover five Plumbers right in the offices of the Democratic National Convention in the Watergate apartment and office complex in Washington, D.C., on the night of June 17, 1972. They wore surgical gloves and carried bugging equipment (tiny microphones hidden in phony ChapSticks), cameras, forty rolls of unexposed film, and $3,500 dollars in brand-new, consecutively numbered hundred-dollar bills.

When the press queried White House Press Secretary Ron Ziegler about this little episode, he dismissed it as "a third-rate burglary." If so, it was the only third-rate burglary to eventually cause the resignation of an American president. At the time, however, Americans paid surprisingly little attention to the news. The campaign went on, with Nixon taking a page from LBJ's 1964 playbook, marginalizing his opponent by making him seem to be a dangerous radical. Effectively caricaturized as the candidate of the "three A's: Acid, Amnesty [for draft dodgers], and Abortion," McGovern was getting the pants beaten off him. One McGovern staffer whispered to a reporter late in the campaign, "I just hope we can avoid a debacle."

★ ★ ★ THE WINNER: RICHARD NIXON ★ ★ ★

And what a debacle it was. Richard Nixon won by the largest plurality of the popular vote, beating McGovern 47,169,911 to 29,170,383 and taking the Electoral College 520 to 17. But the party would soon be

In the Dirty Tricks Hall of Fame, this man deserves a seat of honor.

over, as revelations about Watergate in the ensuing year drove Nixon out of office by August 1974.

Nixon later dismissed Watergate as merely another "political bugging" and, for a cold warrior who had been the victim of a lot of dirty tricks, this was no doubt true. He would admit in his memoirs that "I told my staff that we should come up with the kind of imaginative dirty tricks that our Democratic opponents used against us and others so effectively in previous campaigns." (The campaigns of Kennedy and Johnson were cases in point.)

But, at the time of Watergate, the revelation of the existence of tapes made in the Oval Office let Americans listen in, for the first time, to the sound of their president doing business. And what they heard was not pleasant.

★ ★ ★★ ★ ★★ ★ ★ ★ ★ ★★ ★ ★★ ★ ★ ★ ★ ★ ★ ★★ ★ ★★ ★ ★ ★ ★★ ★

THE DESTRUCTION OF EDMUND MUSKIE AND OTHER TALES OF THE PRIMARIES
Early in 1972, President Nixon, whose approval ratings hovered at only about 48 percent, felt that he was vulnerable to a challenge from a strong Democratic candidate.

So it became the goal of dirty tricks managers like Special Assistant to the President Dwight Chapin to "foster a split between Democratic hopefuls" in the primaries. Teddy Kennedy was not a problem—the last surviving Kennedy brother had pretty much blown his presidential chances by driving a car off a bridge in 1969 and drowning the young woman who was with him.

Going into the New Hampshire primary in February, many predicted the big winner would be Senator Edmund Muskie of Maine (Hubert Humphrey's 1968 running mate)—in fact, most journalists had already anointed him the Democratic presidential nominee. And Richard Nixon viewed Muskie as a formidable candidate.

But then strange things began happening. Suddenly, New Hampshire voters began receiving phone calls from rude black people—phone calls that came late at night or very early in the morning—saying that they had been bused in from Harlem to work for Muskie. And then the conservative editor of the *Manchester Union Leader*, William Loeb, published a letter, purportedly written by an ordinary citizen, that accused Muskie of using the word "Canuck" to refer to French Canadians. In defending himself against this and other slurs, Muskie, standing outdoors before microphones and cameras, began to cry. Or, since it was snowing, perhaps a snowflake had landed in his eye—it's impossible to tell from tapes of the incident.

But Muskie did lose his cool, and many voters wondered if he was unable to handle pressure. He won New Hampshire, but by a much smaller margin than predicted. Only later was it discovered that the "Canuck" letter was written by White House aide Kenneth Clawson.

Things just got worse when Muskie headed for the Florida primary. There, many voters received a letter, written on Muskie campaign stationery, stating (falsely) that Hubert Humphrey had been arrested for drunk driving in 1967. Other letters on Muskie stationery claimed that prominent Democratic senator and presidential hopeful Henry "Scoop" Jackson had fathered a child with a seventeen-year-old girl.

No detail was too small. Posters appeared on Florida highways that read: "Help Muskie in Busing More Children Now." Ads were placed in tiny free shopper's newsletters saying: "Muskie: Would you accept a black running mate?" And, at a Muskie press conference in Miami, someone released a handful of white mice with tags attached to them reading: "Muskie is a rat fink."

The person behind all of this Florida mayhem was Donald Segretti, the dark prince of dirty tricks. Segretti, whose name means "secret" in Italian, was a California lawyer who had been law school pals with several Nixon staffers—in particular, Dwight Chapin, the man who hired him and paid him $16,000, plus expenses, to wreak havoc in the primaries.

Muskie placed fourth in Florida and was finished as a candidate. Segretti's role in the investigations was discovered after the Watergate break-in, and he served four-and-a-half months in prison for misdemeanors associated with illegal campaign activities.

GOT A LEAK? GET A PLUMBER! The Plumbers came into existence at least partially because of the publication of the "Pentagon Papers" by the *New York Times* and *Washington Post*. These top-secret Defense Department papers traced the development of the U.S. involvement in the Vietnam War and showed how covert decisions had been made behind the backs of the American public. Although much of this could be laid at the feet of Democratic administrations, Nixon was concerned that such leaks could establish a precedent that might imperil his own secret decisions.

The leaker of the papers was former Defense Department official Daniel Ellsberg, and the Plumbers were organized specifically to discredit Ellsberg—to "link him to a conspiracy which suggests treasonable conduct," as Nixon aide Chuck Colson put it. Their first operation was to break into Ellsberg's psychiatrist's office, which provided no information on Ellsberg and was done so clumsily that a trail of destruction was left behind.

The clumsiness of this operation was rivaled only by that of the Watergate burgle of the Democratic National Committee offices on June 17, 1972. The group had already broken in on Memorial Day—undetected—to install listening devices. Since the bugs weren't working properly, the Plumbers went back. But this time, they carelessly taped the spring locks on the doors horizontally rather than vertically; the tape was seen by the night watchman, who called D.C. police. Two of the suspects had address books with White House telephone numbers in them and, of course, they carried $3,500 worth of brand-new, consecutively numbered hundred-dollar bills—not exactly your basic walking-around money.

The five burglars had been recruited by E. Howard Hunt and G. Gordon Liddy, who were not present that night. But the trail now led directly to them, to CREEP, and to the White House. From there, the question for the nation in the televised congressional hearings the following year became: Did Richard Nixon approve or know about the burglary? His answer was that he did not, but it was apparent from the Oval Office tapes that at least he knew that such dirty tricks were occurring.

1976

AT A GLANCE

JIMMY CARTER
vs. GERALD FORD

T wenty members of the Nixon administration were convicted after the Watergate dust had settled; that's not including Vice President Spiro Agnew, who resigned after pleading no contest to non-Watergate related tax-evasion charges. Nixon himself might have been indicted had it not been for his appointed successor, Gerald Ford, granting him a "full, free, and absolute" pardon for any crimes he might have committed.

This was not a popular move with the American public, and it came back to haunt Ford in the bicentennial election year of 1976. Under Ford's watch, the country had suffered through significant inflation, rising unemployment, and the shocking end of the Vietnam War, in which American personnel fled the country in ignominy. They also had to deal with Ford's pratfalls—when he stumbled down the steps of Air Force One during official business, no one in the country let him forget it. Nevertheless, he became the Republican Party's nominee after narrowly beating out former California governor and neocon Ronald Reagan in the primaries. Ford's running mate was Senator Robert Dole of Kansas.

Reform laws passed in the wake of Watergate cleared the way for a very untraditional presidential candidate: the former governor of Georgia, Jimmy Carter. With the passage of the Federal Elections Campaign Act (which went by the unlovely acronym FECA), individual campaign contributions were severely capped, but any candidate who could raise $100,000 in fifteen states could qualify for federal matching funds. In 1976, the Supreme Court declared one part of FECA unconstitutional, claiming that contributions were really a form of free speech and thus protected by the First Amendment. Candidates were free to spend as much money as they wanted on their own campaigns, as long as they refused federal matching funds. But the court did continue limits on individual contributions of federal candidates and upheld the part of FECA that called for public disclosure of campaign financing.

Because more money-strapped candidates could now qualify for federal matching funds, the primary season got longer and longer. Also, more primaries abandoned the traditional winner-take-all system in which the candidate who carried the state's primary received all the party's delegates. That meant that a presidential candidate running second or third in a state primary could still take home a proportionate share of delegates.

The result was that a lot of politicians began throwing their hats into the ring, a process that continues to this day. And with so many relatively obscure candidates, Americans relied on television to make sense of them all. The first star of the new age of elections was James Earl Carter, a former peanut farmer and one-term governor of Georgia, who liked to be called "Jimmy." Jimmy Carter was a highly unusual dark-horse candidate. He hailed from the Deep South (no American president had been elected from the South since before the Civil War), was a born-again Christian, and made speeches that were so boring that Senator Eugene McCarthy once called him "an oratorical mortician."

Yet along with his brilliant chief of staff, Hamilton Jordan, Carter understood that early victories in the extended primary process received a disproportionate share of press attention. Therefore, Carter went all-out to win the obscure Iowa caucus—and the next day, the New York Times anointed him Democratic front-runner, a position he was to keep. His running mate was Minnesota Senator Walter Mondale.

THE CAMPAIGN Jimmy Carter ran on the theme that he was an outsider coming to clean up Washington. Most of his speeches began, "Hi, my name is Jimmy Carter, and I'm running for president." Yet the poor country boy did encounter a few problems. For one thing, he had done a Playboy magazine interview, which appeared during the campaign, in which he said: "I've looked on a lot of women with lust; I've committed adultery in my heart many times." This did not go over well with his born-again following. Carter didn't help himself with fellow Democrats either when, in the same interview, he stated that Lyndon Johnson was as guilty as Richard Nixon of "lying, cheating, and distorting the truth." The fact that both these statements were honest doesn't take away from their political foolishness.

Fortunately, Carter was running against Gerald Ford. The candidates held a series of debates—the first presidential debates since 1960 and the first time an incumbent president had ever debated an opponent. Ford's men were careful to keep his klutziness in check, even to the extent of demanding an especially deep well on the podium to hold his glass of water lest he knock it over. But they couldn't control his tongue. America was amazed to hear him say that Eastern European states were not under Soviet domination.

Ford meant to say that his administration refused to accept such a situation as the status quo, but good intentions do not show up under the harsh glare of television lights.

THE WINNER: JIMMY CARTER Not only did Jimmy Carter become president, winning 40,830,763 votes to 39,147,793, a margin of just over 2 percent, but Democrats swept back into power in both the House and the Senate. On January 20, 1977, Carter got rid of his limousine and walked to his inauguration, making a statement that the country had to tighten its belt. Once again, he was delivering an honest message—but it wasn't one voters really wanted to hear.

1980

RONALD REAGAN

★ ★ ★ ★ ★ ★ ★ ★ ★ ★ VS. ★ ★ ★ ★ ★ ★ ★ ★ ★ ★ ★

JIMMY CARTER

"Stop Me Before I Kill Again."

—Sign on California redwood tree after Ronald Reagan
claimed that trees caused more pollution than cars

SLEAZE-O-METER

10
9
8
7
6
5
4
3
2
1

A h, the Carter years. Remember the "killer rabbit" Jimmy had to beat off with a paddle while fishing? Remember the Mr. Roger's cardigan sweaters he wore? Remember the double-digit inflation? Remember that weekend in July 1979 when 75 percent of New York gas stations had to close?

Heading into the election year of 1980, Carter was not having a good time. True, he had brokered the Panama Canal Treaty and the Camp David Accords between Israel and Egypt. But then students in Iran took Americans hostage, the Soviets invaded Afghanistan, and Mount St. Helens erupted.

In addition, Carter was about to run against the "Gipper," Ronald Reagan, former Hollywood actor, former governor of California, and future nonstick Teflon Man. With fifty-one primaries and caucuses, it was a long and extremely nasty campaign, with the mother of all October Surprises at its conclusion.

★ ★ ★ THE CANDIDATES ★ ★ ★

REPUBLICAN: RONALD REAGAN Remember the disgruntled Adlai Stevenson campaign advisor who warned in 1952 that soon "presidential campaigns would have professional actors as candidates"?

Well, the future had arrived. Ronald "Ronnie" Reagan—handsome, smiling, star of such movie classics as *Girls on Probation*, *Knute Rockne—All American*, and, of course, the beloved *Bedtime for Bonzo*—was sixty-nine years old as the 1980 campaign began. He had very nearly beaten Gerald Ford during the 1976 primaries and now ran a well-oiled campaign with a large dollop of secrecy. William Casey, future CIA director, was his campaign manager, and George H. W. Bush, former CIA head, was his vice-presidential candidate.

DEMOCRAT: JIMMY CARTER At age fifty-five, Carter had been worn down by the burdens of a tough presidency and his own miscues. He seemed incapable of grasping that Americans didn't want to hear about a "crisis in confidence," nor did they want anything to do with the severe austerity measures Carter felt were necessary to revive the economy. One image of the Carter White House that resonated with a lot of voters came from the time that Carter, wearing a headband, tried to run a 10K road race near Camp David to encourage physical fitness, and nearly collapsed. To put it bluntly, Jimmy was sort of a drag.

★ ★ ★ THE CAMPAIGN ★ ★ ★

As the campaign began, America's "Misery Index" (a measurement created by a Chicago economist combining inflation plus unemployment) was at an all-time high of 22 percent (in late 2006, it was under 9). Misery is tough on an incumbent, but it leaves a challenger plenty of opportunities. The theme of Ronald Reagan's campaign was "Are you better off today than you were four years ago?" Since the Misery Index was 13 percent in 1976, the answer had to be a miserable no.

Carter's strategy was to be presidential, yet to strike hard at Reagan. A memo written by Carter's media advisor listed how this was to be done:

CARTER	REAGAN
Safe/sound	Untested
Young	Old
Vigorous	Old
Smart	Dumb

Well, Reagan did come across as old and a little foolish. He claimed that the "finest oil geologists" had told him that the United States had more oil than Saudi Arabia. He stated that the eruption of Mount St. Helens released more sulfur dioxide into the air "than has been released in the last ten years of automobile driving." He also loved ethnic jokes. After the New Hampshire primary, reporters overheard him telling one that began: "How do you tell who the Polish fellow is at a cockfight? He's the one with the duck." When reports of this were published, Reagan claimed that he had merely been providing an example of the kind of jokes candidates shouldn't tell. And the Teflon man actually got away with it.

Carter just couldn't win. When he attacked Reagan for having supposedly used code phrases like "states' rights" to imply a racist agenda and for being divisive (under President Reagan, Carter claimed, "Americans might be separated, black from white, Jew from Christian, North from South"), people thought he sounded mean. Reagan, it seemed, just inspired friendly feelings in a lot of people. They didn't want to see him assailed.

The main issue of the election, however, was that Iranian students had captured fifty-three American hostages on November 4, 1979. The country was horrified. A bunch of foreign kids were thumbing their noses at America, and Carter seemed powerless to stop them. His approval ratings during the 1980 campaign sank lower than those of Richard Nixon's during Watergate—one Harris Poll put him at 22 percent.

It didn't help any that a third-party candidate, long-time Illinois Representative John Anderson, was pulling surprisingly well with his moderate National Unity Party. Anderson seemed to many a viable alternative to both Carter and Reagan, but he ultimately did more damage to Carter. Even the new fundamentalists, who were a growing power in the conservative wing of the Republican Party, attacked the born-again president—for being too liberal.

Well, Carter had his debate with Ronald Reagan on October 28 to look forward to, right? Wrong. It was bad enough that a Republican spy stole Carter's secret debate briefing book and provided it to Reagan before the event. But then Reagan proceeded to dominate the debate in his affable, grinning manner, saying, "There you go again, Mr. President," whenever Carter said something Reagan found foolish. Carter didn't help his case by citing his thirteen-year-old daughter Amy as a source on matters of crucial global importance: "I had a discussion with my daughter Amy the other day, before I came here, to ask her what the most important issue was. She said she thought nuclear weaponry."

In the end, the sole hope for a Carter victory was the release of the hostages by Iran, and the Carter administration fought valiantly to achieve it. The Reagan camp, in the meantime, kept warning the public that Carter might try to pull off a grandstanding October Surprise, but the event never materialized (for reasons that will soon be made clear).

★ ★ ★ THE WINNER: RONALD REAGAN ★ ★ ★

Reagan cleaned Carter's clock, 43,904,153 to 35,483,838, and won the electoral votes of all but five states and the District of Columbia. John Anderson took about 5,700,000 votes, a respectable seven-percent showing for a candidate without major funding or the backing of a huge political organization. The victory was so bad that Carter conceded on national television at 9:50 P.M., Eastern Time—only 6:50 P.M. in the Pacific Time Zone, where the polls were still very much open, which infuriated West Coast Democrats running for local office. Carter became the first incumbent Democratic president since Grover Cleveland to fail to retain his office (and even Grover got his back after a second try). Reagan was now president, and the era of "supply side" economics, Irangate, and the "Evil Empire" of the Soviet Union was about to begin.

Oh, yes, and the Iran hostages were released—moments after Reagan's swearing in as the fortieth president.

★ ★

PREVENTING AN OCTOBER SURPRISE In his controversial book *October Surprise: American Hostages in Iran and the Election of Ronald Reagan*, former Carter National Security Council staffer Gary Sick documents in copious detail how William Casey, Reagan campaign manager and later CIA director, stalled the release of the Iranian hostages so that the Carter administration would lose the election.

The Republicans had heard that the Iranians were seeking to negotiate with the Carter administration, which had thrown an economic cordon around Iran, freezing Iranian assets in U.S. banks and asking the international community to respect an arms embargo. Casey knew that the release of the hostages to Jimmy Carter would spell disaster for the Reagan campaign, and he moved swiftly to avert it. According to Sick, Casey used his and George Bush's old intelligence community ties to establish a "back channel" of communications to Iran. Casey met with Iranian cleric Mehdi Karroubi in Madrid in August 1980 and offered military assistance—something Iran desperately needed since Iraq was threatening to invade—if the hostages were not released until after Ronald Reagan was elected. The Ayatollah Khomeini approved the deal.

The Republicans were careful to monitor the situation since they were afraid the Iranians would double-cross them and deal with the Carter administration. Subsequent meetings between Iranian representatives, Casey, and other members of Reagan's campaign team took place in October, and the pot was sweetened: more guns and the unfreezing of Iranian cash in the United States, but only if the hostage release was delayed until after Reagan's swearing in on January 20, 1981, so that Carter would get absolutely no credit. In the meantime, a network of retired military officers who were friends of Casey monitored U.S. air force bases for any sign of unusual activity, which might indicate a Carter deal with some other faction in Iran.

On January 20, the hostages were loaded aboard a plane but forced to wait on the tarmac of Tehran Airport until the very moment of Reagan's swearing in. Then the plane took off for Wiesbaden, Germany. Days later, the Reagan administration began sending military supplies to Iran.

Interestingly enough, Ronald Reagan, when asked in 1991 whether he had any knowledge of these types of secret dealings, said, "I did some things actually the other way, to try to be of help in getting those hostages ... out of there." The questioner asked him, "Does that mean contact with the Iranian government?" to which Reagan replied, "Not by me. No. [But] I can't go into details. Some of those things are still classified."

DEBATEGATE: THE STOLEN BRIEFING BOOK Discussing Carter's 1980 loss, former Carter speechwriter Hendrik Hertzberg pointed out that the debate had been a chief deciding factor, for Reagan came across as a pretty nice guy, not a conservative ideologue: "When people realized they could get rid of Carter and still not destroy the world, they went ahead and did it."

It's an indisputable fact that Carter's top-secret predebate briefing book was stolen and given to Reagan's people before their October 28 debate so that the Gipper would have all the right ripostes to Carter's sallies. But the question remains: Whodunnit?

As recently as 2005, in an interview on National Public Radio, Carter blamed conservative writer George Will. In a scathing reply in his *Washington Post* column, Will, who did help Reagan prepare for the debate, said that there was a copy of the briefing book in the room while he and others were working with Reagan, but Will claims that he did not steal it or use it in his coaching.

Whether or not Will was responsible, there was certainly at least one spy in Carter's midst. A Congressional investigation in 1983 confirmed that Reagan campaign manager William Casey was receiving "classified reports on closely held Carter administration intelligence on the Carter campaign and the Democratic president's efforts to liberate the hostages." And Reagan never denied that the briefing book was stolen. He later said, "It probably wasn't too much different than the press rushing into print with the Pentagon Papers."

To this day, Jimmy Carter swears that someone stole his debate briefing book. But who?

In hindsight, a lot of people wondered how a supposedly impartial journalist like Will could coach Reagan for his debate and then go on *Nightline* the same evening without mentioning his behind-the-scenes participation, praising Reagan's "thoroughbred performance." Although he defended himself at the time, Will now admits his role as Reagan coach was "inappropriate."

NANCY REAGAN, ATTACK DOG: JUST SAY GRRRRR! Prior to 1980, presidential candidates used their wives to enhance their image as stable and well-rounded family men. But in 1980, for the first time in campaign history, a presidential candidate's wife appeared in an attack ad. This televised message from Nancy Reagan aired twice in the last few weeks of the campaign: "[I am upset that President Carter] is trying to portray my husband as a warmonger or a man who would throw the elderly out on the street and cut off their Social Security, when in fact, he never said anything of the kind, at any time, and the elderly people have enough to worry about now. They are scared to death of how they are going to live without this thrown on top of them. That's a cruel thing to do; it is cruel to the people; it is cruel to my husband. I deeply resent it, as a wife and a mother and a woman."

1984
AT A GLANCE

RONALD REAGAN
vs. WALTER MONDALE

Welcome to "Morning in America," as the glowing 1984 Reagan campaign spot described the state of the nation. "In a town not too far from where you live, a young family has just moved into a new home. The factory down the river is working again. . . . Life is better. America is back."

Well, yes and no. In 1984, there were more jobs and the interest rates were down, but the deficit was skyrocketing, tax cuts benefited only the very rich, and religious fundamentalists, intolerant of anyone who didn't share their beliefs, were in the ascendancy. Jerry Falwell of the Moral Majority gave the benediction at the Republican National Convention, calling Ronald Reagan and his vice president, George H. W. Bush, "God's instruments for rebuilding America."

Challenging God's instruments were Jimmy Carter's vice president Walter Mondale and the first female candidate for vice president, New York Congresswoman Geraldine Ferraro.

THE CAMPAIGN The 1984 campaign is one of the most boring on record and reminds many historians of 1956, when another Republican president, Dwight Eisenhower, was running in a time of prosperity. Even Mondale called the pace of the campaign "glacial." Reagan, who had been nearly assassinated in 1981, was loved by most of America, even though there was some speculation that his age (at seventy-three, he was the oldest American president in history) might make him unfit for another full term.

In truth, he often seemed a bit forgetful. At a 1981 meeting of city mayors at the White House, Reagan greeted his Secretary of Housing and Urban

Development, Samuel Pierce, as "Mr. Mayor." He completely forgot the name of his national security advisor, Bud McFarlane. And he was prone to misstatements such as: "Now we're trying to get unemployment to go up. I think we are going to succeed."

No matter. Mondale just lacked Reagan's charisma, and Ferraro's novelty as a woman candidate for high office wore off very quickly when she stumbled on the issue of releasing her real-estate-developer husband's tax returns to the press.

THE WINNER: RONALD REAGAN
In a landslide that hearkened back to FDR's annihilation of Alf Landon in 1936, Reagan took every state except Mondale's home bastion of Minnesota. The popular vote margin was 54,455,075 to 37,577,185, second only to Richard Nixon's victory in 1972. In the Electoral College, Reagan triumphed 525 to 13. Ouch.

1988

GEORGE H. W. BUSH

★ ★ ★ ★ ★ ★ ★ ★ ★ ★ VS. ★ ★ ★ ★ ★ ★ ★ ★ ★ ★

MICHAEL DUKAKIS

*"I will strip the bark off
the little bastard!"*

—Lee Atwater, George Bush's campaign manager, speaking
"off-the-record" to reporters about Michael Dukakis

SLEAZE-O-METE

10
9
8
7
6
5
4
3
2
1

On the face of it, 1988 should have been a campaign about issues. After eight years of Reaganomics, the budget deficit had skyrocketed, the trade deficit was on the rise, and homelessness had become a serious problem in America. On the other hand, inflation had peaked and the Cold War was coming to an astonishing end—almost as if the Gipper himself had scripted the movie.

Plenty of substantial issues for each candidate to sink his teeth into, right? Wrong, punk—and by the way, you sound like you're soft on crime! As it turns out, 1988 devolved into one of the bitterest, dirtiest, meanest elections ever held in this country—an election that set the tone for much of the vicious mudslinging that characterizes Republican-Democrat contests right up to this day.

★ ★ ★ **THE CANDIDATES** ★ ★ ★

REPUBLICAN: GEORGE H.W. BUSH George H. W. Bush had a long resume—rich New England kid, hero of World War II, ambassador to the UN, CIA head, vice president—but Americans didn't feel like they knew him. This was partly because many couldn't understand what the man was saying. He not only mumbled, but he was prone to such elegant malapropisms as "I stand for anti-bigotry, anti-Semitism and anti-racism" and "I'm going to make sure that everyone who has a job, wants a job."

However, he was tall.

DEMOCRAT: MICHAEL DUKAKIS Michael Dukakis, on the other hand, was short—about five-feet-eight-inches—thus proving the truth of the ancient proverb: "It is easier for a camel to pass through the eye of a needle than for a short dude to enter the White House." He did have a pretty good record: as governor of Massachusetts he had turned around that state's faltering economy by bringing in high-tech companies while resurrecting social programs to help the Commonwealth's neediest citizens. (In this he was aided by his far-more-charismatic lieutenant governor, John Kerry.)

Sometimes candidates do the worst damage to themselves. This Michael Dukakis photo op tanked big time.

But in addition to being short, Dukakis was boring—stiff, straight-laced, sincere to a fault—and sported the worst five o'clock shadow since Richard Nixon, the kind that looks like you've just smeared charcoal over your face before going out to trick or treat.

★ ★ ★ **THE CAMPAIGN** ★ ★ ★

While Bush called for "a kindler, gentler nation" and "a thousand points of light," his campaign manager Lee Atwater pursued a strategy of "raising the negatives" by churning out a series of attack commercials. The advertisements portrayed Dukakis as being too liberal on drugs and crime and too much of a girly-man on defense.

Dukakis tried to fight back, but what did he have to propose? Massive cuts in defense spending? Programs for society's needy and disadvantaged? In a decade that made heroes of Rocky and Rambo, the Dukakis platform just wasn't sexy enough. And while the Democrats struggled to formulate a counterattack, Atwater unleashed a sleazy ad campaign to end all sleazy ad campaigns.

It focused on a thirty-nine-year-old black convict named "Willie" Horton. During Dukakis's tenure as governor, Horton had taken part in a weekend furlough program in Massachusetts. Instead of returning to prison, however, Horton fled to Maryland, where he raped a white woman and stabbed her white fiancé. The colors matter here because the Republicans proceeded to make the most racist series of attacks in modern American electioneering history.

To begin with, Republicans renamed Horton. His real name was William. He was known to his mother, family, friends, enemies, cops, and parole officers as William. Newspaper accounts of his crimes referred to him as William. And yet the Republican attack ads called him "Willie."

What kind of attack ads? A few samples:

- "Get Out of Jail Free Card": Modeled after the Monopoly card and distributed to 400,000 Texas voters, this tiny mailbox stuffer read: "Michael Dukakis is the killer's best friend and the decent honest citizen's worst enemy."

- "Pro-Family Letter": This was the Maryland Republican party fund-raising letter that featured photographs of Willie Horton and Michael Dukakis over the headline: "Is This Your Pro-Family Team for 1988?"
- "Weekend Passes": A sixty-second television spot with side-by-side pictures of Horton and Dukakis, looking remarkably alike—and no wonder, since the ad makers used a dark photograph of a weary and unshaven Dukakis with his hair disheveled.
- "Revolving Door": Perhaps most famous of all, this stark black and white TV spot showed convicts marching through a turnstile into jail and immediately back out again. No matter that the "convicts" were out-of-work Republicans instructed not to shave for the day. The point had been made.

★ ★ ★ THE WINNER: GEORGE BUSH ★ ★ ★

With the lowest voter turnout since 1924, Bush took the popular vote 48,886,097 to 41,809,074 and won by a landslide in the Electoral College, 426 votes to 112.

Oops, that's actually 111. One Democratic elector from West Virginia was so disgusted with Dukakis that he cast his vote for vice-presidential candidate Lloyd Bentsen.

★ ★

BUT WAS IT GOOD FOR YOU, TOO? Many Democrats tried to suggest that Bush had indulged in extramarital affairs and pursued shady oil connections, but these charges had no real impact on the campaign. In the end, the most scandalous charge uttered against George Bush came from George Bush himself, speaking in Detroit just weeks before the election: "I have worked alongside [President Reagan] and I am proud to be his partner. We have had triumphs, we have made mistakes, we have had sex . . . I mean, setbacks!"

PRESIDENT QUAYLE Building on fears that vice-presidential candidate Dan Quayle was not qualified to be president, Democrats created a television ad that began with grainy footage of vice presidents Harry Truman and Lyndon Johnson being sworn in as president. The voiceover intoned: "One out of five American vice presidents has to rise to the duties of commander-in-chief. After five months of reflection, Bush's choice: J. Danforth Quayle. Hopefully, we'll never know how great a lapse of judgment that really was." The soundtrack was an ominously thumping heartbeat.

REALLY TANKING Sometimes even the best attempts at publicity can backfire—like the time Michael Dukakis, in an attempt to prove that he was no softie on defense, visited a General Dynamics plant in Michigan for a photo op with a tank. (Memo to future candidates: when poking your head out of the hatch of an MI tank, do not grin and wave, do not wear a tie as well as a silly helmet, and do not, whatever you do, bear a striking resemblance to Alfred E. Neuman.) The photo op was such a disaster, Republicans recycled the footage for an attack ad. "Tank" showed Dukakis riding around and around in circles as a narrator intoned, with more than a touch of incredulity: "Now he wants to be our commander-in-chief? America can't afford the risk."

MOST CONCERNED LETTER FROM A SERIAL KILLER After the Bush campaign claimed in an ad that Chicago mass murderer John Wayne Gacy would be released on furlough if Dukakis were elected, Gacy dispatched an angry missive from prison: "It is an insult to the voting public that [Republicans are] exploiting the name of John Wayne Gacy to scare people into voting for George Bush."

1992

WILLIAM JEFFERSON CLINTON

★ ★ ★ ★ ★ ★ ★ ★ ★ ★ ★ VS. ★ ★ ★ ★ ★ ★ ★ ★ ★ ★ ★

GEORGE H. W. BUSH

"All I've been asked about by the press are a woman I didn't sleep with and a draft I didn't dodge."

—Bill Clinton

SLEAZE-O-METER

10
9
8
7
6
5
4
3
2
1

Just after the successful completion of his one-hundred-hour Gulf War in the fall of 1990, George Bush's approval ratings reached an astonishing 90 percent; he seemed unbeatable. After twelve years of prosperous Republican rule, coupled with extremely weak Democratic presidential candidates, some pundits began to wonder whether the Democratic Party was heading toward political extinction, just as the Whigs or the Federalists.

But as the Bush administration progressed, the approval rating slowly started to fall. War may have made Bush a hero, but he never earned the fanatically loyal following of a Ronald Reagan. He broke his famous 1988 pledge of "Read my lips: No new taxes," which left him open to Democratic attack. Reagan's legacy of a staggering $4 trillion national debt (up $3 trillion since 1980) didn't help much, either. There may have been an explosion of wealth in the top 1 percent of the American population, but one in ten Americans was living on food stamps, and one in eight lived below the poverty level.

The relatively obscure field of Democratic candidates included Iowa Senator Tom Harkin, Nebraska Senator Bob Kerrey, Arkansas Governor Bill Clinton, and Massachusetts Senator Paul Tsongas. But Bush had more than Democrats to worry about. Conservative Christian columnist and former Nixon speech writer Pat Buchanan ran well in the primaries, showing that the religious right would not be denied its share of the action. And the fourteenth wealthiest person in the United States, billionaire Texan H. Ross Perot, decided to hell with federal matching funds, he'd pay for his own campaign—and mounted the most successful third-party challenge since Teddy Roosevelt and his Bull Moose Party in 1912.

★ ★ ★ THE CANDIDATES ★ ★ ★

DEMOCRAT: WILLIAM "BILL" CLINTON If there could be such a thing as a "log cabin" presidential candidate in the late twentieth century, that candidate was William Jefferson Clinton. He was born poor in Hope, Arkansas, in 1946. His father had died in a car accident when he was only three months old, and his stepfather was an abusive alcoholic. Clinton triumphed over all these circumstances to become a Rhodes scholar, attend Yale Law School and, in 1978, become the governor of Arkansas at thirty-two years old.

Married to Hillary Rodham Clinton, Bill Clinton was extraordinarily charismatic—six-foot-two, handsome, empathetic ("I feel your pain"), and a brilliant "policy wonk" with an impressive memory for details. However, according to Republicans, there was the little problem of his being "a pot-smoking, philandering, draft dodger."

Clinton's running mate was another southerner, Tennessee Senator Al Gore.

REPUBLICAN: GEORGE H. W. BUSH By the time the election heated up in the summer of 1992, Bush's approval ratings had dropped to roughly 40 percent. Twenty-one years older than his Democratic opponent, he tried to run on his success in foreign affairs while glossing over his tax increase and the country's huge deficit, but he lacked both charisma and empathy. While Clinton "felt" the country's pain, Bush said, in his weird verbal shorthand, "Message: I care." Focus groups commissioned by the Republican National Committee found that his wife, Barbara, now had higher approval ratings than the president—and his dog, Millie, wasn't far behind.

Even though Bush was told that dumping his hapless vice president, J. Danforth Quayle, would generate a net gain of as much as six points in the approval ratings, Bush wouldn't give up the guy.

★ ★ ★ **THE CAMPAIGN** ★ ★ ★

Gossip had swirled around Clinton's womanizing for years, and it provided plenty of fodder for the campaign. Republican sleaze-meisters whispered that Clinton had had a child with a black woman, and the rumors only got worse from there. He was a rapist. He was a sexual predator. He felt up a woman in the bathroom at his own wedding. And on and on.

The only sexual misconduct charge that stuck with Clinton in 1992 was an affair he supposedly had with nightclub chanteuse and former Arkansas state employee Gennifer Flowers (of whom he reportedly said, "She could suck a tennis ball through a garden hose"). Flowers revealed all in the *Star* tabloid in the winter of 1992. She claimed that their sexual relationship went back twelve years; when Clinton denied this, Flowers held a press conference and played phone conversations she had taped with Clinton, in which they refer to each other quite cozily as "honey." In New Hampshire, the Arkansas governor was now met at every campaign stop by what his staff called "the clusterfuck"— a semicircle of reporters with microphones shouting leading questions.

Clinton worked quickly to control the damage. He appeared on the television news show *60 Minutes* with Hillary, admitted only that he caused "pain in my marriage," and managed to escape unscathed—as he was to do on the issues of smoking marijuana (incredibly, he said he "didn't inhale") and draft-dodging back in the sixties ("dodge" was perhaps too strong a word, but he had avoided military service until he lucked into a high draft lottery number). No wonder Republicans dubbed him "Slick Willie." They hated him passionately and almost hysterically, the same way Democrats loathed Richard Nixon. One wealthy Republican businessman spent $40,000 at the beginning of the campaign digging for dirt that would torpedo Clinton. It did little good.

Bush had another problem, and that was the irrepressible Ross Perot. The historian Richard Hofstadter has written that American third parties are "like bees—once they have stung, they die." In 1992, Ross Perot put a pretty good sting on George Bush.

Perot was quite a character. Born in 1930, the son of a Texarkana, Texas, cotton picker, he founded a data retrieval firm called EDS in 1962 and turned it into a billion-dollar company. Ignoring all traditional avenues of running for president, Perot announced his candidacy on the "Larry King Live" show. He called his campaign organization United We Stand America and crusaded mainly against national debt. With his squeaky drawl, jug-handle ears, and love of pie charts, he was a little like everyone's old high-school math teacher. In some polls he began to lead both Clinton and Bush.

But Perot's campaign began to falter after he made an address to the NAACP in which he referred to them as "you people" and then falsely denied he knew about the case of an Orthodox Jew who had been fired from EDS for having a beard. In July, he abruptly withdrew from the race but returned in September alleging that Republican dirty tricksters had wiretapped his office and threatened to publish nude pictures of his daughter before her wedding. "There has been a ninety-day effort to redefine my personality by a group called opposition research," Perot said. "They're generally known as the dirty tricks crowd."

After Labor Day, Clinton jumped out to a thirteen-point lead in the polls. Desperate Republican strategists even sought advice from two aides to Great Britain Prime Minister John Major, who had won despite a weak economy and poor personal ratings. (Their only suggestion was to plaster pictures of Gennifer Flowers on huge billboards all over the country above the words, "AND NOW HE WANTS TO SCREW THE COUNTRY, TOO.")

Bush tried, in his own way, to attack Clinton and the Democrats. They were "cultural elitists" and "tree huggers" and atheists (they "don't have the three letters G-O-D in their party platform"). With high absurdity, he claimed that if Harry Truman were alive, he would vote Republican, something Truman's daughter Margaret vehemently denied. (Republicans since Ronald Reagan had adopted Truman as a plain-spoken paragon of the presidency, conveniently forgetting how viciously they had attacked him in the 1950s.)

Bush also proclaimed that "my dog Millie knows more about foreign affairs than those two bozos," referring to Clinton and Gore. But it was "THE ECONOMY, STUPID"—as the famous sign plastered in the Clinton-Gore "War Room" read—that the American people were really interested in.

★ THE WINNER: WILLIAM JEFFERSON CLINTON ★

Election Day saw the largest voter turnout since 1960, with Clinton winning 44,908,254 votes to Bush's 39,102,343. Perot, running as an

Republicans accused Bill Clinton of smoking marijuana while in college—and his "I didn't inhale" defense only fueled the flames.

independent, had pulled in nineteen million votes, or almost 19 percent of the total vote—the most of any third-party candidate since Teddy Roosevelt in 1912. He didn't pull in any electoral votes but nonetheless managed the neat trick of hurting Bush and helping elect Clinton—albeit with the lowest percentage of popular vote (43 percent) since Woodrow Wilson beat Taft and Roosevelt (with 41 percent) in 1912. Who knows what would have happened had Perot not dropped out of the race in midsummer?

The forty-six-year-old Clinton, the youngest president since JFK (his boyhood hero), was ecstatic. He couldn't have foreseen that his name would soon become synonymous with JFK for screwing in the White House.

★ ★

OPPO "Oppo"—short for opposition research—had become a separately funded part of the Republican Party by the election of 1992. The program was started by Lee Atwater, briefly chairman of the Republican National Committee, before his death in March of 1991. The opposition resources center, located at the RNC headquarters in Washington, boasted a large room with state-of-the-art data-retrieval computers, a staff of some sixty people, and its own separate budget of six million dollars. Operatives had developed huge files on the likes of Mario Cuomo, when it was assumed he would be Democratic candidate. They also investigated Pat Buchanan, fire-breathing conservative Republican, although it was not considered quite kosher to snoop around in the private lives of fellow Republicans.

Then, of course, there was Bill Clinton.

Oppo men went all over Little Rock, Arkansas, searching for dirt on Slick Willie. They brought twenty years' worth of microfiche on Clinton from Arkansas newspapers and filled thirty file drawers with speculation on his sex life. The problem was that, after the primaries, George Bush wouldn't let them use the sexual gossip they had gathered—some felt he was taking the high road, others wondered if the president felt vulnerable to rumors of his own alleged adultery.

DAN QUAYLE VS. MURPHY BROWN By 1992, Vice President Dan Quayle had already been the butt of a lot of jokes. There was something so callow and ridiculous about the guy, even down to his name, J. Danforth Quayle, and the fact that, as one critic has said, "his pales eyes [look] like windows into an unfurnished room."

In 1992, Quayle picked the lack of "family values" in entertainment as his own particular issue. The music of rapper Tupac Shakur, for instance, had "no place in our society," according to Quayle. Shakur was a relatively easy target, but then the VP made the mistake of going after the phenomenally popular television show *Murphy Brown*. Brown (played by actress Candace Bergen) was an anchorwoman who had decided to give birth to a child out of wedlock. Quayle thundered that bearing a child alone "mocks the importance of fathers" and was an example of the "poverty of values" that afflicted television.

This was not a smart move since even Republicans loved to watch the show, and Quayle, weirdly, was acting as though this sit-com character was a real person. White House staffers decided that Quayle should change his tune and praise Murphy Brown for her courage in having the baby, rather than, say, having an abortion. Bush spared Quayle from this humiliation, and the whole situation died when, in early June, the vice president visited a New Jersey elementary school and corrected student William Figueroa's spelling of "potato," claiming it was "potatoe."

Wrong. But this new source of ridicule sent the *Murphy Brown* controversy spiraling into the old-news file.

1996
AT A GLANCE

WILLIAM JEFFERSON CLINTON
vs. BOB DOLE

There were so many mini-scandals in Bill Clinton's first term, you needed a scorecard to keep them straight. There was "Travelgate," in which several long-time workers in the White House travel office were fired for alleged improprieties and replaced with people with ties to Clinton. Then there was "Filegate," in which the White House head of security improperly requested and received FBI security clearance files on government employees; and, of course, Whitewater, a highly convoluted scandal about a Bill-Hillary Arkansas real estate deal, where no wrongdoing by the president was ever established by Kenneth Starr, the independent prosecutor assigned to investigate it.

In July 1993, Clinton's close friend and deputy White House counsel Vince Foster committed suicide. Some six months later, in February of 1994, Paula Corbin Jones, a low-level Arkansas state employee, sued Clinton for sexual harassment, claiming that as governor, Clinton had cornered her in a room, pulled down his pants, and asked for a blow job ("I will never forget it as long as I live. His face was blood red, and his penis was bright red and curved").

All of this, according to Hillary Clinton, was part of a "vast right-wing conspiracy," and there's plenty of evidence to back up her claim, including indications that at least one conservative tycoon spent years funding efforts to discredit Clinton, to the tune of as much as two million dollars.

Was there any time left to govern the country? It turned out there was. Clinton turned back the challenge of right-wing Republican congressmen by expertly moving to the center on most issues, from balancing the budget (a feat Clinton actually managed) to revamping welfare. When the time came for Clinton to run against Senator Robert

Dole in 1996, he was an incumbent at the helm of a robust economy. Translation: unbeatable, even with his satanic penis.

THE CAMPAIGN Kansas Senator Robert Dole was a wounded World War II veteran with a dry sense of humor, who, at age seventy-two, had spent thirty-five years in Congress and had been Gerald Ford's 1976 running mate. He was too moderate for the mood of the Republican Party and never quite convincingly endorsed the party's positions on abortion, crime, or state's rights. He later said of Clinton that "he was my opponent, not my enemy," a stance that did not endear him to Clinton loathers. On election night, the president took thirty-one states to Dole's nineteen, with a popular vote margin of 45,590,703 to 37,816,307. Ross Perot, running again, garnered about eight million votes.

On January 23, 1996, a triumphant President Bill Clinton gave an eloquent State of the Union address in which he thanked "the person who has taught me more than anyone else over twenty-five years about the importance of families and children—a wonderful wife, magnificent mother, and a great first lady. Thank you, Hillary." Clinton later inscribed an official copy of the speech to a friend: "To Monica Lewinsky, with best wishes, Bill Clinton."

2000

GEORGE W. BUSH

★ ★ ★ ★ ★ ★ ★ ★ ★ ★ ★ VS. ★ ★ ★ ★ ★ ★ ★ ★ ★ ★ ★

AL GORE

"Only Al Gore can beat Al Gore. And he's been doing a pretty good job of that."

—Green Party candidate Ralph Nader

SLEAZE-O-METE

10
9
8
7
6
5
4
3
2
1

D espite being impeached, but not convicted, of the crime of lying to Congress about his liaison with Monica Lewinsky, Bill Clinton left office in 2000 with a 68 percent approval rating—a score even higher than Ronald Reagan's final numbers. It's not that voters approved of the president's extramarital affair or his claim that fellatio didn't constitute sex. The simple matter is that while Clinton was getting his hummer, the economy was humming, too—which left America sighing with relief.

But the Democrats had a challenge ahead of them. Their new candidate was likely to be Vice President Al Gore, who, while undoubtedly smart and honest, lacked Clinton's charisma and political legerdemain. Just as Lee Atwater decided to make Willie Horton Michael Dukakis's 1988 running mate, Republican strategists tried to saddle Al Gore with the hulking shadow of his libidinous president.

First, though, the GOP had to pick a candidate. Big Republican money fell in behind George W. Bush, son of H. W. and the governor of Texas. With the help of his longtime top manager Karl Rove, Bush set out to win the primaries but ran into a roadblock in the form of Arizona Senator John McCain, the former Vietnam POW who took New Hampshire by a sixty-to-forty margin over Bush. The moderate McCain captured the votes of Independents and even some Democrats wearied by Bill Clinton's behavior. His challenge had conservative Republicans worried.

But Bush's men were waiting for McCain in the South Carolina primary, where they dragged out the sleazy old practice of push-polling. Voters in South Carolina were asked: "Would you be more or less likely to vote for John McCain if you knew he had fathered an illegitimate black child?" (McCain and his wife had adopted a Bangladeshi girl.) This technique, which had the fingerprints of Karl Rove all over it, helped derail McCain; he lost in South Carolina, and Bush eventually captured the nomination.

On the Democratic side, Gore had little problem beating his strongest opponent, former New Jersey Senator Bill Bradley, to take the nomination. But two third-party challenges would have serious consequences for Gore down the line: activist Ralph Nader, running as a Green Party candidate, and conservative Pat Buchanan, the Reform Party nominee.

★ ★ ★ THE CANDIDATES ★ ★ ★

REPUBLICAN: GEORGE W. BUSH In 2000 George W. Bush—or "Dubya," as he is affectionately known—was fifty-four years old. Born into a wealthy Republican family (Bush's grandfather Prescott was a U.S senator, and, of course, his father, George H. W., president of the United States), Bush attended Exeter and Yale and received his MBA from Harvard. A real New England Yank. But Bush is forever associated with Texas; it was in that state that he unsuccessfully ran an oil company, unsuccessfully ran for Congress, and partied very successfully. But in 1986, under the influence of the evangelist Billy Graham, Bush gave up drinking and became a born-again Christian, although he never relinquished his warm, fraternal, back-slapping manner, something that endeared him even to those who disagreed with his policies. In 1994, Bush beat Ann Richards to become governor of Texas, and in 2000 he was perfectly situated to seek the presidency. His vice-presidential candidate was Dick Cheney, his father's very conservative secretary of defense.

DEMOCRATIC: AL GORE   Al Gore also hailed from privileged political bloodlines. His father was senator from Tennessee; Gore attended elite private schools and later Harvard. A political junkie, he was fascinated by the electoral process and the history of government but could sometimes come across as stiff, intellectual, and a trifle arrogant, even to friends. The causes he espoused would qualify him for the tag "tree-hugger" in any Republican playbook, including the fight against global warming and a push to pass the Kyoto Protocol, which called for a reduction in greenhouse gas emissions.

Gore's running mate was Senator Joe Lieberman of Connecticut, a religious, conservative Democrat and the first Jewish person to run on a presidential ticket (if you don't count Barry Goldwater, whose father was Jewish).

★ ★ ★ THE CAMPAIGN ★ ★ ★

Almost from the beginning, the 2000 race was neck and neck—but at first glance, it's a little hard to understand why. Gore could lay claim to being a part of an administration that had brought violent crime to a thirty-year low, balanced the budget, created a surplus, and in general kept the country in peace and prosperity. The big problem was Bill Clinton. Gore had been aghast at Clinton's White House "sexcapades" and probably felt it necessary to distance himself from the president— but in doing so, he was distancing himself from the genuine accomplishments of the Clinton administration. Even Karl Rove later said that if Gore had paid more attention to the great shape the country was in, "we [the Republicans] should have gotten our brains beaten out."

Bush's strategists positioned their guy as a man who was out to bring back to America a sense of decency ("there's no question the president embarrassed the nation," Bush told journalists). Bush also became a "compassionate conservative" out to "reform" Medicare and Social Security and fix the environment, just like Al Gore—all of which made more than a few Democrats remember John McCain's remark about Bush during the primaries: "If he's a reformer, I'm an astronaut."

When they realized that Clinton-era scandals were not rubbing off on Gore as well as might be hoped, Bush strategists turned to portraying the vice president as a two-faced liar. They managed to do so quite successfully, creating controversy over most of Gore's political positions, including putting forth the widely accepted (but false) claim that Gore said he had invented the Internet. (Actually, what he said in a 1999 interview was, "During my service in the United States Congress, I took the initiative in creating the Internet." Okay, a bit of an exaggeration. But, according to some people involved in developing the technology, Senator Al Gore was instrumental in approving research funds for the "Information Superhighway," which helped transform it from a military communication system into a worldwide networking and information channel.)

The vice president didn't help his own cause by smirking and rolling his eyes during his first debate with Bush, which made it seem as if he were ridiculing his opponent (Ronald Reagan could get away with "There you go again!" but not the far-less-magnetic Gore).

Democratic strategists were hard at work, too. They resurrected Bush's 1976 bust for driving under the influence in Maine (Bush had gotten off with a $150 fine). And if Gore was a liar, well, Bush was an idiot, a sort of chuckling fool. Bush had once told reporters that his favorite book was the kid's classic *The Very Hungry Caterpillar*. He claimed that Democrats wanted "the federal government controlling Social Security like it's some kind of federal program!" He also said things like "Families is where our nation finds hope, where wings take dreams."

★ ★ ★ THE WINNER (EVENTUALLY): ★ ★ ★
GEORGE W. BUSH

Only some 50 percent of eligible voters turned out on Election Day 2000—November 7, a day that shall live in confusion. By late in the evening, it was clear that Al Gore would win the popular vote (the official tally would be Gore 50,996,582, Bush 50,456,062). The election was close, the difference being a half-million votes, roughly the same margin by which Nixon beat Humphrey in 1968 and not even as close as Kennedy's edge over Nixon in 1960.

The problem, from Gore's point of view, was that pesky Electoral College. To win the 2000 election, a candidate needed at least 270 electoral votes. Not counting the state of Florida's 25 electoral votes, Gore was assured 267 votes, Bush 246. Whichever way Florida went, so went the presidential election.

About 7:50 P.M. EST on election night, major networks, relying on exit polls, announced that the state of Florida (whose governor was George Bush's younger brother, Jeb) had voted for Gore. (Some Republicans later said that calling the election ten minutes before polls closed in Florida kept Bush supporters at home, but there is little evidence of this.) By ten o'clock, Gore, in Nashville, thought he had won the presidency when New Mexico, Minnesota, and Michigan fell into line.

But, gradually, as more returns came in from Florida, the situation changed. At 2:00 A.M., with 97 percent of the votes in, it appeared that Bush had won in Florida. Now Gore made a serious tactical mistake. Anxious to seem statesmanlike and gracious, he called Bush, who was in Texas, and conceded the election. Then he made his way to Nashville's War Memorial Plaza, where he was going to make his concession speech and thank Democratic workers.

Just as he was about to give the speech, news came from frantic campaign staffers that Florida had become too close to call—Bush's margin had narrowed considerably. Gore immediately telephoned Bush and, as the latter put it ruefully, "unconceded."

The following conversation is priceless because it proves that even big candidates sometimes act like squabbling teenagers. Insiders on both sides explain that it went something like this:

Gore: "Circumstances have changed dramatically. The state of Florida is too close to call."
Bush: "Let me make sure I understand. You're calling me back to retract that concession?"
Gore: "You don't have to be snippy about it."
(Bush then explains that his little brother, Florida Governor Jeb Bush, has assured him of victory.)
Gore: "Let me explain something. Your little brother is not the ultimate authority on this."
Bush: "You do what you have to do."

And the election after the election was on. For thirty-six days, no one knew who the next president would be.

★ ★

REPUBLICANS VS. DEMOCRATS In Florida, automatic machine recounts are mandated by law when elections are as close as the Bush-Gore contest. Going into the recount, Bush led by 1,784 votes out of 5.9 million cast. Two days later, after the machine recount, his lead had shrunk to fewer than 300 votes. Democrats then cherry-picked three predominantly Democratic Florida counties—Miami-Dade, Palm Beach, and Broward—and asked for a hand recounting of votes, which was allowed under Florida law.

Republicans argued that of course Gore was going to pick up Democratic votes in these three counties—in all elections, in all states, a few errors are made here and there. No doubt some errors were made in Republican favor in the extremely close contest in New Mexico (which had gone to Gore). Why not pick through votes there?

Bush followers, led by the extremely savvy James Baker, former secretary of state under George H.W. Bush and five-time Republican presidential campaign manager, claimed that the election was over. Bush was the winner, and Gore was the pretender to the throne. The election needed to be certified and done with.

OVERVOTES, UNDERVOTES, AND CHADS Democrats, led by former Secretary of State Warren Christopher, pointed out that this was no ordinary case of a few ballots gone missing. The Votomatic system—in which voters punch out a hole on a paper ballot with a stylus to record their choice and then insert the ballot into a machine—was rife with problems.

In Palm Beach County, the two-page butterfly ballot (which looked like an opened book) was so poorly designed that more than 3,000 of the predominantly elderly, Jewish population had mistakenly punched the hole for ultraconservative Reform Party candidate Pat Buchanan, giving him 2,700 votes more than he won in any other Florida county. (Even Buchanan said that most of these votes were probably cast not for him, but for Gore.) Some voters saw their mistake and punched more than one hole to try to vote for Gore. These were known as overvotes.

There was not necessarily a lot anyone could do about the butterfly ballot errors—the ballot had been designed by a Democrat and approved by both parties ahead of time. But, in other counties, some ballots were only partially punched, leaving a hanging piece of paper (called a chad), which caused the vote not to be counted. This was known as an undervote. There were also ad nauseam "dimpled" or "pregnant" chads, which were still completely attached to the ballot on all four sides and corners, but bulged slightly in the middle, rendering those votes invalid.

In all, Democrats estimated, there were as many as 61,000 disputed undervotes. These had simply not been counted as votes cast, and they needed to be. For it was a matter of law in Florida that a voter's intent to vote be taken into consideration when recounting ballots, even if said voter made a procedural or mechanical mistake (that is, not punching the ballot fully) in casting a vote.

Hence, Democrats said, the hand recount was needed. But Florida Secretary of State Katherine Harris, a co-chair of the Bush campaign in the state, refused to allow the recounts—intent on certifying the election and moving forward. On November 21, the Florida Supreme Court voted to force Harris to let the recount proceed, approving manual recounts in the three Florida counties chosen by the Democrats. The hand count went on, but Republicans sent activists to demonstrate (many of them congressional aides flown to Florida). In Dade County, these "preppy protestors" were so militant that they managed to delay the counting, frightening the exhausted and overwhelmed poll workers.

Hanging chads, swinging chads, dimpled chads, pregnant chads—by the time the 2000 election was over, voters were thoroughly sick of chads.

When the deadline set by the Florida Supreme Court came and went without all votes being counted, Harris immediately declared Bush the Florida winner by 537 votes. But Democrats got another Florida Supreme Court decision not only to reopen the Dade County hand counting but also to hand count ballots for which no choice was recorded for president in all sixty-seven counties in Florida.

AND THE WINNER IS . . . Republican lawyers appealed to the U.S. Supreme Court to hear their case, which the court agreed to do on December 1. In oral arguments, Bush's lawyers claimed that hand counting must be stopped because it failed to provide Bush equal protection under the law—the votes had already been counted, had been recounted automatically as per law, and the Democrats did not have a right to a hand count.

Democrats replied that it was quite odd that the Republicans, fierce state's rights champions, should ask the court to intervene in what should essentially be an issue for the state of Florida to decide.

On December 9, the U.S. Supreme Court ordered a stay of the recount. The decision was made by a sharply divided court, with five conservative justices triumphing over four moderate ones. On Monday, December 11, the Court heard arguments in *Bush v. Gore*. On December 12, they refused to allow the manual recounting to go forward, thus effectively handing the 2000 presidential election to George W. Bush.

SO HOW DIRTY WAS IT? Bush had lost the popular vote but won in the Electoral College 271 to 266, thus becoming president. Historians turned to 1888 to find the last time that a presidential candidate—Benjamin Harrison—did not win the popular vote but won in the Electoral College.

If anything, the 2000 election most closely resembles the Rutherford Hayes vs. Samuel Tilden contest of 1876, which Tilden almost certainly won but had the election stolen from him by Republican "returning boards" in Louisiana, South Carolina, and, yes, Florida. The election was so dirty that Hayes never really recovered and became a one-term president.

In some ways, Republican efforts in Florida were not as sleazy as they have been made out to be. Roadblocks were not put up to keep blacks from voting, as has been reported. But no Republican official in Florida, entrusted with the votes of an entire state, acted in anything other than a partisan manner.

Had the tables been turned, had Democrats controlled the state, would they have acted in a less partisan fashion? No one knows. But other factors that helped Gore lose the election could not be blamed on the Republicans:

Had Gore been able to win his home state of Tennessee, which he did not, the whole Florida issue would have been moot.

Had Ralph Nader or even Pat Buchanan not run third-party challenges, Gore would have won.

Had Bill Clinton not acted as he did while in the White House (or had Gore decided to allow the still-popular president to campaign for him), Gore would probably have won.

And, if Gore and his forces had decided to fight as dirty as Bush's forces did in Florida, they might have won as well. But from the very moment of his too-early concession, Al Gore acted like a gracious loser rather than a tough-minded winner.

A self-fulfilling prophesy, as it turned out.

YOU LOW-DOWN DIRTY RAT! One day during the summer of 2000, a Gore volunteer was watching a Republican ad attacking Gore's prescription drug plan when he saw the word "RATS" flash across the screen. He reported it to Gore campaign officials, who played the ad slowly and also noticed the word, written in big white capital letters, followed by the phrase BUREAUCRATS DECIDE.

Was this an example of the so-called subliminal advertising that had first been tried in the 1950s, the art of hiding secret messages in television commercials? The FCC, while not specifically forbidding this type of advertising, does consider it deceptive.

Democratic Party operatives managed to make the story a cause célèbre. The Republican ad man who created the spot claimed, somewhat lamely, that he had merely flashed RATS because it was the last part of BUREAUCRATS, and wanted to make "a visual drumbeat. . . . You want to get [viewers] interested and involved."

Bush, appearing on *Good Morning, America*, claimed that RATS was meant to be seen—although most watchers did not notice it unless they were warned ahead of time—and further made the whole thing laughable by repeatedly mispronouncing the word "subliminal" as "subliminable."

The Republican National Committee yanked the ad, but it had already run more than four thousand times in different markets across the country.

2004

GEORGE W. BUSH

★ ★ ★ ★ ★ ★ ★ ★ ★ ★ ★ ★ VS. ★ ★ ★ ★ ★ ★ ★ ★ ★ ★ ★ ★

JOHN KERRY

"Our enemies are innovative and resourceful, and so are we. They never stop thinking about new ways to harm our country and our people, and neither do we!"

—President George W. Bush, in a 2004 campaign speech

SLEAZE-O-METER

10
9
8
7
6
5
4
3
2
1

F our years after the election of 2000, the mood of America had changed dramatically. The sexual scandals of the Clinton years now seemed like the high jinks of a bygone generation, as dated as raccoon coats or hippie headbands. In their place was the somber fact of September 11, 2001, when al-Qaeda terrorists flew planes into the World Trade Center and the Pentagon and crashed another plane, intended for the White House, into the ground in Pennsylvania. Three thousand Americans lost their lives.

Bush, who had been limping along, now received approval ratings into the ninetieth percentile, as high as those of his father after the first Gulf War. With broad, bipartisan support, the president invaded Afghanistan and retook it from the Taliban, although American forces failed to capture Osama bin Laden, the mastermind of the 9/11 attacks. The president's approval ratings remained high even after he invaded Iraq in 2003—his rationale being that dictator Saddam Hussein supported al-Qaeda and possessed weapons of mass destruction that threatened the world.

The only problem was that neither of these allegations turned out to be true. As the insurgency took hold in Iraq and more and more American soldiers died, people at home began to question Bush's judgment. And it didn't help any—it never does—that the stock market and the economy were in a post-dot-com nosedive.

As 2004 approached, however, the Republican Party was firmly behind George Bush, to the tune of an $86 million campaign purse even before the primaries—where Bush ran practically unopposed—began.

The Democratic primaries were a different matter, a rough-and-tumble affair. Al Gore had announced in 2002 that he would not be seeking office, which left the field open to the likes of retired general Wesley Clark, Massachusetts Senator John Kerry, former North Carolina senator and trial lawyer John Edwards, and Vermont governor Howard Dean. Dean ran a grassroots campaign based on his early opposition to the Iraq war and support of new health-care initiatives in America. But Dean self-destructed in the Iowa caucus in January 2004, coming in third and essentially ending his campaign with a guttural primal yell that became known as the "Dean Scream." Senator John Kerry rolled to the nomination of his party.

★ ★ ★ THE CANDIDATES ★ ★ ★

REPUBLICAN: GEORGE W. BUSH As progress in Iraq headed south, so did the presidency of George W. Bush. His manic performance shortly after the initial phase of the war ended—landing on a U.S. aircraft carrier wearing a full flight suit and making a triumphant speech in front of a banner that read, "MISSION ACCOMPLISHED"—was beginning to look more and more ludicrous as the fighting intensified. When it turned out that weapons of mass destruction were missing from Iraq, and the U.S. economy continued its dismal slide, the Bush presidency seemed to be in deep trouble.

DEMOCRAT: JOHN KERRY John Kerry began his nomination speech at the Democratic National Convention with the words: "I'm John Kerry, and I'm reporting for duty." This was no casual phrasing, for Democrats had recruited their first war-hero candidate since George McGovern, another vocal opponent of an unpopular war. Raised in an upper-middle-class family in Massachusetts, Kerry attended Yale in the 1960s and then—an unusual choice for someone of his age and background at the time—enlisted in the navy and served two tours as a Swift boat skipper in Vietnam, where he earned a Silver Star, a Bronze Star, and three Purple Hearts.

Kerry was a bit wooden and at times even seemed a little detached. His handlers did their best to present him as a plain-spoken regular guy who loved ice hockey and hunting. But a great deal of Kerry's media attention was devoted to his wife, Teresa Heinz Kerry, the heir to the Heinz ketchup fortune. According to *Forbes* magazine, she was worth about $750 million.

★ ★ ★ THE CAMPAIGN ★ ★ ★

As the fall of 2004 began, political signs began disappearing all over America. One night, you'd plant a candidate's sign in your front yard and by the next morning, poof! It had vanished. In one Pennsylvania town, nearly five hundred Bush/Cheney yard signs were ripped off. Hundreds of Kerry/Edwards signs were taken in Pensacola, Florida, where Kerry supporters responded by hanging Bush signs from tree limbs. There were also thefts in South Dakota, Wisconsin, Washington, Kentucky, Ohio, Colorado, Michigan, and Oregon.

One presidential historian wrote that whenever signs start to disappear, it's an indication of a divided and polarized country engaged in a tough, no-holds-barred election. That certainly describes the 2004 presidential battle. It raged 24/7 via Internet, cable news shows, talk radio, and newspapers. The Democrats were out to win back the presidency from a man they felt had stolen his seat and brought the country into a dangerous and unnecessary war. The Republicans were just as certain that Democrats would make a peace without honor in Iraq, leaving America open to more attacks like 9/11.

Senator John Kerry was supposed to blunt the quadrennial Republican smear that Democrats were not tough enough to face foreign enemies. Even before the campaign began, Kerry had the military bona fides to be able to criticize the president, saying he wasn't aggressive enough in using armed forces to capture Osama bin Laden. Senator Kerry had voted for the use of force in Iraq but later voted against $87 billion of additional military aid to the war effort; Bush's team seized on these facts and tried to brand Kerry as a "flip-flopper." (They were helped immensely when Kerry, trying to defend his position, said "I actually did vote for the $87 billion before I voted against it.")

Bush, in the meantime, ran as a tough guy, the man who told the terrorists, "Bring it on!" He refused to admit to any mistakes. And he said: "You may not always agree with me, but you'll always know where I stand."

Dirty tricks on a fairly minor level began as Kerry was alleged to have had an affair with a young woman (who denied the story). A picture widely circulated on the Internet showed a young John Kerry and the actress Jane Fonda speaking together at a Vietnam War—era rally—but the photograph was a fake. For their part, Democrats sent out scare e-mails claiming that Bush would institute a military draft if reelected.

Kerry and Bush were running almost in a dead heat as Bush's approval rating sank to under 50 percent due to new setbacks in Iran. But on August 4, a self-styled "independent" group, called Swift Boat Veterans for Truth, composed of some of the men who had served on the rivers of Vietnam with Kerry, announced that Kerry "was lying about his [military] record" and that he was "no war hero."

It's hard to understate the importance of the Swifties in the 2004 campaign. They thoroughly muddled the public perception of Kerry's military service and shifted focus away from the important campaign issues. The *Washington Post* published an article showing that one of Kerry's main Swift boat accusers had in fact supported Kerry's account of his wartime service, and Kerry was able to turn back the attacks with some force. But he had spent two weeks of prime campaign time defending himself, and many undecided voters were now unsure what to believe.

Still, Kerry was able to best George Bush in two different debates. And as the race headed for election night, there were predictions that the challenger might pull things off after all.

★ ★ ★ THE WINNER: GEORGE W. BUSH ★ ★ ★

Exit polls agreed that Kerry had a fighting chance. Americans watching the networks during the evening of November 2 saw and heard commentators unanimously quoting exit polls that Kerry would be elected president.

Yet by midnight, Bush was shown as winning decisively, and Kerry conceded the next morning. The official tally was Bush 60,693,281, Kerry 57,355,978, with the incumbent winning in the Electoral College 286 to 251. It was not a huge margin of victory—a little more than 2 percent—but certainly the election was not anywhere near as close as 2000.

★ ★

BATTLEGROUND OHIO Ultimately the 2004 presidential election came down to the state of Ohio, which George Bush won by a margin of 118,601 votes, giving him the state's twenty electoral votes and victory.

But reports of election irregularities began streaming out of the state even before the polls had closed. Representative John Conyers Jr., the ranking Democrat on the House Judiciary Committee (an original member of Nixon's Enemies List), performed the investigation. In his report to Congress in January of 2005, he outlined "numerous, serious election irregularities in the Ohio presidential election, which resulted in a significant disenfranchisement of voters."

To wit: Early in September, two months before the election, Ohio Secretary of State J. Kenneth Blackwell, who—like Katherine Harris in Florida in 2000, was co-chair of his state's Bush-Cheney reelection effort—used an outdated regulation to restrict voter registration. He claimed that the paper registrations needed to be printed on eighty-pound, unwaxed white paper (postcard paper). This might make sense for registrations through the mail, but Blackwell insisted that the regulation covered those delivered in person as well and also that all registrations on different paper were retroactively invalid. According to the nonpartisan Greater Cleveland Voting Coalition, at least 15,000 voters lost their ability to vote because of this.

Among other things, according to Conyers, Republicans engaged in a deceptive direct-mail practice called "caging" to trim Democratic voters off the rolls. In the summer of 2004 the GOP, using ZIP codes, sent registered letters to 200,000 newly registered voters in urban areas more likely to vote for Kerry. Thirty-five thousand people who had refused to sign the letters or whose mail came back marked "undeliverable" were knocked off the voter rolls just two weeks before the election.

Some voters were forced to wait in line for more than twelve hours. Yet there were no long lines in Republican areas. In one county alone, the misallocation of machines reduced the number of votes by an estimated 15,000. Statewide, according to Conyers, African Americans waited an average of fifty-two minutes to vote, compared to eighteen for white Americans.

Voting reforms have been introduced to remedy voter fraud. But with computerized voting expected to come into wide use in 2008—voters will use touch screens on ATM-like terminals—more difficulties can be expected. It's possible that the new villain of election fraud will be an innocuous-looking computer geek.

MUZZLING TERESA Teresa Heinz Kerry, John Kerry's fabulously wealthy wife, was not what anyone would call the ideal campaign spouse. Unlike Laura Bush, whom the president's handlers trotted out at almost every turn, Teresa was not Mrs. All-American.

She was born in Mozambique and moved to New York to work as a translator at the United Nations. In 1966 she met and married Senator John Heinz III, heir to the ketchup fortune. After Heinz died in an airplane crash in 1991, Teresa inherited his vast fortune. She married Kerry in 1995 as a registered Republican, and she remained Republican until her husband ran for president.

Heinz Kerry was often erratic and sullen while on the campaign trail. She once told a reporter to "shove it" and remarked that Laura Bush had never had "a real job." Her biggest controversy took place behind the scenes at the Democratic Convention. After Kerry gave his speech, tradition dictated that he be joined by his vice-presidential running mate. Instead, Heinz Kerry insisted that she go first. "I am the spouse," she said. "I go first." There was no dissuading her verbally, so as Kerry finished his speech, a young campaign aide blocked her with both arms and yelled at John Edwards: "Run!"

BULGEGATE During Bush's first debate with Kerry, many viewers noticed a "bulge" underneath his suit jacket at about the center of his back. It set off much speculation. Some thought it might be a radio receiver. After all, Bush would often give long pauses before answering questions and once said, "Let me finish!" when no one had said anything to him. After the debates, a NASA scientist enhanced images of the area in question and expressed the opinion that what the president was wearing was indeed a receiver.

Others speculated that the bulge was either a bulletproof vest or, possibly, a cardiac defibrillator that Bush was forced to wear after he choked on a pretzel while watching a football game in January 2002.

For the record, the White House claimed that the bulge was "a wrinkle in the fabric."

The year 2004 introduced dirty tricks to the Internet—like a bogus photo of John Kerry speaking with Jane Fonda at an antiwar rally.

★ ★ ★ APPENDIX: ★ ★ ★

Top Ten Classic Attacks in Presidential Elections

S ome things never change—like the ways in which presidential candidates go after each other. Below are ten classic slights, slur, and smears used almost continuously during two hundred years of presidential electioneering.

10. "YOU'RE NOT TOUGH ENOUGH!" This perennial attack suggests that—in a time of war—a candidate will probably turn tail like a yellow-belly chicken. The list of cowardly candidates in U.S. history is enormous: Thomas Jefferson was too soft on France; Franklin Pierce fainted in the heat of battle; Jimmy Carter couldn't stand up to Iran; and many of today's candidates aren't "man enough" to battle the terrorists.

9. "YOU'LL DRIVE US INTO WAR!" The flip side of number 10. These candidates—say, Andrew Jackson, Teddy Roosevelt, Barry Goldwater, George W. Bush—are loose cannons who will drag us into bloody foreign wars and destroy our future, just to prove how tough they are.

8. "YOU'RE TOO OLD!" William Henry Harrison, Winfield Scott, Dwight Eisenhower, Ronald Reagan, Bob Dole—geez, you guys should be out playing shuffleboard! What if you fall asleep with your finger on that big red button? Let the young fifty-five-year-olds take over!

7. "YOU'RE AN EGGHEAD!" Thomas Jefferson, John Quincy Adams, Adlai Stevenson, Eugene McCarthy, Jimmy Carter, Al Gore—all were way too smart for their own good, according to their opponents. Even worse, they were book smart—Jefferson loved architecture, Stevenson read poetry, and McCarthy wrote poetry, for Christ's sake.

6. "YOU'RE AN IDIOT!" On the other hand, candidates like Lewis Cass, William Howard Taft, Herbert Hoover, Alf Landon, and George W. Bush must have fallen down and bumped their heads when they were young. In the case of Gerald Ford, many Democrats speculated that he'd played too much football without a helmet.

5. "YOU'RE A SLUT!" Apparently Thomas Jefferson, Grover Cleveland, Warren Harding (a rare Republican target for this attack), Woodrow Wilson, John F. Kennedy, Gary Hart, Bill Clinton, and John Kerry just couldn't keep their minds on business when the ladies were around.

4. "YOU'RE CLEARLY NOT HAVING SEX WITH ANYONE!" On the other hand, Americans do want their presidents to have a little red blood. It's bad form for the commander-in-chief to appear dry, shriveled, and sexless, like James Madison, Benjamin Harrison, Calvin Coolidge, Richard Nixon, and even Jimmy Carter, despite the lust in his heart.

3. "YOU'RE AT LEAST A LITTLE BIT GAY!" Not that there's anything wrong with it. But many felt that James Buchanan and Adlai Stevenson "played for the other team," and party operatives did their best to spread rumors.

2. "YOU'RE DRUNK ALL THE TIME!" This favorite attack was used most notably against Ulysses S. Grant, but it was also leveled at the likes of Henry Clay, Franklin Pierce, Teddy Roosevelt, Warren Harding, and George W. Bush. Of course, Bush was clean and sober by the 2000 election, but who cares. Once a souse, always a souse.

1. "YOU'RE INSANE!" Shrinks publicly stated that both William Jennings Bryan and Barry Goldwater were neurotic and paranoid; Horace Greeley died in an asylum right after Election Day 1872; Thomas Eagleton received shock treatments; and Nixon—well, all you had to do was look at the guy's 1952 Checkers speech. Diagnosis: Bonkers.

INDEX

Ackerman, Kenneth D. *Dark Horse: The Surprising Election and Political Murder of President James A. Garfield*. New York: Carroll & Graff, 2003.

Aitken, Jonathan. *Nixon: A Life*. Washington D.C.: Regnery Publishing, Inc., 1993.

Ambrose, Steven E. *Eisenhower: The President*. New York, Simon & Schuster, 1984.

Auchincloss, Louis. *Theodore Roosevelt*. New York: Henry Holt & Company, 2001.

Boller, Paul E. *Presidential Campaigns: From George Washington to George W. Bush*. New York: Oxford University Press, 2004

Brands, H. W. *Andrew Jackson: His Life and Times*. New York: Doubleday, 2005.

Brodie, Fawn M. *Thomas Jefferson: An Intimate History*. New York: W.W. Norton, 1974.

Bourne, Peter G. *Jimmy Carter: A Comprehensive Biography from Plains to Postpresidency*. New York: Scribner, 1997.

Calhoun, Charles W. *Benjamin Harrison*. New York: Henry Holt & Company, 2005.

Cannon, Lou. *President Reagan: The Role of a Lifetime*. New York: Simon & Schuster, 1991.

Dallak, Robert. *Flawed Giant: Lyndon Johnson and His Times, 1961-1973*. New York: Oxford University Press, 1998.

Dean, John W. *Warren G. Harding*. New York: Henry Holt & Co., 2005.

Dershowitz, Alan M. *Supreme Injustice: How the High Court Hijacked Election 2000*. New York: Oxford University Press, 2001.

Donald, David Herbert. *Lincoln*. New York: Simon & Schuster, 1995.

Donovan, Robert J. *Conflict and Crisis: The Presidency of Harry Truman, 1945-1948*. New York: W.W. Norton & Co, 1977.

Ellis, Joseph J. *American Sphinx: The Character of Thomas Jefferson*. New York: Alfred A. Knopf, 1997.

Ellis, Joseph J. *His Excellency: George Washington*. New York: Alfred A. Knopf, 2004.

Ferling, John. *Adams vs. Jefferson: The Tumultuous Election of 1800*. New York: Oxford University Press, 2004.

Goldberg, Robert Allen. *Barry Goldwater*. New Haven: Yale University Press, 1995.

Goldman, Peter, et al. *Quest for the Presidency 1992*. College Station: Texas A&M University Press, 1994.

Goodwin, Doris Kearns. *Team of Rivals: The Political Genius of Abraham Lincoln*. New York: Simon & Schuster, 2005.

Greenfield, Jeff. *The Real Campaign: How the Media Missed the Story of the 1980 Campaign*. New York: Summit Books, 1982.

Howe, George Frederick. *Chester A. Arthur: A Quarter-Century of Machine Politics*. New York: Frederick Unger Publishing Co., 1957.

Jamieson, Kathleen Hall. *Dirty Politics: Deception, Distraction and Democracy*. New York: Oxford University Press, 1992.

Jamieson, Kathleen Hall. *Packaging the Presidency: A History and Criticism of Presidential Campaign Advertising*. Third Edition. New York: Oxford University Press, 1995.

Johnson, David E., & Johnny R. *A Funny Thing Happened on the Way to the White House: Foolhardiness, Folly and Fraud in Presidential Elections, from Andrew Jackson to George W. Bush*. New York, Dallas: Taylor Trade Publishing, Lanham, 2004.

Ketchum, Ralph. *James Madison: A Biography*. Charlottesville: University of Virginia Press, 1971.

Klein, Joe. *Politics Lost: How American Democracy Was Trivialized by People Who Think You Are Stupid*. New York: Doubleday, 2006.

Kutler, Stanley I. *The Wars of Watergate: The Last Crisis of Richard Nixon*. New York: W.W. Norton & Co, 1990.

Lorant, Stefan. *The Glorious Burden: The History of the Presidency and Presidential Elections from George Washington to James Earl Carter, Jr*. Lenox, MA: Author's Edition Inc, 1977.

Leech, Margaret. *In the Days of McKinley*. New York: Harper & Brothers, 1959.

McCoy, Donald R. *Calvin Coolidge: The Quiet President*. New York: Macmillan & Co., 1967.

McCullough, David. *John Adams*. New York: Simon & Schuster, 2001.

McCullough, David. *Truman*. New York: Simon & Schuster, 1992

McFeely, William S. *Grant: A Biography*. New York, London: W.W. Norton & Co., 1981.

Martin, John Bartlow. *Adlai Stevenson of Illinois: The Life of Adlai E. Stevenson*. Garden City & New York: Doubleday & Co., 1976.

Miller, Douglas T. & Marion Nowak. *The Fifties: The Way We Really Were*. Garden City, New York: Doubleday & Co, 1977.

Morgan, Ted. *FDR: A Biography*. New York: Simon & Schuster, 1985.

Morris, Edmund. *Theodore Rex*. New York: Random House, 2001.

Nagel, Paul C. *John Quincy Adams. A Public Life, A Private Life*. Cambridge, MA: Harvard University Press. 1997.

Patterson, James T. *Restless Giant: The United States from Watergate to Bush vs. Gore*. New York: Oxford University Press, 2005.

Phillips, Kevin. *William McKinley*. New York: Henry Holt & Co., 2003.

Pringle, Henry F. *The Life and Times of Howard Taft: A Biography*. New York, Toronto: Farrar & Rinehart, 1939.

Reeves, Thomas C. *A Question of Character: A Life of John F. Kennedy*. New York: The Free Press, 1991.

Robinson, Lloyd. *The Stolen Election: Hayes versus Tilden—1876*. Garden City, NY: Doubleday & Co.1968.

Roseboom, Paul H., and Alfred E. Eckes Jr. *History of Presidential Elections: From George Washington to Jimmy Carter*. Fourth Edition. New York: Macmillan Publishing Co, Inc., 1979.

Seigenthaler, John. *James K. Polk*. New York: Henry Holt & Company, 2003.

Shephard, Edward M. *Martin Van Buren*. New York and Boston: Houghton, Mifflin & Company, 1899.

Sick, Gary. *October Surprise: American Hostages in Iran and the Election of Ronald Reagan*. NewYork: Times Books, 1991.

Slayton, Robert A. *Empire Statesman: The Rise and Redemption of Al Smith*. New York: The Free Press, 2001.

Smith, Richard Norton. *An Uncommon Man: The Triumph of Herbert Hoover*. New York, Simon & Schuster, 1985.

Stephanopoulis, George. *All Too Human: A Political Education*. New York: Little, Brown & Co., 1999.

Toobin, Jeffrey. *A Vast Conspiracy: The Real Story of the Sex Scandal That Nearly Brought Down a President*. New York: Random House, 1999.

Toobin, Jeffrey. *Too Close to Call: The Thirty-Six Day Battle to Decide the 2000 Election*. New York: Random House, 2002.

Walworth, Arthur. *Woodrow Wilson*. New York: W.W. Norton & Co., 1978.

White, Theodore H. *Breach of Faith: The Fall of Richard Nixon*. New York: Atheneum, 1975.

Wicker, Tom. *One of Us: Richard Nixon and the American Dream*. New York: Random House, 1991.

★ ★ ★ ACKNOWLEDGMENTS ★ ★ ★

I would like to thank Jason Rekulak, my astute and generous editor. Not only was this book his brainchild, but he has made many helpful suggestions along the way which have immeasurably improved it. Every writer should be so lucky.

I'd also like to thank Mary Ellen Wilson, for her meticulous fact-checking, especially when it came to tracking down accurate vote totals (a surprisingly difficult task). Doogie Horner's energetic page design perfectly matches the patriotic yet risible spirit of America's presidential elections, as do Mike Fink's spirited illustrations.

I read innumerable books and articles while researching this book, but I relied heavily on Stefan Lorant's *The Glorious Burden*, Paul Boller's *Presidential Campaigns*, Kathleen Hall Jamieson's books *Packaging the Presidency* and *Dirty Politics*, and Paul H. Roseboom and Alfred E. Eckes Jr.'s *History of Presidential Elections: From George Washington to Jimmy Carter*. These books are treasure troves of information on all aspects of presidential politics, and I highly recommend them.

Finally, I'd like to thank my friend Eric Thoroman, whose brain I picked on matters presidential during our long runs in New Jersey and who first introduced me to Lorant's glorious *The Glorious Burden*.